The Best American Short Plays

2011–2012

The Best American Short Plays

2011–2012

edited with an introduction by
William W. Demastes

APPLAUSE THEATRE & CINEMA BOOKS
An Imprint of Hal Leonard Corporation

The Best American Short Plays 2011–2012
Edited with an intoduction by William W. Demastes

Published in 2013 by Applause Theatre & Cinema Books
An Imprint of Hal Leonard Corporation
7777 West Bluemound Road
Milwaukee, WI 53213

Trade Book Division Editorial Offices
33 Plymouth St., Montclair, NJ 07042

Printed in the United States of America
Book interior by UB Communications

ISBN 978-1-47687-734-1 [cloth]
ISBN 978-1-47687-733-4 [paper]
ISSN 0067-6284

www.applausebooks.com

contents

introduction

"I Know Not Seems": Theater's Legacy of Appearances

William W. Demastes

"Seems, madam? Nay, it is. I know not 'seems.'" So begins Hamlet's maddening entry into a world of illusion, mistaken identity, and self-delusion. Hamlet's dilemma—struggling to distinguish between seeming and being, trying to tell what is real and what is illusion—has plagued humanity since we developed that first spark of consciousness. T. S. Eliot suggested that it would be better to be a pair of ragged claws—scuttling across the floors of silent seas—than a human being burdened with the task of separating fact from fiction. If you think about it, this single issue is really the root of all human problems. Does she love me, or does she just want my money? Should I trust him, or is he leading me to ruin? Is he bluffing? Is she lying? We simply don't have the tools to tell what is going on behind that trust-me smile or that furrowed-brow look of sincerity.

Hamlet, however, doesn't seem to suffer from any such uncertainties, supremely confident that he has "that within which passes show." Of course, anyone who knows the play knows that Hamlet gets massively entangled in a deadly world of deception and illusion as the play moves forward. And his early confidence in his ability to distinguish reality from its mirror image soon fades, even to the point that he succumbs to that most extreme version of the dilemma, the problem of self-deception. Does his behavior prove him a coward? When he puts on his antic disposition, who is he really fooling?

As with Hamlet, there is always that problem that we, too, will become victims of our own deceit. Hardly a single one of us has not wondered, "Am I a generous person or a nice person, or a smart or witty or charming or good-looking person?" And most of us have likely answered yes to all the above at some point in our lives. And most of us tend to hold to the point even when overwhelming evidence suggests otherwise.

Putting on an act. Doing make-believe. For better or for worse, that's what we do. While we do admittedly suffer a great deal at the hands of these powers of deception, make-believe also provides a great deal of color and depth to life and living. Deception and trickery are in fact so central to our lives that we invented theater to explore their effects and consequences, working to understand them even as we fall victim to their ingenious devices. Put another way, theater becomes the place where make-believe, paradoxically, serves our unquenchable pursuit of truth. Playwrights seek truth by creating worlds of illusion, actors seek truth by pretending to be people other than who they are, and audiences go to the theater to be swept into other worlds, fully prepared to suspend their disbelief in the process, provided what they see is in some way "true to life." Hamlet himself is attracted to the theater—the play's the thing, after all, for him and his schemes—and uses it as one of his tools to strike through the mysteries of appearance and illusion. *Hamlet* is brilliant for many reasons, but one very big reason is that it reveals theater for what it is: the heart and soul of the human condition, bound as we all are in the life-and-death struggle to distinguish fact from fiction. Nature red in tooth and claw has nothing so deadly in its Darwinian arsenal of danger than the tools of deception.

Of all the art forms that humanity has crafted, theater is by far the most suitable laboratory for the study of this great art of deception. It is a place where we test our ability to separate truth from illusion by determining who's the good guy, who to believe, how the play will end. And it's the playwright's task to provide enough clues throughout to lead us to a generally unexpected conclusion that in hindsight is perfectly logical, reasonable, probable. The play should test our discernment, and while we may expect to be deceived, we also expect that the deception should serve to sharpen our skills for future challenges. The theater is the place where we welcome deception, and in the process it's the great safe haven where we can test our ability to distinguish seeming from being, truth from fiction, without the fear of consequences we would experience out in the real world. For humans, theater is a most suitable survivalist testing ground.

The plays in this volume deal with deception, as all plays do. But there's a certain twist to the matter of illusion/reality that encourages paying special attention to the entwining of truth and fiction in each one of the following selections. From haunting to hilarious, they exercise our powers of perception and refine our abilities to separate fact from fiction. In the process, here's hoping we will return to the world better able to distinguish a hawk from a handsaw, keeping pace with Hamlet himself as he strives to separate illusion from reality.

Jules Tasca's *Play Development or If* Hamlet *Had Been a Reading* opens the volume by turning to *Hamlet* itself, this time in a rehearsal being scrutinized by a test audience. Besides the comedy generated by this misinformed interest group, Tasca humorously reminds us of the ever-present human failing of self-deception. Do these would-be critics, directors, and playwrights hear what they're saying? Thankfully, self-deception is not always fatal. *Elzbieta Erased* by John Guare, on the other hand, is a haunting theater piece that works its way through the troubled life of a true acting talent suffering in a world of far more dangerous types of deception, self-generated and otherwise. *Warner Bros.* by Andrea Sloan Pink follows the trail of self-deception by presenting a cast of simple people struggling to achieve their dreams in the epicenter of the modern world's dream factory. Pink observes of her work, "This play is a polemic against Hollywood's siren song. Behind the glamour and romanticism, the film industry's brutality makes it a place where humans are fungible." Pink, like Tasca and Guare, presents portraits of self-deception that serve as cautionary tales to all. Interesting and intriguing in their own unique ways as they each deal with a common industry of illusions, these playwrights all serve the theater well as they present different perspectives on the nearly institutionalized nature of deception and make-believe.

Assumptions by Lynne Bolen takes a different look at the issue of deception, ingeniously blurring reality and illusion by layering the play with actors who are first merely acting but then turn into actors who are acting actors. The hall-of-mirrors trickery capitalizes on theater's singular strength—its power of illusion. In a similar act of theatrical "trickery," *Starf*cker* by Adam Pasen highlights an unsavory term (starf*cker—obviously charged despite the attempt at censorship) and utterly alters its connotation so that by the end of the play the term reconstitutes itself as a signifier of innocence and integrity. A new reality suggests itself before our very eyes. In the case of both plays, the playwrights capitalize on audience predispositions and use the destabilizing forces of theater to test the certainties of our prepositions, with notably destabilizing effect.

Claudia Barnett's *Lillie Meant Murder* is based on a true story where a man pretends to marry a woman and secure all the rights and privileges of such a union. The deception is unearthed with grave consequences in this play, generating an engaging play where form and theme impressively converge.

Gift of an Orange by Charlene A. Donaghy is based on a Tennessee Williams short story, "Gift of an Apple." Though Williams's story is set in the desert Southwest, Donaghy returns Williams to Louisiana, filling the tale with the all the exoticism found in Williams's spiritual home of New Orleans. The play's theatrical mood is magical (almost literally) as it takes us into backwater bayous where strange hauntings should prevail but where human truths reconfigure an alien world through unexpected emotions.

White or the Muskox Play by Jonathan Fitts was invoked by a series of events surrounding the death of the author's grandfather, who was the most influential man in Fitts's life. This play is in many ways an exorcism for Fitts, but in its way it presents the hauntings that affect us all in our daily lives. Life rarely exists in our twenty-four-hour, sunup to sundown world, but is governed by currents flowing beneath worldly surfaces. And they require our attention. This play reminds us of the multiple dimensions of reality—often thought of as mere illusion—at work in our lives.

The Cowboy by Patrick Holland is haunting in its own way. The work is perfectly crafted to present a collection of improbabilities leading to a fantastic accident that generates the feeling that the accident was no accident at all. The messy lives of three women come together in an unexpectedly appropriate manner, overseen by the silent hand of a character known as the Cowboy, begging the question: What forces lie beneath daily events beyond our control and even understanding?

A Little Haunting by A. K. Abeille and David Manos Morris is another supernatural venture, though this one is far less ominous, except perhaps for the central character. And it's far more wacky, capitalizing on multiple dimensions of reality and illusion in a way only the theater can capture.

Ichabod Crane Tells All by Lawrence Thelen takes advantage of the monologue form to study the inner workings of self-deception. Disturbed by recent onslaughts of campaign advertising, Thelen wondered, "Can someone if they repeat a lie long enough and loudly enough actually convince others it's true?" Expanding that question to a matter of history itself, he asks, "Is history what it is, or only what you say it is?" The play puts the case to its audience, who get to hear Ichabod Crane's masterful spin on an age-old tale, interrupted by the arrival of the Headless Horseman, who ironically represents the appearance of that ever-present force that attempts to keep us on the straight and narrow.

Bulgarian Rhapsody by Rich Orloff is a hilarious romp somewhat reminiscent of Shaw's comic masterpiece *Arms and the Man*. Inspired by a news article reporting post-Communist struggles in Bulgaria, Orloff took the suffering and combined it with simple human resilience, extending the fusion to a farcical extreme. Amid the farcical shenanigans, however, lies a logic of its own. And in the play's absurdity lies a homage to the human spirit, which in this case transcends any sort of sincerely penned treatise or report or news article.

Like several plays in this volume, *Change of Venue* by Judd Lear Silverman is based on a news story. This one was about a man who visits a local bordello only to find that he knew his intended partner better than he expected. Needless to say, the matter of self-deception abounds in this play, but so does the matter of regeneration: How might a change of venue create a revitalization of dead-end circumstances?

The Wager by Neil LaBute is a work commissioned by Theater Breaking Through Barriers in New York City, to be included in an evening of six plays about disability. LaBute destabilizes audience expectations several times through the course of this short piece, making it uncomfortable throughout to settle on the matter of where we should stand, until the end when standing becomes a sort of joke unto itself.

A Waffle Doesn't Cure Insomnia by Erica Bennett presents the genuine humanity of two characters whose first impressions may lead an audience to presume anything but humanity. It's an extended duologue inspired by actual insomnia experienced by the author and a friend, with Bennett observing, "If there is any semblance between my love for my friend and the play, it's the love between the characters of Heyzeus and Mou-Mou." Life courses through the living at levels far beneath the surfaces we daily observe.

There are of course surfaces that severely restrict the development of living at any level. *Wife Shop* is Angela C. Hall's response to what she calls "the ubiquitous media portrayals of women as commodities." She reports that her play uses a strategy similar to that employed by Luis Valdez (*Los Vendidos*), "to 'send up' a number of stereotypes that have dogged women in general, and to address the highly racialized and sexualized imagery that has plagued African American women in particular." The discomfort among the hilarity generated by presenting the racialized/sexualized stereotypes results in yet another layer of truth generation, the layer that acknowledges what we witness is wrong and deserves serious reconsideration.

If racialized and sexualized stereotypes are dangerous forms of oppression, so is the generally well-intentioned stereotype that A. R. Gurney addresses in *The Interview*, another play commissioned by Theater Breaking Through Barriers. Gurney reports that he "was struck by the pride and intensity of the actors whose various disabilities gave a special urgency to their performances." What Gurney presents in his short piece breaks through one stereotype by revealing that circumstances sometimes labeled hindrances can in fact blossom into decided strengths.

Come Again, Another Day by Cary Pepper has an eerie Pinteresque quality about it, refusing to move very far from between the walls of the room on the stage. A very unusual encounter in that room leads to personal assessments of two lives, which Pepper announces, "became a meditation on life, death, and dying, and how often our lives (and well-being) hang by that precarious, mercurial thread that can be snapped, cut, or unraveled—or not—at any moment, in so many different ways." Security, stability, and personal control are perhaps the greatest of our personal delusions, ultimate deceptions worthy of similar meditation and reflection.

Take My Land . . . Please by John F. Richardson is in no way Pinteresque, but is rather a meditation and reflection with a decidedly irreverent twist. Splashed with comic anachronism, this play is Richardson's rewrite of the "bad rap" given to the Native Americans who sold Manhattan to the Europeans: "I'm convinced there's a deeper truth behind the historical record. My play is an attempt to set that record straight." It's not entirely clear what record is being set straight, but it's not a real cause for concern.

YouTopia by Chaney Kwak ends the volume with a look into the not-so-distant future at the self-generated destruction of the idea of the private citizen. Kwak reports: "Originally I tried to write *YouTopia* as a short story, but every draft felt false. I realized that the story I was trying to tell couldn't work without the immediacy of live actors, defying the very idea of the virtual world we're building." I suggest that Kwak's confession applies equally well to all the works in this volume: they are each suited to the theater in ways that would be diminished had they not found their way to the genre represented here in The Best American Short Plays. Illusion, deception, self-delusion, and make-believe—for better and for worse—are the fabrics of our lives and the life's breath of the theater.

Play Development or If *Hamlet* Had Been a Reading

Jules Tasca

Jules Tasca

Jules Tasca is an award-winning playwright who has over 130 produced and published plays in the Unites States and abroad. His play *Art Lover* was produced as part of the Philadelphia International Festival of the Arts. His latest publication is *Chekhov's Ladies*, an anthology of Chekhov's short stories adapted for the stage. *If Hamlet Had Been a Reading* is Mr. Tasca's fifth selected play to be included in The Best American Short Plays series.

··· production history ···

This newly written work has yet to be produced.

characters

WILL SHAKESPEARE, a depressed playwright

5 ACTORS, nondescript

5 AUDIENCE MEMBERS, four nondescript, one gay

• • •

[*The lights come up on several actors dressed in Elizabethan style. Before them is an audience of several people sitting on benches. They also are attired in Elizabethan outfits. The* ACTORS *finish reading the last few lines of Shakespeare's* Hamlet. *A pause.*]

ACTOR 1   And that is the end of Will's new piece . . .

[*Polite applause. The* ACTORS *rise and join the* AUDIENCE MEMBERS *on benches.*]

WILL   [*Rising from the bench.*] Yes, thank you . . . great reading. Thank you so much.

ACTOR 1   You're welcome, Will. Please take a seat up there and we'll get some feedback.

WILL   Of course.

[WILL *sits in the area vacated by the* ACTORS. *There's a long pause.*]

ACTOR 1   Who'll start?

WILL   Yes, please do.

AUDIENCE 1   Well . . . it is long.

ACTOR 2   I agree.

AUDIENCE 2   It's overly long, Will.

WILL   I understand.

ACTOR 3 Yes, it needs vast cutting.

WILL You think?

ACTOR 3 Will, may I make a suggestion?

WILL Yes, go on.

ACTOR 3 The ghost. The ghost bothers me.

ACTOR 2 I agree.

ACTOR 3 I don't know, Will. It's . . . it's gimmicky, you know? I think you're better off letting Hamlet discover the murder through—I don't know—somebody who saw Claudius kill Hamlet's father. Say, one of the guards . . . Bernardo, say . . . it's just a suggestion, because, you know, the ghost is just a device . . .

ACTOR 2 I agree.

WILL I thought . . . I'd hoped that the ghost would add tension to the play, and, after all, it is the ghost of his father, which makes the revelation more poignant and that . . . that . . .

AUDIENCE 3 Well, while they're waiting for the ghost to appear to Hamlet, what was that long looming passage about a dram of evil and fortune's star all about? It seemed more of an essay. It seemed extraneous.

ACTOR 2 I agree.

AUDIENCE 4 Will, and I mean this constructively, some of that scene seemed showy.

WILL Showy . . .

AUDIENCE 4 To me, yes. You made Hamlet too . . . too . . . intelligent. An A student. . . . He'd work better as a revenge character if he were a B or B-character with a hotter temper. Right now he's all talk, talk, talk, muse, muse, muse, ponder, ponder, ponder.

AUDIENCE 5 Also, he constantly broods.

ACTOR 2   I agree.

AUDIENCE 5   The play's a gloom and doom enough piece now, Will. I mean, you've made Hamlet so melancholy, you almost wish he would kill himself.

AUDIENCE 3   Will, maybe Hamlet could consult a priest.

WILL   A priest . . .

ACTOR 3   In the castle there would be a priest, a spiritual advisor.

ACTOR 2   I agree.

AUDIENCE 2   A priest could be a double agent—a spy for Claudius.

ACTOR 1   That's not a bad idea. There would be a priest around somewhere. Who married them? The uncle and the mother?

WILL   I didn't think it necessary to show the actual ceremony.

AUDIENCE 3   I'd like to ask about this madness business. Why does Hamlet have to pretend he's mad? It's never explained. Why can't he do what he's doing at Elsinore—which is a lot of dawdling—without going about with one shoe on and one shoe off? I think you have to explain it.

ACTOR 2   I agree.

AUDIENCE 1   Will, he also seems to go mad pretending to go mad. I think you need to clarify this in your rewrites.

ACTOR 1   There is a lot of ambiguities in Hamlet's character. You need, Will, to get him off the fence with his thoughts.

ACTOR 3   Just to follow up on that idea, I'm curious about—what's the girl's name?

WILL   Ophelia?

ACTOR 3   That's right, Ophelia—I hate that name, but that's beside the point. I don't think we know if Hamlet loves her or not.

AUDIENCE 1 It wasn't clear to me either.

ACTOR 3 Yes, the relationship needs to be defined more.

ACTOR 2 I agree.

ACTOR 3 A love scene wouldn't hurt, Will.

AUDIENCE 1 That's a great idea because one minute he's saying, get thee to a nunnery and at the grave scene he's whining that he loves her more than 40,000 brothers could.

ACTOR 5 I read that part and I'm still in a dither over who she is.

AUDIENCE 3 He's right. You need to set Hamlet's character more firmly, so we can get a handle on him.

ACTOR 5 As an actor, I didn't know what to play, Will—love? Hate? Distance? Closeness? Perturbation?

ACTOR 2 I agree.

AUDIENCE 2 Will, I don't want to tell you how to write your play, but perhaps you could cut Ophelia out altogether.

ACTOR 3 That's not a bad suggestion.

ACTOR 2 I agree.

AUDIENCE 2 I mean, this Ophelia goes deranged because her father's killed? That's not how derangement occurs. It's not. Does it? Am I wrong? My father was killed in the Spanish Armada Battle and I mourned, yes, but to start singing snatches of old ditties off-key and babbling in a stream, I don't think so . . .

WILL It was Hamlet, the man she loved, who killed her father and . . .

AUDIENCE 1 True. Yes. Polonius. He's tedious, Will.

ACTOR 2 I agree. I would take the suggestion, Will, to cut Ophelia, and if you do . . .

ACTOR 5 I pray you do . . .

ACTOR 2   Then you won't need Polonius either.

AUDIENCE 2   That's so, but then who does Hamlet stab behind the tapestry?

ACTOR 1   It could be anybody—Bernardo.

ACTOR 3   Come, come, why would Bernardo be in the Queen's chamber?

ACTOR 5   Why not? Everyone else seems to get in there.

ACTOR 1   Bernardo could be there to kill Hamlet for Claudius.

WILL   The idea was that Laertes comes back to avenge his father's killing.

AUDIENCE 4   Then you make Bernardo, instead of Ophelia, Laertes's brother.

ACTOR 5   Or his best friend, if I might add my two farthings here. I think the relationship between Horatio and Hamlet is ever so, so, so understated, Will.

ACTOR 2   I agree.

ACTOR 5   I would love to see this pairing developed, because I think Horatio is on Hamlet's tail at every turn and right now in this first draft it's begging to come out of the block of marble, Will. Horatio wants to be more than a yes man for this glorious protagonist. I wonder what would happen if Horatio's real feelings were—so to speak—fleshed out.

AUDIENCE 2   Will, might I add, there could be fewer set speeches on suicide.

AUDIENCE 3   Yes, that to be or not to be meditation is a month too long. He could say suicide in a rhyming couplet and make the same point.

ACTOR 2   I agree.

ACTOR 5 Cutting the long soliloquies, Will, would give you more time to spend on mother Gertrude. That bitch has driven that sweet boy to—well—talk to himself. You have an excellent scene in the bedroom where he rips her a new one. I want more of that, Will.

WILL More . . .

ACTOR 2 I agree.

WILL I see.

AUDIENCE 1 And lose the ghost in the bedroom scene.

AUDIENCE 2 I thought he was cutting the ghost.

AUDIENCE 1 If he keeps the ghost, I'm saying, he should, but let Gertrude see the ghost, too. Will, you should write a gripping scene for Gertrude and her cuckolded husband. Those two have to have it out.

ACTOR 2 I agree.

WILL That would throw the play off its arc.

ACTOR 1 Just think about it, Will, that's all, just think about it.

ACTOR 2 I agree.

AUDIENCE 1 Will, Rosencrantz and Guildenstern. They have to do more.

AUDIENCE 5 Which ones were they?

AUDIENCE 1 School chums from Wittenberg.

AUDIENCE 5 I was just thinking, Will, it would truly spice up your plot if one of them ran off with Ophelia.

ACTOR 2 I agree.

AUDIENCE 4 I thought he was cutting Ophelia.

ACTOR 1 We don't know if he is. We're just suggesting that Will cut Ophelia.

AUDIENCE 1 Nobody's said a word about Claudius. For my money, Will, Claudius is your most interesting character.

ACTOR 2 I agree.

AUDIENCE 1 Sure. Look at him, he killed his brother to steal the Queen. He committed incest, marrying his brother's wife. He took over Denmark on his own. This man has Machiavelli hostage in his balls, gentlemen. Will, I think it's Claudius's play.

WILL Claudius's play . . .

AUDIENCE 1 Yes. King Claudius, a tragedy. He is the meat of the story. Hamlet's just a visitor who walks about spouting philosophical screeds. Claudius is not petrified like Hamlet is. When you start to rethink this, Will, consider giving Claudius the ink instead of Hamlet.

ACTOR 2 I agree.

AUDIENCE 2 I liked the gravedigger scene. He's funny. It was my favorite scene. I would keep that scene in the rewrites minus the Yorick skull. Too gruesome.

AUDIENCE 5 I'd like to comment on the ending, the Fortinbras character.

WILL Yes . . . Fortinbras.

AUDIENCE 5 Yes. Fortinbras is nothing but *deus ex machina*, Will, or *Norway ex machina*.

ACTOR 2 I agree.

AUDIENCE 5 We never see this character in the play and all of a sudden, bold as a bare ass, he shows up to take over Denmark. He's not a character who rises organically from the storyline.

ACTOR 1 He could be cut, too, Will.

ACTOR 2 I agree.

[*As the lights begin an* adagio *fade.*]

ACTOR 1   Who was Voltimand?

ACTOR 2   He was a courtier.

ACTOR 3   Wasn't that Osric?

ACTOR 4   There's no Osric in the play.

ACTOR 5   I beg your pardon, but I read Osric.

ACTOR 4   Oh . . .

AUDIENCE 1   Did Osric have anything to do with Rosencrantz and Guildenstern?

AUDIENCE 2   We don't know. We don't need to know.

AUDIENCE 3   I still think the play needs a priest, Will.

AUDIENCE 4   Or a Bishop.

AUDIENCE 5   Have you thought, Will, of turning *Hamlet* into a comedy?

WILL   It hadn't occurred to me. Many of the things and remarks you made never occurred to me and I thank you heartily for all your suggestions. You've been so helpful.

ACTOR 2   I agree.

ACTOR 5   About the play within the play—the mousetrap—Will, is it possible to turn it into a musical? I'm just asking.

[*The stage is dark now.*]

ACTOR 1   [*In the dark.*] Will, put that bench down!

[*We hear a crash and a cry of pain.*]

• • •

Elzbieta Erased

John Guare

John Guare

John Guare is the Tony, Obie, and New York Drama Critics Circle Award-winning playwright of *House of Blue Leaves*, *Six Degrees of Separation*, *Landscape of the Body*, *A Few Stout Individuals*, and *A Free Man of Color*. He co-edits the *Lincoln Center Theater Review*, is a council member of the Dramatists Guild and a trustee of PEN America, and has received the Gold Medal in Drama from the American Academy of Arts and Letters.

··· production history ···

Elzbieta Erased was commissioned by the Atlantic Theatre Company, New York, and originally premiered on May 18, 2011, acted by John Guare (A) and Omar Sangre (B), then played at an art gallery on Vinalhaven Island, Maine, before the portrait that figures in the play. Is it scheduled to open at the Atlantic Theater, New York, May 2013, as part of an evening called 3 Kinds of Exiles, comprised of three one-act plays by Guare.

•••

[*A bare stage. Two actors appear.*]

A   If you go to the office of Andre Bishop—

B   the artistic director of Lincoln Center Theater—

A   you'll see on his wall a life-size painting of a woman who dares you to look away.

[*Projection #1 of the painting.*]

B   Look at that pose. Sexy—

A   Inviting—

B   Sad—

A   Defiant—

B   Seductive—

A   Lost.

B   Foreign.

A   Definitely foreign.

B   She is, as they say, of a certain age.

A   But the way she shows her leg is the way of a woman who has not given up on life.

B Is that Helen Mirren?

A Excuse me. It's not. It's a woman with an unpronounceable name—
Czyzewska.

B Spell it out. C-Z-Y-Z-E-W—

A Don't! We don't have that much time. She was the most popular
young actress in Poland in the 1960s.

B Classically trained at the Drama School in Warsaw.

A Specializing in the work of the Polish romantic tragedies of the
nineteenth century.

B [*In Polish, declaims the opening lines of "Pan tadeusz."*]
Litwo! Ojczyzno moja! ty jesteś jak zdrowie
Ile cię trzeba cenić, ten tylko się dowie,
Kto cię stracił.

[*Projection #1 out. Projection #2: ELZBIETA in Erotique.*]

A Young Polish women spoke like her—

B Dressed like her.

A They copied her hairdo.

B She appeared on television.

A She sang songs.

B She was the star actress at the leading theater in Warsaw.

A And then her life changed.
[*Projection #2 out.*]
The *New York Times* put great value on its Warsaw bureau, Poland
being the only Iron Curtain country that would tolerate the
presence of American journalists.

B In January 1965, they sent their current top young reporter, David
Halberstam—

A Who had won a Pulitzer Prize for his Vietnam reporting—

B To man the Warsaw bureau of the *New York Times*.

A One of his first assignments is to cover Arthur Miller, who is in Warsaw to attend rehearsals for his play *After the Fall*.

[*Projection #3: Arthur Miller in Warsaw talking to students.*]

B Miller talks to students about—

A Censorship—

B Critics—

A *The Misfits*, the screenplay he wrote for his wife, Marilyn Monroe.
[*Projection #3 out.*]
He described it as being—

B About "a certain type of person vanishing everywhere, a person not dependent on society but who lived by himself, and that in itself is a little sad."

A Do Miller and Halberstam recognize each other? Two tall, virile, craggy-faced, deep-voiced Jewish American intellectuals. Miller cannot stay for the opening.

B The Dramatyczny Theatre—the epicenter of theatrical life—invites David to the opening night.

A The theater had built a box with its own private entrance and lobby in case Joseph Stalin should ever appear in Warsaw and decided he wanted to see a show. Stalin never came. The box was now used for special visitors. David sits there.

B David already saw that theater meant something different in Poland. Back in America, theater meant Broadway—

A "The best damn musical I've seen in years."

B A hit comedy.

A "An orgy of laughter."

B An occasional serious drama.

A "A thunderbolt of emotion."

B The theater where David sat tonight was custodian of Poland's cultural identity.

A A place where classics could be kept alive and even subversively re-interpreted.

B The theater was a place of discussion.

A Of communion.

B In a totalitarian regime, a place of freedom. If theater in Poland was a temple—

A These actors were its priests. *After the Fall* begins.

B The translator accompanying David translates quietly.

[*Polish, then English.*]

"Chciałem tylko powiedzieć dzień dobry," I just wanted to say hello.

A David feels at home watching Miller's dissection of the boiling activity of New York life in the McCarthy era. And then Maggie— the Marilyn Monroe character—appears.

[*Projection #4: Elzbieta at her most beautiful.*]

B [*Polish.*] *"Przepraszam, czy nie widział pan człowieka z dużym psem? Czy mogę usiąść koło pana? Poczekam sobie, a pan będzie myślał?"*

A What is she saying?

B "'Scuse me, did you see a man with a big dog? Could I sit with you? While you're thinking?"

[*Back to Polish.*]

"Bo ja stałam tam i przyszedł jakiś człowiek z dużym psem i włożył mi smycz do ręki i poszedł sobie . . ."

A   Who is she?

B   Elzbieta Czyzewska. Shhhhhh.

A and B   [*First in Polish, then English.*] *"Maggie, pani jest bardzo piękna. Chciałbym, żeby pani bardziej o siebie dbała"* / You're very beautiful, Maggie. And I wish you knew how to take care of yourself.

A   David approaches her at the opening-night party. "Who are you?"

B   "Everyone in Poland knows who I am. And you don't? What a refreshing feeling."

[*Projection #4 out.*]

A   They start to see each other. He struggles to understand her few words of English and in that struggle hears music.

B   "My father murder in war. My mother send my sister—me—to nuns, to orphanage fill with children—in same boat! I become actress. You see me and don't know who I am."

A   David asks her to marry him.

[*Projection #5: News item. "Poland blocks wedding."*]

B   The Polish government tries to block the marriage.

[*Projection #5 out.*]

A   Why? Because every piece David sends back to New York is critical of Poland and its regime.

B   "Young people in Poland are not attracted by the Communist Party."

A   "Poland cool to President Johnson's plea for better relations."

B   On June 13, 1965—

A and B   They are married.

[*Projection #6: ELZBIETA and David's wedding photo.*]

A   After the wedding, David and Elzbieta drive to the Tenth Anniversary Stadium where thousands of fans await her.

[*Projection #6 out. Projection #7* ELZBIETA *on magazine cover.*]

B She receives the Golden Mask Award as the most popular star in Poland. Poland at her feet. An American on her arm.

[*Projection #7 out.*]

A Not just an American, but the very avatar of American capitalism, a Jew working for the *New York Times*.

B In what will be his last dispatch from Poland, Halberstam writes:

A "This is the particular tragedy of Polish daily life, a country struggling against itself. Because its population is strong, restless, and dissatisfied, the government cannot relax; because the government cannot relax, the population remains restless and alienated. It is the subject worthy of a very great novel, but if Poles are writing it now, they are writing it for their desk drawers."

B On December 27, 1965, Poland kicks David out of the country.

A Will she leave with him?

B Should she?

A "Come with me? Don't leave me. Come?"

B "I would not be a defector like Nureyev. Hadn't Grace Kelly left her country to become the wife of the prince of Monaco? I am no Madame Butterfly. My Pinkerton will take me back to America where—dream of dreams—we will live in New York City on East 61st street."

A A block known as the Gold Coast. The fairy tale will have a happy ending.

B And life begins in New York.

A They see people like Gay and Nan Talese.

B William and Rose Styron. Styron is charmed by the way she mangles English.

A   They go to Elaine's. The whole *Paris Review* crowd.

B   "Hello! Hello!" I *am* Princess Grace!

A   They have a second home in Nantucket. Life is very buoyant.

B   But there are no acting parts.

A   Her accent makes the English she speaks impenetrable.

B   "C-Z-Y-Z-E-W-S-K-A. In America my name sounds like a bad hand in Scrabble."

A   In 1967 David publishes a piece in *Harper's* magazine condemning life in Poland. "The business of getting up on a grey and dark day thinking dark thoughts about life . . . to ignore as best he can the government and the official life, to pretend if he can that these things don't exist."

B   The piece infuriates the Polish government.

A   But Mr. and Mrs. Halberstam are thousands of miles away on the Gold Coast.

B   At the same time Andrej Wajda, the great Polish director, announces a new film to be called *Everything for Sale*. He asks Elzbieta to star.

A   Hurrah! She comes back to Poland in January 1968 to play the lead in this story of the incestuous world of actors living in fantasy. She loved Wajda. They shared a devil-may-care attitude towards the steel fist of life in a Communist regime where your real life happened in your dreams. Elzbieta has returned! We will forgive her! "Welcome home! All is forgiven!"

B   [*Then in Polish.*] *Witaj w kraju! Wszystko wybaczone!*

[*Projection #8:* ELZBIETA *in* Everything for Sale.]

B   The subtitle reads: "*Do you like playing parts that are sad or funny?*"

A   She completes her filming.

[Projection #8 out.]

B   Will she stay? Surely she will not leave!

A   On April 13, 1968, she returns to New York.

B   At the Warsaw airport, passport control strip-searches her.

A and B   *[Polish and English.] Pani nazwisko? / Who are you?*
Przecież każdy wie, jak się nazywam. Wasze dziewczyny chcą wyglądać
tak, jak ja. Mówić jak ja. / Everyone knows who I am! Your
girlfriends look like me. Speak like me.
Powód wyjazdu? / Why are you leaving?
Jadę do męża. / To be with my husband.
Akt ślubu poproszę? / Do you have your proof of marriage?
Ślub był brany w Polsce? / Were you married in Poland?
Czy są jakieś inne dokumenty? / Do you have any other papers?
Czy małżonek jest żydem? / Your husband is a Jew.
Czy Pani małżonek jest żydowskim szpiegiem? / Is your husband a Jew
in the secret police?

A   The officials finally stamp her passport.

B   Poland grows smaller beneath her as her plane goes higher in the sky.

A   A few days later, the Polish newspapers and state-controlled television
denounce Elzbieta.

B   Miss Czyzewska "was for many years Poland's best-known actress,
having created unforgettable roles. I say 'was' because two years
ago, she married David Halberstam, the American journalist, and
left the country . . . for publishing dirty libels against our country."
She "was an excellent actress but her husband's article had
discredited her in the eyes of her admirers."

[Projection #9: News item damning wife of U.S. writer.]

A   She will not be allowed to return to Poland.

[Projection #9 out.]

B *Everything for Sale* will not be seen in America for nineteen years.

[*They switch lecterns.*]

A It was now 1973.

[*Projection #10: Photograph of John Wulp and John Guare.*]

A John Wulp, who would paint that portrait years later, and John Guare, a playwright, were starting a theater on Nantucket. Would there be a place in it for Elzbieta? They went to see her at her home on Coffin Street.

[*Projection #10 out.*]

A This legendary beauty must have now weighed in at three hundred pounds.

B Elzbieta chain-smoked long black cigarillos. What she was saying was hidden in a fortress of flesh. What could she play even if you could understand her? Wulp suggested she could teach the apprentices. David was irate.

A "A star of her magnitude, even if it was behind the Iron Curtain, does not work *behind* the scenes of the Nantucket Stage Company." No one saw her again that summer.

B Salvation! It's 1974. Wajda will come to America to New Haven, to the Yale Rep, to re-create his successful Polish production of Dostoevsky's *The Possessed* with a cast of American actors and Yale students.

A Wajda's production showed Dostoevsky's Russians trapped in a suicidal avalanche.

B The production touched a nerve in Poland.

A The Poles had a deep and precise knowledge of Russia.

B They lived with it every day.

A Wajda thumbs his nose at the Polish officials who had let him come to America.

B He casts Elzbieta as the wife who's been driven mad by love.

A She has slimmed down. You saw her former beauty, what David, what Poland fell in love with.

B She was acting! In English! "He called me his dove. He gave me a ring. He said, 'Look at it in the evening and I'll come to you in your sleep.' But my brother took my ring and drank it up. And now I'm alone every night. Every night."

A She and Wajda talk about home. She asks:

B "Why do you stay in Poland? Stay here."

A Wajda says:

B "Poland is my past and my future. . . . I want to take part in something vital. I have dreamt this all my life. . . . This is my hope."

A The *New York Times* called Wajda's production "extraordinary" and singled out a "wonderfully physicalized performance by the Polish star Elzbieta Czyzewska."

B A small part in the production is played by a student named Meryl Streep.

A Wajda returns to Poland. Elzbieta becomes a fixture at Yale Rep, playing in Strindberg's *The Father* with Rip Torn.

B Their daughter was played by that young Meryl Streep.

A It was about this time that her marriage to David started to crumble. By the end of 1975, she and David had split.

B There were rumors of domestic abuse. But not by David. No, by Elzbieta.

A Did she remember her speech from *The Possessed*?

B "You were ashamed of me. . . . Your very face changed. . . . No more kind words—just impatience, anger, the knife. . . . You want my death because I am in your way. . . . Assassin!"

A Did David remember that the Marilyn Monroe character's first line in *After the Fall* was her screaming at the Arthur Miller figure, "Liar! Judge!"

B [*In Polish.*] Kłamca! Oskarżyciel!

A They divorce.

B She does not see any of David's friends.

A She moves to a fourth floor walkup on 59th Street between the bridge and Bloomingdale's.

B William Styron calls occasionally to ask her details about life in Poland.

A She adorns the walls of her new apartment with silk scarves, transforming it into an Arabian tent.

B Her only companion is a Yorkie.

A Which she never takes out. As she smokes a long black cigarillo and sips a glass of red wine—

B She puts the dog into a wicker basket attached to a great length of rope.

A She lowers the basket four stories below to the garden of a neighbor she does not know.

B The dog does its business—

A Sniffs around and hops back into the basket—

B Which she then pulls back up to her apartment.

A Does she read about life in Poland in the *New York Times*?

B No *New York Times*!

A Nor does she write letters.

B In spite of being warned that the Polish secret police is wiretapping phones—

A   She calls friends back home.

B   A fellow actress, Halina Mikolojska.

A   "Hello, Halina!"

B   Their conversations steer clear of any controversy—

A   Namely all the things she wants to know—

B   Needs to know.

A   In 1979 William Styron publishes *Sophie's Choice*.

B   The book is written from the point of view of Stingo, a young Southern writer.

A   "I encountered Sophie in the flesh for the first time and fell, if not instantaneously, then swiftly and fathomlessly in love with her. . . . wonderfully negligent sexuality."

B   He hears Nathan, her lover, scream at her.

A   "You dumb fucking Polack. When are you going to learn to speak the language?"

B   Sophie: "Please don't go, Nathan. We need each *other*. Don't go!"

A   Nathan: "I need you like death."

B   At the end of the first chapter, Stingo realizes "with a dreamer's fierce clarity that she was doomed."

A   All her friends are sure when this is made into a movie, Sophie will be Elzbieta's part. "Elzbieta, don't you think this part was written for you?"

B   Silence. In 1979, Elzbieta got good news. Magda, her twelve-year-old niece, coming from Poland with a children's choir on an international tour, was given permission to go to Nantucket for one day and meet her aunt. Elzbieta had seen no one in her family now for eleven years.

A By chance, John Guare happened to see her walking along the Madeket Beach, her arm around Magda, gesticulating wildly. What was Elzbieta telling this child? What does one generation pass on to the next? Guare would write a play expressly for Elzbieta, who would play a Polish nanny in charge of a young American girl. He would set the play in nineteenth-century Nantucket.

B Now it's August 1980. Poland is on the front page of the *New York Times*, of every paper in the world!

A Dock workers, led by an electrician named—

B Lech Walesa

A Protesting high food prices, do the impossible.

B Lech Walesa scales the walls of the Lenin shipyard at Gdansk and calls a strike.

A Within two weeks, the strike sweeps to twenty other cities.

B On August 31, the Polish government negotiates with the workers and allows them the right to strike.

A The Solidarity movement soon has ten million members.

B Elzbieta is astonished. What's happening? Is this the first step toward freedom in her country? Can she go home?

A She tries to call her friend Halina for more news. She can't get through. She keeps calling.

B Does she think of Adam Mickiewicz's *Ode to Youth*, written in 1820 but still to the point.

A and B [*English, then Polish.*] "Hail, hail thou dawn of man's new liberty! / Salvation's sunrise will disperse the night." // "*Witaj, jutrzenko swobody / Zbawienia za tobą słońce!*"

A She has hope.

B   In 1981, actors did a workshop performance in New York of Guare's play *Lydie Breeze*.

A   She was magical.

B   "This night. This beach. We are what we are for only a few moments in our lives. My moment came loving you. You in me. That's all I have."

A   In December 1981, General Jaruzelski takes charge of Poland and declares martial law.

B   The new government arrests Walesa and other Solidarity leaders.

A   Elzbieta calls Wajda. No answer.

B   She calls her friend Halina. A voice on the other end of the line tells her Halina has been imprisoned.

A   The play for Elzbieta is ready for production. Louis Malle will direct.

B   At a party a few days before rehearsals, Elzbieta got drunk and out of control.

A   Louis Malle called the playwright.

B   "I will not direct the play if she is in it. Make a choice. Her or me."

A   "Elzbieta? The part I wrote for you is no longer yours."

B   Silence. "Fine," she said, lighting a long black cigarillo.

A   The playwright changed her role to that of an Irish girl. The actress who played the part was very good. It wasn't the magic of Elzbieta.

B   And then production began on the movie of *Sophie's Choice*. The part went to Meryl Streep.

[*Projection #11: Meryl Streep as Sophie.*]

A   Elzbieta had never been considered. Meryl won the Oscar for Best Actress.

[Projection #11 out.]

B Did Meryl have Elzbieta's voice in her head when she played Sophie?

A Was Meryl giving Elzbieta's performance?

B No, no, no. Meryl worked very hard with a vocal coach on getting her Polish accent right.

A Her friends didn't care. Meryl had stolen her part.

B They needed Elzbieta as their own personal tragic heroine, deepening their lives.

A At this time, a young Polish actress named Joanna Pa-cu-la.

B Pacula.

A We pronounced it Pa-cu-la—arrives in New York and shows up at Elzbieta's door.

B Joanna knows no one in America.

A She worships Elzbieta, who is still whispered about in Poland.

B Elzbieta takes her in.

A She learns what's happening in Poland.

B Solidarity is outlawed. Halina is out of prison. Because of his work with Solidarity, the government will not allow Andrej Wajda to make films in Poland. He has moved to Berlin, where he is working in television. Elzbieta has a friend.

A Elzbieta shows the young woman New York—

B Teaches her how to dress—

A Passes on hard-earned knowledge—

B Things that had been taught her—

A By the nuns—

B By Wajda—

A By her friend Halina—

B What it means to be an actor—

A How to behave with these Americans.

B She introduces her to everyone she knows.

A What fun!

B They are friends. Until—

A Joanna gets the lead in a Hollywood thriller called *Gorky Park*—

B Thanks to people she met through Elzbieta.

A Joanna moves to Hollywood—

B And ditches Elzbieta.

A "Elzbieta, she *used* you!" All her friends say that.

B Silence. She lights a cigarillo.

A She becomes an increasingly maddening friend.

B Midnight calls.

A Drunken suicide threats.

B "What reason to live? I am so alone."

A "You're not alone. Come to us. Stay."

B She'd arrive, carrying a bottle of brandy.

A "Oh. Please go."

B "Don't leave me! I cannot be alone!"

A Her calls to Poland become more erratic and dangerous to the people she phones.

B Numbers are not answered.

A Numbers are changed.

B Numbers are not in service.

A   She now lives in a small walkup on West 43rd Street near 7th Avenue.

B   On the street she finds a black dog—

A   A skipperje—

B   A dog bred in Holland to live on a barge and warn its captain of any arrivals.

A   She names the dog Halinka after her imprisoned friend.

B   She and the dog become as inseparable as she and Halina were in Warsaw.

A   Halinka barked and growled nonstop at anyone who dared approach Elzbieta.

B   People stayed away.

A   But people still believed in her.

B   In 1986 Janusz Glowacki, a Polish playwright living in New York, wrote *Hunting Cockroaches* for her about Polish émigré actors living in New York. She'll be perfect!

A   Arthur Penn would direct it at the Manhattan Theater Club. He did not know Elzbieta's work.

B   They meet. Elzbieta behaves in a lifeless manner, cold, distant, charmless.

A   He chooses Dianne Wiest for the role. Had Elzbieta botched her audition on purpose?

B   Her friends became a Greek chorus commenting on her downward spiral.

A   "The most famous émigré in history is Medea. What nearer and dearer thing for the childless Elzbieta to slaughter than her talent."

B   A young Polish director comes to New York to interview Elzbieta for a film he wants to make about Elzbieta and that treacherous young actress.

A It'll be a Polish *All About Eve*.

B She tells him everything.

A She tells her friends she will be playing the Bette Davis part.

A and B [*English, then Polish.*] "Fasten your seat belts. It's going to be a bumpy night." / "*Zapnij pasy. To będzie noc pełna wrażeń.*"

B Finally, nineteen years later, in 1987, *Everything for Sale* finds a release in America!

A She will be seen!

[*Projection #12:* ELZBIETA *in the film.* "*Do you prefer to play parts that are sad or funny?*"]

B The film opens.

A Disaster.

[*Projection #12 out.*]

B In 1987, the film about Elzbieta and the actress is made.

A It is called *Anna*.

B The nationalities have been changed—

A From Polish—

B To Czech.

A The role of the older actress went to an American named Sally Kirkland, who learned an accent.

B Sally Kirkland is nominated for an Academy Award for Best Actress.

A Sally Kirkland does not win.

B In 1989, Lech Walesa, the former dock worker, now freed from jail—

A Now the winner of the Nobel Peace Prize—

B Soon to become the President of Poland—

A   Visits New York City as a hero. When he sees Elzbieta at a reception in his honor, he says:

B   "Mrs. Czyzewska, why did you leave Poland? I was in love with you! And hoped to marry you someday!"

A   Elzbieta smiles and bows to him.

B   In 1989, she learns her friend Halina has died in Poland.

[*They switch lecterns.*]

A   And then in 1990 people saw her—

B   And she was different.

A   She had stopped drinking.

B   Elaine Stritch had become fascinated by this tortured soul and helped her.

A   Elaine Stritch? *That* Elaine Stritch?

B   Yes, Elaine Stritch had rescued her. Elzbieta was sober.

A   In 1990, Elzbieta won an Obie for Mac Wellman's *Crowbar*, playing a nineteenth-century actress come alive in an abandoned twentieth-century theater.

B   She won a prize for playing a ghost.

[*Projection #13: The life-size portrait of* ELZBIETA.]

A   John Wulp painted this portrait in 1995.

B   She came to his studio carrying a suitcase.

A   She put on this red dress.

B   This shawl.

A   She began dancing.

B   The painting did not sell. For starters, no one had a room big enough to hang it.

A   Andre Bishop had a large empty wall in his office at Lincoln Center. He'd hang the painting there till it found a buyer. It's still there.

B   She would show up at Andre Bishop's office.

A   She would sit and smoke and stare at the portrait for hours.

B   Has she ever appeared there?

A   No.

B   So she's hanging in a theater where she's never worked. Typical Polish destiny.

[*Projection #13 out.*]

A   The Berlin Wall comes down. The Soviet Union breaks up. She could go back home.

B   Elzbieta chose *Six Degrees of Separation* to make her return.

A   She called Andrej Wajda:

B   "Does Poland have any young black actors?"

A   "Yes. I am teaching an African Polish student named Omar Sangare at the Academy where you studied. His mother is Polish. His father is from Mali. Omar is also a member of the company at the theater where you played *After the Fall*."

B   "When she called, I thought it was a joke. Czyzewska calling me from America? I had heard of her. She belonged to another time. She sent me and the theater a copy of the play. Yes! *We would do Six Degrees of Separation!*"

   [*Six Degrees in Polish.*]

   "*Szósty stopień oddalenia!*"

A   She would return to the very theater in which she had triumphed in *After the Fall*.

[*Projection #14: The theater with the banner announcing the play.*]

B Reporters flocked to see her.

A "Do you still dislike the Polish culture you had turned your back on?"

B Silence.

A "Why did you leave Poland when you were so famous?"

B Silence. She thought they'd be friendly.

A "What awards have you won?"

B An Obie.

A "No Tonys? No Oscars? What is an Obie?"

B Rumors of her drinking had preceded her.

A "Are you drinking?"

B "I have not had a drink for five years."

[*Projection #14 out.*]

A The theater would house her.

B They gave her a cot in the lobby to Stalin's box.

A Rehearsals began.

> [*Projection #15:* ELZBIETA *and Omar Sangare in a scene from* Six Degrees.]

> "Imagination. That's God's gift to make the act of self-examination bearable."

B "Wyobraźnia. To dar od Boga, który sprawia, że próba samego siebie jest do zniesienia."

> The new theater people had no memory of her bravura style of acting, even feeling there was no truth in it.

A The director cut all references to Sidney Poitier. Poitier was not known in Poland.

[*Projection #15 out.*]

B She was still a figure of controversy.

A Her old fans came to see her.

B "Should she have left?"

A "Should she have come back?"

B Some said she is magnificent.

A Some said she's not as great as we thought.

B She received very unfair notices.

A She became sick during the run but did not miss any performances. No one came backstage to see her. She stayed on her cot in the lobby leading to Stalin's box. She did not drink. After a few months, she received a letter.

B "Your contract is up. You must vacate Stalin's lobby immediately."

A The director kept the play running and erased—replaced Elzbieta with his wife. She came home.

B "I went back to Poland to learn, for better or worse, I am an American."

A She returned to her walkup on West 43rd Street.

B Condé Nast had begun constructing a sixty-seven-story office building directly behind her on West 42nd Street.

A One morning, a steel beam plunged down vertically from the top of the construction site and pierced through Elzbieta's building, slicing her small apartment, the entire building, in half.

B Amazingly, no one was killed.

A She was at home when it happened. "It must have been terrifying."

B She lights a cigarillo. "No. It was another event to happen on another day."

A The city gave each of the dispossessed tenants two hundred dollars to buy a cell phone until they could return to their apartments.

B Elzbieta spent her two hundred dollars on a pair of new shoes. Very high, skinny heels. Tiny straps.

A Not the best pair of shoes for a homeless person.

B She stayed on sofas of various people she knew. She did not drink.

A She played the maid in *Hedda Gabler* with Elizabeth Marvel at New York Theater Workshop. She sat at the side of the stage for the entire performance, smoking.

B Beth Marvel felt as if Elzbieta herself was controlling the events of Hedda's life.

A Beth became fascinated by this mysterious silent creature and came to John Guare with an idea to make an evening about Elzbieta's life. In it, Beth would ask Elzbieta all the questions she never got a chance to ask during the run of *Hedda Gabler*. John would make it into a play for the two women. They made a date with her.

B "Yes. I would like this very much."

A Elzbieta met them at a café on West 43rd Street.

B She carried a manila envelope—

A Which she opened.

B She showed them photos of herself as a girl—

A A teen—

B A young actress—

A All her stage roles—

B Articles in fan magazines—

A 45-rpm records of her singing—

B   Stills of her in films. "*Erotique*, a three-minute experimental film that put me on the map. Look at my Golden Mask Award!"

A   "Yes, this is interesting but we wanted to focus on your life after you met David and moved to America."

B   "Who would be interested in that? My life in Poland—that would be wonderful. I could wear these clothes and sing these songs. They are like the bubblegum pop of today."

A   They finished lunch silently. Later, John Guare wondered if David Halberstam had supported Elzbieta all these years on the proviso that she never speak about their life together.

B   In 2007 David Halberstam was killed in a traffic accident.

A   She came raging to John Guare's apartment.

B   "Did you see that obituary in the *New York Times*? A short-lived marriage to a Polish actress? Since when is eleven years short-lived? I will not be the official skeleton in the closet of David Halberstam! I'm going to that funeral."

A   "No. You'll make a scene. It's not fair to his wife, to his daughter. Your marriage is truly over. Going to the funeral doesn't do anything for anyone, including you."

B   She didn't go.

A   She didn't drink. Before she died of esophageal cancer at the age of seventy-two, she clutched her pack of black cigarillos in her hospital room and said:

B   "My only friend."

A   Her obituary in the *New York Times* mentioned her legendary bad luck.

B   She had a sparsely attended memorial at Actors Studio in April 2010.

A   Elzbieta's niece, Magda, now a beautiful woman, had come to New York to collect Elzbieta's ashes. John Guare asked her what

Elzbieta had said to her that day when she was a child in Nantucket.

B "Probably exhorting me to always be a lady."

A Guare remembered something Elzbieta had said years before.

B "I'm looking at that person I was. I'm dancing with David because he shows off my dress so nicely, and it's like walking in the mountains, whistling and knocking a little pebble in front of you because you're so joyful. And then that pebble goes down the mountain and starts an avalanche, and you find yourself descending with that avalanche and you say, I was only walking in the mountains. I didn't mean for that whole thing to happen."

A Magda took Elzbieta's ashes back to Warsaw. The government gave her the distinction of allowing her to be buried in the Lane of Honor, a place reserved for Polish heroes.

B The papers did not consider her burial a newsworthy event.

A Thirty or so people came to the service.

B Actors, playwrights.

A Did Andrej Wajda come?

B Maybe he hadn't heard about it.

A The mourners were heard grumbling:

B "How dare she be buried in the Lane of Honor?"

A "She was the opposite of a hero."

B "She thought only of herself."

A "No one was more talented but many were more loyal."

B The actor Daniel Olbrychski, who had played opposite her in *Everything for Sale*, cried out that he hoped Elzbieta was not seeing this miserable performance with such a low number of spectators.

As they buried her, he recited her favorite poem. Elizabeth Bishop's great poem.

A "W sztuce tracenia nie jest trudno dojść do wprawy"

B "The art of losing isn't hard to master."

A I hope she's at peace.

B How did she hold together for so long?

A What did she have to stay sober for? What did life hold for her?

B You don't understand her kind of courage.

[*Polish for* "courage."]

Odwaga.

A Had David Halberstam identified her brand of courage—*odwaga*—all those years before in his infamous *Harper's* magazine piece that had sealed Elzbieta's fate? "Courage is a matter of someone who is really and truly afraid and yet carries on, as in war, someone who knows fear and yet gets up and keeps going each day. Courage in the totalitarian society is the ability to wait. . . ."

B To wait. Yes.

A For what?

B Freedom.

A and B [*English then Polish.*] "Hail, hail thou dawn of man's new liberty!/ Salvation's sunrise will disperse the night." // "*Witaj, jutrzenko swobody / Zbawienia za tobą słońce!*"

[*Projection #16: The portrait appears.*]

B Look at her portrait.

A Her name is Czyzewska.

B C—

A   Z—

B   Y—

A   Z—

B   E—

A   W—

B   S—

A   K—

B   A.

A   David looks at her. "Who are you?"

B   "Everyone in Poland knows who I am. And you don't? What a refreshing feeling."

[*Projection #18: The portrait. Zooms in on close up of her head, then her face, then her eyes. Then darkness.*]

• • •

Warner Bros.

Andrea Sloan Pink

Andrea Sloan Pink

Andrea Sloan Pink wrote and produced *The Best and Brightest*, a televised film festival of early works by American film directors. Her first play, *The Physiology of Solar Flares*, received a full production in the Francis Ford Coppola One-Act Festival at UCLA. Andrea's *Hollywood Trilogy* of plays includes *Les Hollywood Hills*, *Warner Bros.*, and *The Golden Age*. Her other plays include *Origami*, *Ode to Provence*, *Light*, and *The Horse Latitudes*. She received her BA and MFA in screenwriting from UCLA School of Film and Television. She earned her Juris Doctorate from UCLA School of Law in intellectual property. She is an award-winning poet, playwright, and essayist.

··· production history ···

Warner Bros. received a staged reading on January 28, 2012, at the Empire Theater, Santa Ana Artists Village, California.

> Producer: Eric Eberwein, OCPA Discoveries
>
> Director: Jenni Dillon
>
> **TINA**   Jennifer Pearce
>
> **LOLA**   Christine Krumme
>
> **STU**   Joseph Hernandez
>
> **WILL**   Adam Ferry

time

One summer in the 1980s

setting

The Warner Brothers lot in Burbank, California

The Office: Cheap secretarial furniture and push-button telephones. A large metal Rolodex sits on one desk. The other holds a dictionary and porcelain Woodstock pencil cup.

Stu's Cadillac: A bench seat from an old Caddy thrown onstage. A dashboard with 8-track tape would be super.

Mulholland: The suggestion of a hill with sagebrush or tumbleweeds. A fan offstage can create wind if you're feeling fancy. Likewise, a rear-stage floor of slowly twinkling lights can suggest the city.

characters

> **TINA**, 20s. Attractive and smart. Her clothes might be business poetic.
>
> **LOLA**, 20s. Beautiful enough to be an actress or model. Dresses provocatively.
>
> **STU**, 30s. Dumpy. Solid. Does not have the looks or the moves.

WILL, 20s. A writer. You know how writers dress: 501s, T-shirt, beat-up leather jacket.

• • •

···scene 1···

[TINA *sits at a desk.* LOLA *sits on the floor. She sorts a stack of head shots she has piled between her legs.*]

TINA   He says to me, I knew I should have married you. And I'm thinking, what the hell are you talking about? It's not as if you ever kissed me!

LOLA   But you think he's handsome, right?

TINA   Of course he's handsome. Everybody thinks he's handsome. I guess he's handsome.

LOLA   Yeah, and you know he'll make a lot of money.

TINA   And? What's your point?

LOLA   Don't you want to be rich?

TINA   Of course! But he's got a long face, plus that hair! And who's he trying to fool with that mustache?

LOLA   But Duke's gonna be rich. You know he's gonna be rich.

TINA   Maybe. But how am I ever gonna forget that he used to drive an orange Gremlin?

LOLA   Good point. You think you're too good for him and it's gonna come back and bite you in the butt.

TINA   Maybe.

LOLA   And you're gonna be wishing.

TINA   I doubt it. I'm going to make it on my own. I don't need him or any other guy.

LOLA   Just wait. You're going to see.

···scene 2···

[TINA *and* STU *sit on the bench seat of his old Cadillac. And I'm not talking about a romantic, old, nostalgic Cadillac. I'm talking about a piece of shit Cadillac that's too big an old man car for a guy this young to drive. They pass a joint between them.*]

TINA   You sure Rich isn't going to know?

STU   How's he going to know?

TINA   Like maybe he's going to smell it?

STU   If he does, he'll probably just ask me for some.

TINA   What the hell is that?

[TINA *motions to the 8-track.*]

STU   What?

TINA   That.

STU   8-track deck.

[STU *pulls out a box filled with 8-track tapes.*]

TINA   Seriously.

STU   What? Was that before your time? I got my whole life in here.
[STU *rummages through the box.*]
"Smoke on the Water." Neil Young. This is good shit.

TINA   You don't think this is a problem, do you?

STU   What?

TINA   Well, like the fact that we're sitting here at 8 o'clock in the morning getting stoned.

STU   What's the problem with that? Anyway, speak for yourself. I'm not getting stoned.

TINA   You don't think it means something?

STU   Like what?

TINA   Like maybe we're not happy?

STU   I'm just taking the edge off.

TINA   At my high school, we had a name for people like you.

STU   Yeah?

TINA   Loadie. Stoner.

STU   We had a name for people like you.

TINA   Yeah?

STU   Stuck-up bitch.

TINA   Nice. So there's this guy—I think he likes me. At least Lola thinks he likes me.

STU   She would know.

TINA   He keeps asking me out.

STU   Then go out with him. Not like I want the competition or nothing.

TINA   Nah. I just got to wait and see.

STU   Man, I got a headache.

   [STU *reaches across* TINA, *brushing her. He bops the glove box with his fist. The door drops open. He grabs a bottle of Tylenol and shakes a few into his hand.*]

   Oh shit! Here comes Rich!

TINA   Time to hit the phones.

[STU *pops pills into his mouth and swallows. They scramble out of the car.*]

···scene 3···

[TINA *stands alone in the office.*]

TINA   And when I'm driving to work—I mean, I got this crappy car. Totally unromantic. I wanted a Karmann Ghia and instead I ended up with a diesel Rabbit off of auction. Life is like that, you know? Anyway, when I'm driving to work, the sun is always too bright when I come over Barham. I get on the 101 at Highland and then I've got to do this five-lane switch over to get to the exit, and it's like every time I think I'm going to die on my way to the friggin, pointless, dead-end job, and then I crest over Barham and I'm coming down to the lot, and if the light passes over, I can see it, the wall painters. They'll be there in the early morning light, under the water tower, dangling off the wall in a harness and they'll be painting the sunglasses on Tom Cruise's face in super-size and I just think, isn't that the coolest thing? Isn't that the coolest thing to see the guy painting the billboard for a movie that's coming out of my studio even though all I'm doing is answering some guy's phone?

[*The phone begins ringing.* TINA *answers.*]

Good morning, John Daniels's office. Please hold. Good morning, John Daniels's office. Please hold for John Daniels.

[TINA *picks up one of the lines.*]

Yes, Mr. Daniels wants to know when his VCR will be repaired. Uh-huh. Uh-huh. I'll tell him. Yes, I tell him next time to take the porn tape out before he brings it in. Mr. Daniels's office, please hold. Mr. Daniels's office, please hold. Drinks at Trumps. Dinner at Morton's. New tires for the Jag.

[TINA *hangs up the phone.*]

We've got to have the story meeting on Rich's boat once a month so he can write the whole boat off on his taxes. We're sitting down there on deck, and the boat's tied to dock in Marina del Rey, and the wind is whipping and we're all huddled together in the cold, shouting at each other over the gusting wind about the announcements in *Publishers Weekly*.

[*The phone rings again.* TINA *answers.*]

Oh, hi, Duke. No, I can't go out tonight. I have to do John's expenses.

[TINA *hangs up phone and crosses to a window looking out on the lot.*]

What is the value of something old? People look at this lot with its crumbling ghost town and huge sound stages full of used backdrops and they just see the face of it. They don't see the Polish brothers, Hirz, Aaron, Szmul, and Ithzak. Those were their secret names, their hidden names. To the outside world, they were Harry, Albert, Sam, and Jack. They started with a single projector, showing silent films at the Cascade Theater in Pennsylvania. These sound stages were built in 1928. How many hopefuls toiled here, pounding away at a wooden framed backdrop, dreaming of getting into the union? This whole place is a ghost town. You feel their spirits moving through the offices, through the old lath and plaster walls. It's the same dust the cowboys rode through when they shot *High Noon*. I don't have a romantic view of it. No, I don't. As far as I'm concerned, hope has a bitter aftertaste.

··· scene 4 ···

[*An evening after work. The lights are low in the office.* TINA *and* LOLA *lie on their backs on the floor. They have been drinking.*]

TINA and LOLA [*Singing.*] Whatever Lola wants
Lola gets
And little man, little Lola wants you
Make up your mind to have no regrets
Recline yourself, resign yourself, you're through
I always get what I aim for
And your heart 'n' soul is what I came for.

TINA Ah, man, I should have learned my lesson.

LOLA What?

TINA Never get drunk on Kahlua and cream.

LOLA Deadly.

TINA I can't fall asleep and the room is spinning.

LOLA Hey, remember that guy at Ports?

TINA Steve Koffler?

LOLA Yeah. He pushed me into the bathroom when you went to get a drink.

TINA Don't tell me that! You are ruining my night! You didn't do anything, did you?

LOLA What's anything?

TINA You didn't! I wasn't gone but a couple of minutes!

LOLA Oh man, I remember it.

TINA Bitch!

LOLA Don't call me that! That hurts my feelings! You know you love me!

TINA That was my guy!

LOLA Was.

TINA You are such a dishonest—slut.

LOLA Not like it was a one-night stand!

TINA What, so this went on?

LOLA It's not like I'm a cheap—

TINA Oh no, no, no. Whatever Lola wants, Lola gets.

LOLA [*Singing along.*] Whatever Lola wants, Lola gets.

[TINA *smacks at her playfully.* TINA *and* LOLA *are laughing happily as lights fade.*]

···scene 5···

[STU *sits alone in the car.* TINA *looks around furtively before climbing in.*]

TINA   Don't your friends back home give you a ration for being a
secretary?

STU   I'm not a secretary. I'm an executive assistant.

TINA   Still.

[TINA *lights a joint with the car cigarette lighter.*]

STU   Are you kidding me? As far as they know, I am a big success. I'm
living out here in California, in the palm trees and sunshine and
working in the movie biz. I'm the biggest thing that ever happened
to them. I'm the king!

TINA   Yeah!

STU   They're stuck out there on the South Side a' Chicago. Ever been?

TINA   No.

STU   Those guys is nothing but a bunch of losers. All just hanging out
in Hughey Watson's backyard drinking Pabst.

TINA   But don't you wonder if, you know, there's something more?

STU   No. I recommend that you don't either. Not if you want to be
happy like me.

TINA   I don't know.

STU   Next time you have that thought, get a cat. Get a cat. That's my
advice.

···scene 6···

[TINA *alone in the office.*]

TINA   Some days, when I'm alone, I take my lunch out to the ghost
town. I walk down the back lot, onto the dusty street with the

Western facades. I've got my cheap black pumps on and they're getting dusty, but do I care? And I get up onto the boardwalk, and the wooden boards are creaking beneath my feet and I push open the swinging door of the saloon. It's cool and dark in there, and I pull up a crate and sit down. Once my eyes adjust, I can see the millions of layers of faded wallpaper on the walls, each one like another year passing by. I open up my bag with my banana and my yogurt and I'm thinking about gunslingers and my future and how I'm gonna get there, and I don't know why I'm crying, but it's just so hard, so hard to see.

···scene 7···

[TINA *is crying. She sits on the floor with her back slumped against the desk.* LOLA *enters.*]

LOLA   What happened?

TINA   [*Crying.*] He called me stupid! He kept screaming, "You stupid—, You stupid— You'll never make it here!"

LOLA   What? John?

TINA   He got a call from an agent at CAA and I kept him on hold too long and he hung up and that was it! He just started yelling at me!

LOLA   Bastard. Quit. Quit!

TINA   I can't quit!

LOLA   Well, you can't put up with this, him berating you, abusing you.

TINA   No. He was right. I should of—

LOLA   What?

TINA   I should have known to put him through. Just, like, one second sooner. I know who he is. Shit, I used to work at CAA! I should have put him through!

LOLA Don't be ridiculous. You're blaming yourself. You told him he was on the line, right? He knew he was on the line.

TINA But I should have gone in. I should have made him get off.

LOLA There's nothing you could have done. You can't make him get off. John's an adult. He's mad at himself. That's why he's yelling at you. He knows he screwed up.

TINA Everything he said about me is true. You're right, I should quit.

LOLA Hell no! Let him fire you!

TINA I don't want to get fired!

[TINA *starts crying again.*]

LOLA Come on, look! Look. Look at me! And here she is, ladies and gentlemen, Miss Placerville, Lola Philabenautry! Sounds of crowds roaring.

[LOLA *struts like a victorious beauty queen.*]

TINA What was your talent again?

LOLA Classical accordion. I played Chopin and stuff.

TINA That is so cool.

LOLA I mean, screw the bastard. Really. You are too smart for him.

···scene 8···

[STU *and* TINA *in the car.*]

TINA Don't you want to move on?

STU Sure, but you gotta pay your dues.

TINA But you've paid yours, right? You've been here six years.

STU Rich says they're gonna move me up soon. They pay me good.

TINA I don't know how long I can hold on.

STU What am I gonna do, quit? Just 'cause things aren't moving as fast as I want?

TINA I don't know.

STU You see *The Graduate*?

TINA Sure.

STU One day I'm gonna make a film like that. Just a small film, you know? No action or nothing. But important.

TINA I just don't see how you get there from here.

STU What are you talking about?

TINA You know, from what we're doing and all.

STU Are you kidding me? Rich Goldstein is one a' the biggest producers in this business! We are learning this thing from the inside out! Every phone call, every whisper, every maneuver, we are there!

TINA Yeah, I guess.

STU Just you wait! One day, one day we're gonna get our day in the sun!

···scene 9···

TINA He caught me in a moment of weakness.

LOLA So you said yes?

TINA Uh-huh.

LOLA Oh my God. How was it?

TINA I said I'd go with him to this thing, this awards event. There we were, at the Egyptian Theater, Duke, me, Duke's boss, and his wife. And I'm wearing my one dress.

LOLA The Joseph Magnin?

TINA Yeah. The one I bought on sale. And the wife's got this Judith Leiber purse in the shape of an Oscar, covered with hundreds of little gold crystals. That thing must have cost as much as an entire month of my salary.

LOLA Wow. You're so lucky.

TINA And they're telling me how great Duke is, as if he's their long-lost son. And he keeps looking at me, you know, like is this having any effect?

LOLA So?

TINA So what?

LOLA So did it?

TINA What? Make me fall in love with him?

LOLA Yeah.

TINA Not exactly. I just don't feel it.

LOLA So what happened?

TINA So the ride home was really tense, right.

LOLA Uh-huh.

TINA And then we get to my door.

LOLA Oh my God. I can't believe it. You did it. He put the moves on you.

TINA We're standing there on my porch, under the porch light, and he moves in, and that's when I see his mustache twitch, just this tiny little—twitch, and I suddenly have in mind one of those caterpillars, the black and red ones? And the next thing I know, I'm saying, "I have to go in now. I have to get up early to have my teeth cleaned."

LOLA Ow!

TINA That pretty much took the wind out of his sails.

LOLA Oh my God! I have to remember that one! Except, I usually want to get laid.

TINA I just couldn't—my brain said yes, but my body said no.

LOLA He is going to spend the rest of his life getting back at you.

TINA It's just that I've known him forever. If I do it, I have to be all in. It's not as if it will be easy to extricate myself.

LOLA You don't think you could just—get a taste?

TINA It's radioactive. One kiss with him would have a half-life of a million years.

···scene 10···

[*Morning light.* TINA *sits alone in* STU's *Cadillac. She smokes a joint and stares thoughtfully out the windshield. After some time,* STU *gets in. He is carrying a cardboard file box.*]

STU Hey.

TINA Hey.

STU I heard about your date.

TINA News travels fast.

STU Probably just as well.

TINA Yeah.

STU I never saw you two together anyway.

TINA Me neither.

STU That's because I know you're secretly in love with me.

TINA Right. Why aren't you in there?

STU Rich isn't coming in today.

TINA That's weird.

STU That's what I thought when he asked me to clear his calendar.

TINA What's in the box?

STU Nothing.

[TINA *hands* STU *the joint. When he takes it, she grabs off the box lid. First she takes out a red college dictionary. Then a Woodstock character pencil cup.*]

TINA Hey, this is your pencil cup.

[STU *grabs back the box.*]

STU Gimme that.

TINA What is this shit?

STU My stuff.

TINA This isn't yours.

[TINA *pulls out a bunch of matchbooks.*]

STU Just get out of the car, okay?

TINA Did they can you?

STU I got somewhere to go.

TINA Really? Why do you have Rich's matchbooks in here?

STU Get out.

TINA They fired you, and Rich didn't even have the decency to come in? After all these years?

STU I gotta headache. Do you mind?

[STU *motions for her to get out. She doesn't budge. He bops the glove box and it falls open. He takes a couple of Tylenol from the bottle and downs them. They both sit in stunned silence.*]

Up until yesterday, I had hope. I really thought I was gonna do it. That somehow, everything was gonna go my way. But last night, I had this weird feeling in the pit of my stomach, and I just thought, you know what, Stu, what if it doesn't? What then?

TINA And what was your answer?

STU I didn't have one. It was just this big, ugly blank. It had never occurred to me before. And I realized, all the holding on, all the waiting, all the stuff I've given up, the parties I didn't go to because I was working. What was the point of all that? I'm never gonna make a film. I'm never gonna get the chance. Look at me. I'm thirty-two years old and paunchy and—it is never gonna happen for me.

TINA It could. What are you going to do?

STU What do you mean, what am I going to do?

TINA You're gonna give it more time, right? You're almost there, right?

STU No.

TINA Stu, you can't give up now. You've got important work to do. You're the only one who can do it. Who else can tell your story?

STU You don't get it, Tina. No one is interested in my story.

TINA You'll get back on your feet. I'll set you up with my friend at CAA. You want me to call Duke? He's connected.

STU No. I'm going back to Chi-town.

TINA You gonna tell them?

STU Hell no. I'm going to give them all matches from Uncle Rich. They're gonna lift me up on their shoulders. They're gonna carry me around Hughey Watson's backyard and they're all gonna shout, "Hail King Stu! All Hail King Stu!"

[STU *begins to cry softly.*]

TINA Don't, Stu. Come on.

[TINA *tries to comfort him, awkwardly at first, and then wrapping her arms around him. He rests his head on her shoulder like a dog who hasn't laid his head down in years.*]

It's gonna be okay.

[STU *pulls back. He looks up at her. After a long moment, she kisses him gently on the lips.*]

STU   That wasn't—a sympathy kiss, was it?

TINA   No. Not entirely.

···scene 11···

[*Sunset light of orange and magenta color the evening sky. STU sits alone in his Cadillac. He puts an 8-track in the deck. Simon & Garfunkel's "Sound of Silence" begins to play.*]

···scene 12···

[TINA *sits at her desk. STU's desktop is empty. LOLA enters. She sets a tall stack of scripts on TINA's desk.*]

LOLA   I've been thinking.

TINA   Yeah?

LOLA   My parents—they have a spot for me.

TINA   And?

LOLA   I think I'm gonna take it. We own the hardware store in Placerville. It's on the main street.

TINA   Sounds kinda cute.

LOLA   Yeah. Things aren't really working out for me here. You know. So I think I'm gonna do it. Change a' pace.

TINA   Change a' pace can be good.

LOLA   Yeah. Right. That's what I think.

TINA   When you going to do it?

LOLA   I already have, sort of. Gave my notice.

TINA   Wow.

LOLA   Wow.

TINA   You sure?

LOLA   Yeah—at least I think I'm sure. Hey, if I hate it, I figure I can come back and sleep with Duke.

[WILL *enters. He carries a folded slip of paper.*]

TINA   Can I help you?

WILL   I'm Will Fortunary. I have a 2:30 with John Daniels.

LOLA   Look, Tina. I'll talk to you later.

TINA   Yeah. Sure. We'll catch up.

[WILL *consults the paper again.*]

WILL   Am I in the right place? I'm not interrupting anything, am I? My agent told me to come here.

[LOLA *exits.*]

TINA   You're in the right place. John's running a little behind schedule. Have a seat. I'll let him know you're here.

WILL   Yeah. Thanks.

[WILL *sits uncomfortably.*]

TINA   John—Will Fortunary is here to see you. Okay. I'll let him know. [TINA *hangs up phone.*]

He said it will be a few minutes. He's on a call with NBC.

WILL   No problem. I'm just glad I made it to the right place. I've never been out here before.

TINA   Kind of hard to find. You got through the gate okay?

WILL   Yeah. No problem.

[TINA *and* WILL *sit in silence for a long time. It is uncomfortable.*]

TINA   Look, I'm really sorry. You want me to buzz him again?

WILL   No. Busy guy. I'm sure he's got a lot of important things to do.

[*They sit in silence again.* WILL *unfolds and refolds the paper many times.* TINA *picks up the phone, then sets it down. The silence is squirmy and painful.*]

TINA   I'm sorry. This never happens. Why am I lying? This happens all the time.

WILL   Maybe I should reschedule?

[WILL *gets up.*]

TINA   Wait—don't leave.

WILL   I knew I should not have come. I was going to cancel—

TINA   You know, I used to lie all day long for John. He's in a meeting. He loves your script. Whatever. I just can't do it anymore.

WILL   Um, I'm sorry to hear that?

TINA   Look, I know this is none of my business, but you know, you might be wasting your time out here. John could be on the phone for hours, and well, you may as well be home writing.

WILL   This is kind of career suicide for you, isn't it?

TINA   Yeah. I guess you could say that.

[TINA *opens her desk drawer and pulls out her purse.*]

You can wait if you want, but I'm not staying.

···scene 13···

[*Darkness except for stars. A hilltop is suggested by* WILL *pulling* TINA *up to the crest. City lights twinkle in the distance. A strong wind blows from offstage.*]

WILL   Are you freezing? Here, take my coat.

TINA   You'll be cold.

WILL   It's okay.

> [WILL *gives her his coat. He immediately starts shivering.*]
> Man. It's freezing.

TINA   You okay? Really?

WILL   I'll be fine.

TINA   I never realized it was so big. When you're down it in, it just feels so crowded and tight.

WILL   That's why I like to come up here.

TINA   It just goes out and out, doesn't it?

WILL   If you look out there, that's the valley. And over there, that's the beach. I love Mulholland. You can see everything. It's like the spine of the city, this great, writhing beast.

TINA   That must be downtown over there? And Century City?

WILL   On the left is the west side, the right, the valley. The have and have-nots.

TINA   So, which side are you going to live on?

WILL   Depends on who you ask.

TINA   I'm asking you.

WILL   I'm a writer.

TINA   Yeah?

WILL   Nobody knows nothing. You hear the one about the Polish actress?

TINA   No.

WILL   She slept with the writer.

TINA   I see.

WILL   Look, the wind is getting stronger. You can almost lean in to it. Try it.

TINA   Really?

WILL   Come over here, near the edge.

[*They both move to the edge of the hill. The wind gusts their hair. They lean into the wind and it suspends them over the city.*]

We're flying, Tina. We're flying.

[WILL *reaches over and takes her hand.*]

TINA   Big winds bring change.

[*They kiss.*]

···scene 14···

[TINA *on an empty stage.*]

TINA   When we buried Stu, it was like the air going out of a balloon. Turns out that Stu was Jewish and we all chipped in and got a plot for him at Rose Hills. His mom came out. She had no idea where he'd been living. Rich showed up at the cemetery, the douche bag. That night I went up to the top of Mulholland. When you looked out, you could see Rose Hills in the distance. And in the foreground was the lot. You could tell because it was a big black void surrounded by all those little lights, everybody with their families tucked neatly in their homes. You could barely make out the sound stages in the moonlight. The lot. That's what we used to call it. We spent that summer living on the lot. After that, nothing was the same. Lola left for Placerville, and Rich's contract didn't get renewed. Someone else moved into our offices. The desks were thrown onto the scrap heap. One day, years later, after I made my film, I had a meeting on the lot. It was so weird coming back. I had to get a pass to get through the gate. All during the meeting, I never heard a word they said. I couldn't wait to get out of there. All I wanted to do was go back. Afterwards, I didn't go to my car like you're supposed to. I walked down that Western street. I went into the saloon. It was cool and dark. I looked for a crate to pull up but there weren't any. I looked out from the darkness into the bright L.A. light. We didn't all get our day in the sun.

[*Neil Young's "Heart of Gold" comes up as lights fade to black.*]

• • •

Assumptions

Lynne Bolen

Lynne Bolen

Lynne Bolen is a playwright, director, producer, and actor. She is a member of New Voices Playwrights Theatre in Orange County, California, and has served as an officer on the board of directors for several years. Bolen was a member of the former Vanguard Theatre Ensemble. Her plays have been produced in California at the OC Pavilion Performing Arts Center, Chance Theater, Vanguard Theatre, Gallery Theatre, STAGEStheatre, Cabrillo Playhouse, Empire Theatre, Mysterium Theater, Stage Door Repertory Theatre, and the MUZEO museum. She has directed over fifty plays and has produced dozens of shows. As an actor, Lynne has appeared in numerous stage productions and films, and she starred in an award-winning American Film Institute movie that toured the world for over two years. A graduate of UCLA, she holds an MBA and an MS.

···production history···

Assumptions was first performed in *Summer Voices*, eight one-act plays produced by New Voices Playwrights Theatre in September 2011 at the Mysterium Theater, Anaheim, California. The play was directed by Terry Winkler.

cast

> **GRACE**, 30s, female
>
> **ANDRE**, 30s, male
>
> **JASON**, 20s–60s, male

time

Present

set

A table and two chairs

• • •

[ANDRE *is sitting at the table, reading a document in a file folder.* GRACE *opens the door and enters, dressed in a tight jacket and skirt, and high heels.*]

GRACE   Hello.

ANDRE   [*Quickly closes the folder.*] Hi.

GRACE   [*Offering her hand.*] I'm Grace Lee.

ANDRE   [*Rises and shakes her hand.*] Grace, hello. Andre Washington.

GRACE   A pleasure to meet you, Andre.

ANDRE   Likewise. Please, um, have a seat.

GRACE   Thank you.

[*They both smile and sit with an awkwardness.*]

ANDRE   So . . . Grace Lee.

GRACE   I know. You were expecting me to be Asian.

ANDRE   What? No.

GRACE   Really, it's okay. I'm used to it. It's happened my whole life.

ANDRE   I'm sorry. It's just that Miranda said you went to UCLA and are really smart . . .

GRACE   . . . And with that plus my last name Lee, you put two and two together.

ANDRE   It was a possibility. I apologize for assuming. Me of all people, right?

GRACE   What do you mean?

ANDRE   The pot calling the kettle *black*, you're thinking?

GRACE   I'm sorry, but I'm just not following . . .

ANDRE   [*Teasingly.*] Didn't you assume I was black?

GRACE   You look white to me. Why would I assume you're black?

ANDRE   Before we met. My name is Andre Washington. Admit it. You assumed I was black. Really, it's okay. I'm used to it. It's happened my whole life.

GRACE   [*Smiling apologetically.*] Well, it was a possibility. Washington just seems like an African American name.

ANDRE   Yeah, like George Washington.

GRACE   Like *Denzel* [*Den'-zel*] Washington.

ANDRE   It's Den*zel* [*Den-zel'*].

GRACE   Same thing.

ANDRE   Not to Den*zel*. You see, his father's name was *Den*zel, and to differentiate, his name is pronounced Den*zel*.

GRACE   Subtle difference. You're quite the expert.

ANDRE   Well, I like to keep track of all my Washington brothers.

GRACE   Good for you, Andre. So have you known Miranda long?

ANDRE   Yeah, we met at Berkeley. She is one classy lady.

GRACE   Miranda has a great sense of humor. I assume she told you a bit about me.

ANDRE   Miranda speaks very highly of you. She thought we would get along well. What did she tell you about me?

GRACE   She said that you are very charming, and very wealthy.

ANDRE   Miranda is right.

GRACE   What else did she say about me?

ANDRE   She said that you wouldn't disappoint me.

GRACE   Miranda is right.

[*Beat.*]

Did you make your money legally, Andre?

ANDRE   You cut right to the chase, Grace.

GRACE   One of my strengths.

ANDRE   I started a dot-com company and it was bought out for a fortune before the bubble burst. All perfectly legal.

GRACE   I like a man who beats the odds.

ANDRE   [*Flirty.*] I think we are going to get along just fine.

GRACE   [*Smiles.*] So, Mr. Washington, shall we get down to business?

ANDRE   Let's do it. Ms. Lee, I would like to engage your services. Miranda said that you're the best.

GRACE   And the best is very expensive.

ANDRE   No worries, I can afford the best and will pay whatever *high price* you normally charge your clients.

GRACE   So you'll hire me at my usual rate?

ANDRE   Whatever it takes. You come highly recommended by Miranda.

[*He offers his hand, and they shake.*]

GRACE   [*Stands and removes her jacket.*] All right, let's get started.

ANDRE   I can't wait.

GRACE   How do you plan to plea?

ANDRE   Not guilty, counselor.

GRACE   I assumed so. But tell me, Andre, did you kill Vivienne Louise Anthony on the night of May 13?

ANDRE   No, I did not.

GRACE   Your DNA was recovered from the crime scene.

ANDRE   That doesn't mean I killed her.

GRACE   You were ID'd in a police lineup.

ANDRE   I'm innocent.

GRACE   The evidence against you is overwhelming. The reason I agreed to take this case is because Miranda asked me to. Tell me what happened, and I can work a plea deal that'll keep you off death row.

ANDRE   I told you I'm innocent! Why the hell don't you believe me? Why does everyone assume I'm guilty?

GRACE   Not assumptions, Andre, but implications based upon forensic evidence and witnesses.

ANDRE   People shouldn't jump to conclusions. Just because I'm rich, people are jealous and want to take me down. People are . . . the police are . . . the district attorney . . . Just because the district attorney is . . . Shit!

GRACE Dammit! Not again!

JASON [*Emerges from the audience.*] Cut!

ANDRE Sorry, Jason. Keep the camera rolling. I'll pick it up.

GRACE Focus, for God's sake!

ANDRE Knock it off, you screwed up the last scene.

GRACE Only because you fed me the wrong lines.

JASON Hey, kids, stop the constant bickering. Camera's rolling, let's go. Okay, settle. Ready, and—action!

ANDRE People shouldn't jump to conclusions. Just because I'm rich, people are jealous and want to take me down. Just because the district attorney assumes I killed Vivienne doesn't mean I did.

[*Earnestly pleading.*]

Do you believe me, Grace?

GRACE Things are not always what they seem to be. I guess I shouldn't assume.

ANDRE If you believe me, Grace, I know we can beat this case together.

JASON Cut! Okay, everyone, take five.

GRACE [*To* JASON.] He keeps blowing his lines. I assume we'll be shooting this scene again after the break?

JASON You assume correctly. I need *more* from both of you. Hold tight, I'll be back in a minute.

[*Exits.*]

GRACE [*To* ANDRE.] You'd better get it right next time. And step it up! Jason wants "more" from you.

ANDRE   Actually, he said he wants "more" from *you*.

GRACE   It's obvious he meant you. You need to bring "more" when you say you're innocent, and then you need to explode when you say people jump to conclusions.

ANDRE   I have a director. Don't tell me how to act. Try working on your own acting. You're supposed to be sexy when you talk about getting down to business. Who'd want to hire a cold fish like you?

GRACE   Cold fish! Really? You're crazy. Jason loves what I'm doing. He hasn't asked me to change anything. This is ridiculous. I can't work like this. Jason! Jason!

ANDRE   Stop being such a damned diva. It was embarrassing the way you went on about the lunch catering.

GRACE   The food has been terrible on this shoot. In fact, everything has been terrible on this shoot. Especially you.

ANDRE   And you.

[*Beat.*]

GRACE   Please, can we just get through this awful scene without another take?

ANDRE   If you bring "more."

GRACE   Truce. Seriously, I don't want to be here all night. I'm tired and I'm hungry. Craft services suck.

ANDRE   Truce. [*They shake hands firmly at first, but he holds on.*]

So . . .

[*Flirty.*]

After we wrap tonight, how about the two of us going out for a cold glass of beer and some grilled ahi tuna?

GRACE   How about a cold glass of milk and some tuna casserole?

ANDRE   With crushed potato chips on top?

GRACE It's the twins' favorite! And frozen peas.

ANDRE Ah, the glamorous movie-star life.

GRACE And after dinner, chapter three of *Captain Billy and the Gypsy Princess*.

ANDRE [*Speaking with a pirate accent.*] Aye, and 'tis a saucy lass is the princess beauty. Arrr!

GRACE The twins love your pirate-speak. It's your best acting of the day.

ANDRE It's my favorite role of the day.

[*They lovingly smile at each other.*]

JASON [*Enters.*] Okay, kids, back to one. I assume you'll nail it this time.

GRACE [*She puts on her jacket and moves toward the door.*] You know what happens when you *assume*.

JASON Yeah, my actors get to wrap for the night.

ANDRE and GRACE [*Suddenly look at each other, earnestly.*] Let's do it!

[*They give each other a high five.*]

JASON Assume [*Sarcastically.*] your positions. Back to one.

    [GRACE *exits.*]

    All right, everyone, settle. Quiet on the set. And—action!

GRACE [*Enters.*] Hello.

ANDRE [*Quickly closes the folder.*] Hi.

GRACE [*Offering her hand.*] I'm Grace Lee.

ANDRE [*Rises and shakes her hand.*] Grace, hello. Andre Washington.

[*Lights fade.*]

• • •

Starf*cker

Adam Pasen

Adam Pasen

Pasen recently completed his PhD in playwriting at Western Michigan University under Steve Feffer. His full-lengths include *Badfic Love* (WordBRIDGE 2012), *Board Fold: A Tale of Retail* (Reva Shiner Comedy Award Finalist), *Tea with Edie and Fitz* (Dead Writers Theatre Collective), and *Vanity Fair* (Remy Bumppo Adaptation and Translation Series). Youth plays *Study Group* and *Butterfinger* are available from Heuer and Brooklyn Publishers. *Starf*cker* previously appeared in *Poems & Plays* #20 (Spring/Summer 2013).

···production history···

*Starf*cker* won the 2012 ACTF Ten-Minute Play Award from the Kennedy Center. It was a finalist for the Theatre Oxford National Ten-Minute Award and received a reading in Oxford, Mississippi, in May 2012. It was also recently announced as a Northnorthwest selection through Western Washington University.

···

[*Nighttime in L.A. The courtyard of an enormous Hollywood mansion.* BOY *enters in his In-N-Out Burger uniform, holding a box and singing the chorus of "Star Star" by the Rolling Stones.*]

BOY   You're a starf*cker, starf*cker, starf*cker, starf*cker, star . . . yeah! You're a starf*cker, starf*cker, starf—

[*Setting box down, taking in mansion.*]

Whoa. Well, it's no Sherman Oaks . . . psst!

[*Pause. The door cracks and* GIRL *peeks out, grinning.*]

GIRL   Oh my God. Oh. My. God. Oh my God?

BOY   Okay, okay, I get it, chill!

GIRL   No way! I'm going to blog about this all day tomorrow!

BOY   Easy, it's a blog, not a blah-blah-blog . . .

BOTH   Haaaaah!

GIRL   But seriously, can you believe I'm here, in *his* mansion? It's like the mother lode—my first score above Sunset!

BOY   It's not that big a deal.

GIRL   Are you kidding? You're talking to a girl whose most high-profile hookup to date has been Mario Lopez in a Starbucks bathroom. This is a fucking *milestone*.[1] Tomorrow I might be a kept woman

---

[1] If Mario Lopez is no longer topical, replace with the current middling actor du jour.

with her own place in the Hills, and then it's bye-bye to my crappy apartment next to yours in our crappy complex in the Valley. This could be the last time we ever see each other. *Ever.*

[*Beat.*]

Well, maybe I can keep you on as my, like . . . producer.

BOY Hey, don't patronize me. I came to L.A. to be a famous screenwriter and it'll happen!

GIRL I mean . . . I don't know how seriously I can take someone who uses "famous" and "screenwriter" in the same sentence.

BOY All right, fine. But I'll still be rich.

GIRL I know! And I can't wait so I can screw your brains out. Maybe you can join us.

BOY No thanks! I only engage in orgies with actors whose aggregate film score on Rotten Tomatoes is above 20 percent. I mean, seriously? Him? He's only done, like, *one* good movie in his *life* . . . that indie pseudo-romance where at the end he goes to the girl's place and delivers that huge speech to the door about how he realizes he loves her, but you don't even know if she hears because they don't show if she's behind the door or not, and then while he stands there waiting they just fade to black and you never find out.

GIRL I haven't seen it. So? Do you think she's behind the door or not?

BOY I think it's irrelevant. I think that even if she does hear his confession, she stays inside with her new rich boyfriend and her guaranteed security because that's how life works.

GIRL Mmm. It makes me sad that you think that.

BOY Why? I thought you hated romance.

GIRL Not onscreen.

[*Beat.*]

BOY So where is he now?

GIRL   Taking a shower.

BOY   Did you—

GIRL   No! I mean. Not yet. I said if he got clean enough, I'd get him dirty again after. See, he listed his quirks in *Maxim* last month and said he couldn't take a shower for less than an hour, so I knew I'd have time to call you and for you to get here with . . . the *item*. And you should *see* this shower, it's got, like, fifteen different nozzles. It'll be awhile . . .

[*Draping herself over* BOY.]

I might even have time for a little pregame, in fact. You look so dapper in your In-N-Out Burger uniform, I'm almost tempted, what do you think?

BOY   You couldn't blog about it.

GIRL   [*Peeling off.*] True. Too bad. Oh well, back to Plan A then.

[*Pointing at the box.*]

Is that it?

[BOY *nods.* GIRL *smiles and turns away.*]

BOY   So . . . uh . . . how did you end up at Plan A's place again?

GIRL   [*Tying her shirt in a knot at the waist.*] Oh my God! How did I not tell you on the phone . . . okay, so I was at that launch party for—I don't even remember, new movie-review website X, and I was trying to wrangle a three-way with Ellen DeGeneres and Portia de Rossi[2] . . .

BOY   Ballsy.

GIRL   [*Pulling hair into pigtails.*] Ironically. Anyway, it was going pretty well, but then I made some comment about letting Anne Heche[3] watch and it was all downhill from there. So I'm all dejected, and I walk back to the bar to get another appletini, and some guy bumps

---

[2] Or current Power Lesbian Couple.
[3] Or the highly publicized former lover of half of Power Lesbian Couple.

into me and spills his drink all over my Jimmy-Choos—which are on rental, of course . . . and I'm about to go five shades of ballistic and I turn around and it's him! Like—*him!* Like, him that I passed five new billboards for on the cab ride over!

BOY I only counted three—

GIRL [*Taking off pants.*] And he's just *so* sweet and *so* apologetic and, can he get my name and number so he can pay the bill? And then we get to talking and I tell him how much I loved his last film—I did, I totally said "film" . . . and next thing I know we're here and I tell him to shower and then call you for my "favor" and now here we are!

[*Pause, in her underwear from waist down.*]

So—are you gonna give it to me?

BOY What? Oh!

[BOY *picks up the box and gives it to her.* GIRL *sets the box on the step and pulls out a plaid schoolgirl skirt. Pulls it on over the next few lines.*]

Yeah, explain the rationale to me again?

GIRL Oh . . . right. Okay, same *Maxim* article as the shower quote, they ask him his biggest turn-ons and he says any girl in a Catholic schoolgirl uniform.

BOY I can't believe you don't think it's pseudo-sleazy and cliché to have a schoolgirl fetish.

GIRL It *is* sleazy and cliché! Have you met me? That's the point. I'm just glad I actually had one of these—from that Halloween party I went to last year in Venice Beach, I mean . . .

BOY What'd you go as, old-school Britney Spears?

GIRL Senator's Wet Dream.

[*Doing a little spin.*]

How do I look?

BOY   Uh . . . wet dreamy.

GIRL   Sweet talker. I knew there was a reason I trusted you with the keys to my place. Who else could I call who would leave straight from work, grab some random . . . *tchotchke* from my bureau, and brave the 405 to bring it to me? You're the nicest person I know.

BOY   Look, don't act like we have some special bond or something. I'm probably listed as "boy" on your phone. You only gave me your keys because I'm your one neighbor who's so low on the social totem that you can ask me with, like, relative *impunity* to stop in and feed your goldfish while you spend the weekend boning some D-Lister.

GIRL   D-Plus. I have standards.

BOY   You should be careful . . . what if I sneak into your place at night and do something weird like put little stuffed animals in bed with you to help you sleep?

GIRL   Aww! That's, like, such a bizarre fusion of cute and creepy, I don't know what to call it . . .

BOY   Uh, how 'bout "cute-py"?

GIRL   Nah, "cute-pee" makes it sound like you have adorable urine.

BOY   Maybe I *do*.

BOTH   Haaaaah!

[*Pause.* GIRL *hugs* BOY. *They continue to talk without breaking apart. As the scene continues, they unconsciously begin to sway and finally dance.*]

GIRL   Thanks. So . . . what are you writing these days?

BOY   Oh, just some studio specs. Boy gets girl, that kinda thing. Something that'll sell.

GIRL   I hear writers lift scenes from their lives. Would you use this in your movie?

BOY   Wouldn't make a good scene. No conflict. The characters don't seem to want to *get* anything from each other. All they do is spew cutesy banter back and forth—

GIRL   Right—that's how you know they belong together!

[*Pause.*]

In the movie. Besides, what's so great about trying to get something from somebody? How's that artistic? That's just like real life. There's nothing I find more fascinating than watching two people just—*coexist* . . .

[*Short pause.*]

My grandparents were like that. We'd go to their house for Easter and the aunts would take all the kids out for ice cream, but I'd stay behind and just watch them together. He had that disease, what's it call—uh . . . *emphysema*. He had to use this breathing apparatus thing and couldn't do much for himself. So she'd shuffle over with his dinner and say, "I don't know what I ever did to end up with a wheezy old fool like you." And he'd say, "Maybe that's all a dried-up husk like you deserves." And the whole time, just these big grins on their faces. Them against the world.

[*Short pause.*]

So different from my parents.

[*Beat.*]

BOY   So can I ask *you* a question?

GIRL   Sure.

BOY   Why do you sleep with these people?

GIRL   Who?

BOY   Famous people. I mean, sort-of famous people. Is the sex better? Is it like famous sex?

GIRL   It's not about the sex.

BOY   What's it about?

GIRL   It's about *that look*. I don't know. You know some girls move to LA to be actresses? I came so I wouldn't have to ever see that look again.

BOY   And that is?

GIRL   It's just a look I always saw on boys' faces back home. I'd meet someone interesting and we'd hang out and talk and . . . just have fun, you know? Whatever—pass the time. And then one day, I'd turn and they'd have *that look* on their faces, and it . . . it just . . . it killed me, because I knew I couldn't keep . . . that it wasn't fair to . . .

BOY   You ran away because you think everyone was in love with you? How terminally narcissistic. You could *totally* be an actress!

GIRL   Some people are emotionally equipped to hurt people. I'm not. I was built to be hurt. It's . . . cleaner. And I figured, where can a person who winds up systematically destroying anyone who makes the mistake of caring about them go to fit in?

BOTH   Los Angeles.

BOY   So what do you . . . want him to do?

GIRL   [*Short pause.*] I want him not to call. I'm looking forward to crying myself to sleep because I know he's not thinking of me. And somewhere down the line it would be nice to see him at an event or something and know by his expression that not only does he not remember my name, he doesn't know he's *supposed* to know my name because he has no idea we've even *met*. It meant so little to him that I don't exist. That I was a complete—ghost fuck.

BOY   You would like that?

GIRL   I would *relish* it.

BOY   You're weird.

GIRL   I didn't claim I was going to win any normalcy contests. PS, what was that *you* were singing when you walked up . . . "Starf*cker?"

BOY   What were you, like, listening at the door?

[*Pause.*]

Yeah, I was. The Stones. Classic. Only it's not called "Starf*cker," it's called "Star Star." 'Cuz good ol' Mick Jagger knew it would never get any play if it was called "Starf*cker," so now we've got, like, a pornographic song with the title of a nursery rhyme.

[*Beat.*]

Huh, you're kind of, like, the same but reversed. Like, if you were a song, you'd be called "Starf*cker" but the words would be all innocent and deep.

GIRL   Thank God nobody listens to lyrics anymore.

BOY   Yeah, then you might have to give up your hard-earned cynicism.

[GIRL *halts.*]

GIRL   I am not a cynic. A cynic doesn't believe love *exists*. I'm not, like, the Catholic Church with the heliocentric model of the universe . . . I am *susceptible* to empirical evidence—and I've *seen* love. I told you, my grandparents.

[*They begin moving again.*]

But I believe in the lottery too . . . that doesn't mean I think I'm going to win.

[*Beat.*]

We're dancing.

BOY   We are.

GIRL   That's so old Hollywood.

BOY   Careful or you'll fall in love with me.

GIRL   Never.

BOY   So why dance with me?

GIRL   Because you're the most beautiful man I know who doesn't try to kiss me.

BOY   What if I said I wanted to sleep with you?

GIRL   I'd take you home with me this second.

BOY   What if I said I wanted to *maybe* sleep with you someday but right now I just wanted to hold you and tell you how beautiful I think you are?

GIRL   I'd never talk to you again.

   [GIRL *laughs and looks at* BOY. *He has "that look." She pulls away.*]

   I should get back inside.

BOY   Was it my two left feet? Call me "Fred A-Scare," right? Haaaaah! [*Pause.*]

   Do you wanna grab some coffee tomorrow, tell me all about it?

GIRL   Busy day. I don't know, maybe. We'll see, okay?

BOY   Yeah . . . uh, sure. Night.

GIRL   Night.

   [GIRL *opens door. Pauses and turns back.*]

   Hey, Doug?

BOY   Yeah, Kelly?

GIRL   [*Pause.*] Thanks for feeding the fish.

[GIRL *gently shuts the door. Long beat.*]

BOY   I lied to you. About the end of that movie. What I think happens. I lied. I think she is behind the door listening. I think that while the credits are rolling she runs out and kisses him and tells him she never wants them to be apart again. Because when people fall in love, they make exceptions for each other. I think they end up happily ever after. I've never been more sure of anything in my life.

[BOY *stands facing the door. He continues to watch it. Very slowly, the lights fade to black.*]

• • •

Lillie Meant Murder

Claudia Barnett

My thanks to the Faculty Research & Creative Activity Committee at Middle Tennessee State University for the grant that helped me write this play.

Claudia Barnett

Claudia Barnett wrote her most recent play, *Witches Vanish*, as the fall 2011 resident playwright at Stage Left Theatre in Chicago. She teaches playwriting at Middle Tennessee State University. Her book *I Love You Terribly: Six Plays* was published by Carnegie Mellon University Press in 2012.

···production history···

Lillie Meant Murder was first produced by Independent Actors Theatre (artistic director Emily A. Rollie), Columbia, Missouri, as part of the fourth-annual Short Women's Play Festival, March 9–11, 2012. It was directed by Elizabeth Braaten Palmieri and stage-managed by Emma Squire with the following cast:

LILLIE   Brooke Underwood

BOLLANDER   Matt Ingram

HAGGERTY/JUDGE   Nathan Bryant

DRUMMER   Nick Page

historical note

This play is based on two brief articles in the *New York Times:* "Lillie Meant Murder" (May 22, 1888) and "The Judge Thought Her Justified" (May 26, 1888). It's also inspired by an unrelated story in which the following line appears: "Something in the way the youth walked attracted [policeman] Luddy's attention. He followed" ("Finds Wealthy Girl Disguised as a Boy," June 11, 1910).

two notes

1. The role of the drummer was added by the first director of the play, Elizabeth Braaten Palmieri. It worked so well that I've added it to the script. The point is to add rhythm and pacing. The drummer should feel free to improvise and could also, if necessary, be replaced by a recording.
2. ** in the text indicates a line from the original source material.

characters

LILLIE, Lillie Richmond, 30. She wears a man's suit and false mustache. Played by a ballerina.

BOLLANDER, Thomas J. Bollander, 40. A real-estate dealer. Played by a tap dancer.

HAGGERTY, Special Policeman Haggerty.

JUDGE, Judge Woodman.

DRUMMER, Set off in a separate space.

setting

Chicago. May 21, 1888. A street that turns into a courtroom and back into a street.

For the street, the stage is bare except for some poles to suggest buildings and trees. For the courtroom, a podium appears. On top of it is a xylophone.

• • •

[*At rise: The* DRUMMER *drums.* LILLIE *enters dancing to the beat, as if in a ballet. She dances from pole to pole, twirling around each one, carefully inspecting her surroundings. After a few moments,* HAGGERTY *enters surreptitiously. He hides behind a "tree" and observes her. Finally,* LILLIE *stops dancing and hides behind a tree herself, waiting.* HAGGERTY *keeps his eye on her, but she does not notice him.* BOLLANDER *enters, tap-dancing across the stage. Just as he passes* LILLIE, *she pulls a pistol from her pocket, twirls it once, aims. (The gun should be obviously fake, for instance, bright orange.) When she is about to fire,* HAGGERTY *grabs her. A shot fires into the air, just missing* BOLLANDER, *who throws himself to the ground.*]

HAGGERTY   Ah-hah. I knew something was off here.

[*He pulls the mustache off* LILLIE.]

A woman in men's clothes.

LILLIE   Is that a crime, officer? They fit so well and comfortably; they made me want to dance.

HAGGERTY   Dancing in the street? That's unlawful, too. I'll have to write you up. Where'd you get that suit?

BOLLANDER   [*Rising and addressing* HAGGERTY.] She tried to kill me, and all you care about's her clothes?

HAGGERTY   Your name, sir?

BOLLANDER   *My* name? I'm the victim here. You want *her* name: Lillie Richmond. Write that down. Take her to jail.

LILLIE   Lillie Bollander.

BOLLANDER   Lillie *Richmond*. My name's Bollander; hers ain't.

LILLIE   I am that man's wife. I signed a written contract with him and thought it was a legal marriage. He lived with me nearly two years on the strength of it. He deserted me, and I tried to kill him.**

HAGGERTY   So in addition to impersonating a man and dancing in the street, we add concubinage to the charges.

BOLLANDER   And attempted murder.

LILLIE   He's the one committed a crime.

BOLLANDER   Officer, this woman's been stalking me and spreading gossip for weeks, and now she's tried to kill me.

HAGGERTY   So basically a domestic dispute. Not a concern of the police. Are those your clothes, Mr. Bollander?

LILLIE   Of course they're not his clothes. Look at the size of him. Now look at me.

HAGGERTY   Is that your pistol, sir?

LILLIE   I'm not a thief.

BOLLANDER   Just a would-be murderess.

HAGGERTY   Since you two are so well acquainted, allow me to introduce myself: Special Policeman Haggerty of the Chicago, Milwaukee, and St. Paul Railway.

LILLIE   We're not on a railway; we're on a street corner. So aren't you out of your jurisdiction? Please, Special Policeman Haggerty, let me go.

HAGGERTY   Don't you worry, miss. The patrol wagon will be here in short order to take you to the station.

[HAGGERTY *pulls a whistle from his pocket and blows. At the sound of the whistle,* LILLIE *leaps into the air and pirouettes.* HAGGERTY *catches her when she lands. They stand a moment in stunned silence.* BOLLANDER *taps his feet impatiently.*

The sound of a siren as the street turns into the courtroom. LILLIE *dances and* BOLLANDER *taps his feet as* HAGGERTY *exits. The* JUDGE *enters and takes his place behind the podium and bangs his gavel.*]

JUDGE Order. Order in the court.

> [*He bangs his gavel again. This time, he uses it to play the xylophone. He plays a scale and checks his docket.*]

> Next case: Bollander versus Richmond.

> [BOLLANDER *tap-dances angrily toward the podium.* LILLIE *approaches, taking tiny steps en pointe. The* JUDGE *clangs a few more notes.*]

> Miss Richmond. You've been arrested on the charge of impersonating a man.

BOLLANDER And attempted murder.

JUDGE Let's deal with the lesser charge last. Miss Richmond, you're dressed in men's clothes, thereby challenging the status quo, the hierarchy of the sexes, the sanctity of marriage. How do you plead?

LILLIE Guilty.

JUDGE Guilty? Don't you want to offer an excuse? Extenuating circumstances? After all, you do look fetching in that suit.

LILLIE I dressed like a man so that Tom wouldn't notice me on the street when I went to shoot him.

JUDGE You tried to be unobtrusive, but you attracted the attention of the police.

LILLIE I was dancing. Couldn't help it. I suddenly felt so free.

JUDGE Because you were about to kill Mr. Bollander?

LILLIE Because of the clothes. No whale bones, no cinched waist, no itchy lace. I could take giant steps.

JUDGE I'd hardly think you'd need whale bones, Miss Richmond, with your slim figure. Have you ever danced before?

LILLIE   Oh no, Judge. It just suddenly hit me—the impulse, I mean.

JUDGE   I see. Won't you demonstrate a few steps, as evidence.

BOLLANDER   I object.

[*He taps his feet. The* JUDGE *ignores him.*]

JUDGE   Miss Richmond?

[*He plays a tune on the xylophone.* LILLIE *leaps up and performs a brief dance that ends with an arabesque.*]

LILLIE   Ta-da!

JUDGE   Thank you, Miss Richmond. That was very convincing. Now, Mr. Bollander, what on earth did you do to cause this young woman to resort to such measures?

BOLLANDER   What did I do? She tried to kill me!

[*He taps his feet to the sound of drumming.*]

JUDGE   I'm beginning to suspect you deserved it. When did you first become acquainted with the accused?

BOLLANDER   Two years ago.

JUDGE   Under what circumstances?

BOLLANDER   I took her to dinner.

JUDGE   But not dancing?

BOLLANDER   Never.

JUDGE   That may have been your mistake. Then what happened?

BOLLANDER   I tired of her; she told lies about me.

JUDGE   Lies, Miss Richmond?

LILLIE   He means I went to his real-estate office and introduced myself as his wife, but that's not a lie. It's the truth.

JUDGE   You are Mr. Bollander's wife?

LILLIE   I have the certificate of marriage right here.

[*She takes a paper from her pocket and hands it to the* JUDGE.]

BOLLANDER   That's not a certificate of marriage, Judge.

[*The* JUDGE *inspects the paper.*]

JUDGE   It certainly is not. It's a slapdash imitation. Miss Richmond, Illinois is not spelled with three Ls.

[*The* JUDGE *holds up the paper and points out the typo on the "State of Illllinois" letterhead.*]

LILLIE   Oh my.

JUDGE   It seems to me you're guilty of misreading, Miss Richmond. Now, Mr. Bollander, you also signed this piece of paper.

BOLLANDER   Yes, Judge.

JUDGE   Yet you knew it was a forgery.

BOLLANDER   I wouldn't call it a forgery. It was more of a game—like how children play pretend.

JUDGE   You had a pretend wedding for fun.

BOLLANDER   That's it. Exactly.

JUDGE   Was it fun for you, Miss Richmond?

LILLIE   Oh no. It was a solemn occasion. I'd waited all my life.

JUDGE   Did you wear white?

LILLIE   Oh yes, the works. Silk stockings, white lace. I'd thought we were married. We cohabitated after that. He took two years to tell me 'twas a lie.

BOLLANDER   How could you not have known? No minister, no witnesses, no justice of the peace?

LILLIE   You can't blame me for believing you. I was really quite in love.

BOLLANDER   I was rather in love myself.

LILLIE   But then you fell out of love and dumped me in the street.

BOLLANDER   Sorry, Lillie, but you know how it was: Things got stale, routine, a bore.

JUDGE   Mr. Bollander, how can you look at this delicate nymph and use such discourteous words to describe her? You're guilty of faulty vocabulary.

LILLIE   Oh no, it was that way, Judge. His words aren't wrong. I was different then. Dull.

JUDGE   What's changed?

LILLIE   Being married made me weary. But when I aimed my gun at Tom, I realized I could wear men's suits forever and keep dancing.

[*A drumroll.* LILLIE *dances.*]

BOLLANDER   This change is charming, apart from the violence. I wonder if we could try again. Lillie, may I have this dance?

[*The* JUDGE *plays the opening notes of the wedding march on his xylophone.* BOL-LANDER *begins to tap-dance, expertly, stops in front of* LILLIE, *and bows.*]

LILLIE   I don't think so, Thomas. Our styles are ill suited.

[*The* JUDGE *bangs his gavel on the podium.*]

JUDGE   Order. Order in the court. Miss Richmond, when you shot at Mr. Bollander, did you mean to kill him?

LILLIE   Oh yes, Judge.

BOLLANDER   Lock her up! She's a menace to society.

JUDGE   Would you do it again?

LILLIE   Not if I could dance instead.

JUDGE In that case, the charges against you are dismissed. You're free to go.

LILLIE Thank you, Judge.

[LILLIE *dances happily away from the men and around the courtroom.*]

BOLLANDER But she's guilty on all counts!

JUDGE I haven't yet ruled on the charges against you, Mr. Bollander.

BOLLANDER There aren't any charges against me.

JUDGE Well, there ought to be, but if there aren't, you're free to go as well.

[BOLLANDER *begins to tap-dance toward the door. The* JUDGE *strikes up a Brazilian tune on the xylophone.*]

Let's all go . . . samba!

[*Music plays. The* JUDGE, BOLLANDER, *and* LILLIE *dance with abandon. The courtroom turns back into the street.* HAGGERTY *emerges from behind a tree and blows his whistle loudly. The* JUDGE *and* BOLLANDER *freeze, while* LILLIE *leaps into the air and pirouettes.* JUDGE, BOLLANDER, *and* HAGGERTY *rush toward her as if to catch her, but* LILLIE *lands on her own two feet and dances happily away.*]

• • •

Gift of an Orange

Inspired by Tennessee Williams's short fiction piece "Gift of an Apple," written in 1936, published in *Tennessee Williams Collected Stories*, 1985.

Charlene A. Donaghy

Charlene A. Donaghy

Charlene A. Donaghy's plays have been produced in New York City, Boston, and around the United States, with recognition in Great Britain and Canada. Her publications include *Best American Short Plays*, *Estrogenius*, and *Into the Eye*. Donaghy teaches playwriting and theater at University of Nebraska and Lesley University. She is a member of the Dramatists Guild.

··· production history ···

Gift of an Orange was originally produced by New Urban Theatre Laboratory for its premiere in Boston (September 6–16, 2012) and at the Provincetown Tennessee Williams Theater Festival (September 20–23, 2012). It was directed by Jackie Davis; set design by Megan Tracy Leddy and Luke Sutherland; lighting design by Michael Clark Wonson; stage manager Samantha MacArthur. The cast was:

OSHUN   Dayenne C. Byron Walters

TAUREAN   Richard B. Caines, III

JAKE   James Bocock

MUSICIANS   Pete Hennig, Liz Rapoza, Ukumbwa Sauti, Terry Orlando Jones

characters

OSHUN, a woman of Creole descent. She is dark-skinned, plainly clothed, 45 years old. She is scarred by life. OSHUN speaks with a Southern Louisiana accent.

TAUREAN, an African American man, 19 years old. He is muscular and handsome, looking older than his years. He is dusty from walking. TAUREAN does not have an accent.

JAKE, burly Caucasian man, 55 years old. His clothing and mannerism reflect a rugged life working on the oil rigs.

time

A hot summer, late afternoon, 2011

setting

Buras, Louisiana

instrumentation

A Jembe drum can be used to personify OSHUN's desires.
A flute can be used to personify TAUREAN's emotions.
A chime can be used to represent the magic.

• • •

[*A dry, worn-down yet neat yard of a trailer. Two exits: one into the trailer, one to the wood pile and road. A weathered table, two armchairs, metal washtub, and hose are present. A small voodoo altar is set with a worn New Orleans Saints cap, a photograph of a young man, a knife, and various voodoo items (candles, bells, feathers, colorful cloth, etc.). Honey, herbs, gourds, and other natural items are present, for sale. Central to the yard is a lush, blossoming orange tree yard, springing from a small patch of dark, rich earth circled by stones. It is a sharp contrast to the rest of the worn-down yard.*]

···scene one···

[*Faint birdsong is heard. OSHUN, humming to a blues beat, dances in from the trailer carrying a wooden bowl, a straight pin, a glass of water. She gathers herbs, spices, and an orange from the tree. She is barefoot, wearing a light cotton dress with a waist pocket.*]

OSHUN

> I'M A VOODOO WOMAN SINCE I BEEN BORN,
> MOTHER NATURE'S BOUNTY, THE PACT I'VE SWORN,
> LOAS BE MY GUIDES TO THE SKY AND EARTH,
> I CALL DOWN THE SPIRITS: JOY, PAIN, REBIRTH.

[*She continues to hum tune. OSHUN crosses to table with items. She breathes on the herbs, places all items in the bowl, pricks her finger, lets the blood drip into the water, mixes. She crosses with bowl to tree and sprinkles the ingredients at the base. She begins to dance about the tree in wild abandon.*]

Mother Earth, while I yet alive, it upon you I put my trust.
Mother Earth, who receive my body, we are addressin' you.

[*She dances a few moments, then plucks an orange from tree, crosses to Saints hat, picks it up, breathes it in, lovingly pets hat. Speaks to herself, smiles sadly.*]

How you like oranges, my bébé boy. One thing always grow out here, no matter what. 'Course, I help it along. Yes, I do.

[*She puts hat back, rips open the orange, and eats. TAUREAN enters dressed in jeans, T-shirt, and sneakers, carrying a worn backpack. OSHUN watches*] *him. He hungrily eyes the items in the yard, sees the tree, and stops. After a moment he starts to walk away. Smoothes the front of her dress.*]

You want to buy somethin', you?

[TAUREAN *stops.*]

TAUREAN   I don't have any money.

OSHUN   Huh. You *and* me. That why I'm sellin' my . . . things.
[*Beat.*]
C'mon over here, maybe you find somethin' you like.

TAUREAN   I just need something to eat.

OSHUN   Been a might since you had somethin' good to eat?
[TAUREAN *nods.*]
Where you walkin' from, you?

TAUREAN   Up New Orleans way.

OSHUN   You walk sixty miles into the bayou?

TAUREAN   Mostly. Hitched some but didn't have any money to give for gas and didn't want to ride with drunks. Besides I can take care of myself.

OSHUN   What you doin' up there, you?

TAUREAN   Looking for a job.

OSHUN   No money. I says you didn't find one.

TAUREAN   I will. Have to.

OSHUN   C'mon over here. I give you somethin'.

TAUREAN   No. Thanks.

OSHUN   Look to me like you might need a few things, including that job.

TAUREAN   You got one?

OSHUN   I'll think on it. Come. Sit. Be a might before you see another
   body along this here road. C'mon. I not a gator, I won't bite.

   [TAUREAN *backs up a step.*]

   Didn't your mama teach you manners?

TAUREAN   [*Defensively.*] You don't know nothing about my mama.

OSHUN   only meant that I'm invitin' you to my table. Come on now,
   sit on down.

TAUREAN   I don't have time to hang around here.

OSHUN   Well then, I guess I best be quick about . . . feedin' you.

   [*She motions him to the table. He hesitates, then slowly crosses and sits.*]

   That more like it.

[*Pause as she stares at him.*]

TAUREAN   I was hoping to find more people out this way.

OSHUN   Me too.

   [*Beat.*]

   It a quiet place but it comin' alive again. There be peoples wander
   back, not as many like before.

TAUREAN   Nothing like before.

   [*Beat.*]

   I need to find work, maybe a fishing boat.

OSHUN   Fishin' jumpin' a might again but still a ways to go.

TAUREAN   I'll find something. Take care of myself. Maybe try my hand
   at roughnecking on the oil rigs.

   [*Beat.*]

   Need to be on my way soon and see what's out there.

OSHUN   Roughneckin' on the rigs? How old you be, you?

TAUREAN   Old enough.

[OSHUN *reaches across the table, runs a hand down his cheek. He backs his face away. She smiles.*]

OSHUN   You got soft skin, but I 'spect you are . . . old enough. Maybe just, though.

  [OSHUN *takes bowl, crosses to the orange tree.*]

  Don't matter much. No fishin' boats hirin' right now. Oil work still 'bouts the new rigs buildin' up. That good for me, more people comin' out this way, be wantin' my advice and goods, but they ain't hirin'.

TAUREAN   You give advice?

OSHUN   I do.

TAUREAN   Like Dear Abby?

OSHUN   Not quite. Mine come with cards and cat bones.

TAUREAN   What?

OSHUN   You born here 'bouts?

TAUREAN   Yeah.

[OSHUN *rips a few oranges, crosses back to table.*]

OSHUN   Then don't you go actin' dumb. You knows what a woman fixin' to do with cards and cat bones.

TAUREAN   I heard stories. I never seen—

OSHUN   You wanna see from me?

  [TAUREAN *shrugs his shoulders.* OSHUN *chuckles.*]

  Mmm-hmmm.

[*Pause.*]

TAUREAN   Are you any good with advice?

OSHUN   I am.

TAUREAN   And other stuff?

[OSHUN *walks around* TAUREAN, *smiles.*]

OSHUN   I'm good with everythin'. What you want, you?

TAUREAN   I mean, other stuff with cards and bones, maybe connecting people.

OSHUN   What people you want connection with, you?

> [TAUREAN *rises, crosses away from her, hugs himself.*]

> Most my advice sought by folks what have sadness in their lives. You too vibrant for that.

TAUREAN   [*Turns to face the orange tree.*] I wish that were true.

OSHUN   They look good, no?

TAUREAN   They look perfect. I don't think I've ever seen oranges quite like them.

OSHUN   Stay with me a bit. I give you one.

TAUREAN   I'm heading on down the road, see what I can find.

OSHUN   I already told you, no work down there.

TAUREAN   Don't seem to be any here, either.

OSHUN   I could find lots of things to keep you here.

> [*Beat.*]

> I tell you what, you see that wood pile? It need stackin'. You do it, I pay you.

TAUREAN   With more than an orange?

OSHUN   Once you nibble on something so juicy, you might not want anything else, chère.

TAUREAN   I'll need more.

OSHUN   Maybe I fixin' to give you more.

TAUREAN   I don't know—

OSHUN   Yes, you do. A good day work might just bring pleasure to both of us.

[OSHUN *motions for* TAUREAN *to exit to woodpile: he does as she watches him. Lights fade.*]

··· scene two ···

[*Lights up: afternoon sun begins to slip away.* OSHUN *stands by table, wringing out* TAUREAN'*s damp shirt.*]

OSHUN

I'M A VOODOO WOMAN, CAST YOUR LOVE TO ME
ALL ELSE DISAPPEAR, I BE WHAT YOU NEED
CALL DOWN THE SPIRITS, TWINE AN ACHE WITH YOU
MY CHARMS BREW IN YOUR BODY, I BE YOUR ONLY
VIEW.

[TAUREAN *enters, shirtless, wet with sweat, crosses around the orange tree, looking at it.*]

I wash it out a bit but don't have no dryer. Hang it over the chair, take a short time in this heat.

TAUREAN   I can wear it wet.

OSHUN   It stick to you. No comfort there.

TAUREAN   Who says I'm looking for comfort?

[OSHUN *snaps out the shirt, hangs it over a chair.*]

OSHUN   You been stackin' a few hours. The rest of the wood can wait and I owes you an orange.

TAUREAN   I've been wondering about these oranges. You notice this tree the only thing all blooming in your yard?

[OSHUN *takes a knife from her pocket.*]

It's like nothing else alive out here except these oranges.

OSHUN   Trust me, chère, I'm alive. Very much alive.

TAUREAN   Nothing is *growing* except this orange tree. Why is that?

[OSHUN *shrugs and takes an orange from the bowl on the table.*]

OSHUN   Why question it? Just come over and enjoy.

TAUREAN   It don't feel right. I feel—

OSHUN   *I* feel.

TAUREAN   What?

OSHUN   You come over here now and I pay you.

TAUREAN   I'm just gonna take my shirt and go.

OSHUN   Go to what, you?

TAUREAN   Go farther south.

OSHUN   I didn't say where. I say to what.

TAUREAN   To a job. Maybe people down there.

OSHUN   I'm not people?

TAUREAN   I'm *not* curious about you.

[OSHUN *laughs, cuts orange with knife, sniffs deeply as the aroma fills the air.* TAUREAN *sniffs.*]

OSHUN   Smell even better than they look, no?

TAUREAN   I gotta go. I just need my shirt.

[OSHUN *takes a slice of orange, crushes it.* TAUREAN *begins to cross to his shirt, but she cuts him off, brings the orange to his mouth. He tries to move around her, but she places one hand on his chest, stopping him.*]

OSHUN   Bite. Take it. I give them somethin' special.

TAUREAN   I don't need nothing special from you or anyone else. I can take care of myself.

[OSHUN *bites the orange slice, juice runs down her fingers.*]

OSHUN Just a taste.

[*She slides the hand from his chest to caress his cheek. He tries to move away.*]

TAUREAN Get away from me.

OSHUN I give you work and this how you pay me, you?

TAUREAN *You* were supposed to pay *me*. Guess not, huh?

OSHUN One bite and I will.

TAUREAN One bite?

OSHUN If that's all you want.
>[*She tickles his lips with the orange, his lips part. Singing.*]
>I'M A VOODOO WOMAN
>[*She smiles and feeds him.*]
>Good. Yes?

TAUREAN Tastes like an orange. Don't look like you're gonna give me what I need.

OSHUN [*Singing.*] CAST YOUR LOVE TO ME

TAUREAN I'm going.

[TAUREAN *tries to move around* OSHUN; *she counters his movements, stopping him.*]

OSHUN One more bite.

TAUREAN You said only one.

OSHUN You need more.

TAUREAN I don't think so.

[TAUREAN *pulls away from* OSHUN, *picks up his shirt, starts to exit.*]

OSHUN [*Singing.*] ALL ELSE DISAPPEAR.
>[*Stops singing.*]
>Take this for the road. It already cut up.

TAUREAN   I'm fine.

OSHUN   All I asks is you take the orange.

TAUREAN   That all?

[OSHUN *gives* TAUREAN *the orange slices. He turns to exit, takes a slice, eats it.*]

OSHUN   ALL ELSE DISAPPEAR, I BE WHAT YOU NEED.
WHAT YOU NEED. WHAT YOU NEED.

[TAUREAN *stops.*]

TAUREAN   It tastes . . . different. Sweeter. Deeper.

OSHUN   More?

TAUREAN   [*Growing weak.*] I said only one . . .

OSHUN   That all you want, you? Really?
[*Sings.*]
CALL DOWN THE SPIRITS, TWINE AN ACHE WITH YOU.

TAUREAN   [*Weaker.*] I don't . . . I don't know.

OSHUN   More.

[TAUREAN *turns to* OSHUN. *He swoons. She guides him back to the chair: he does not resist. She sits on the chair arm, rips open another orange, feeds him.* TAUREAN *looks up at her.*]

TAUREAN   I never tasted an orange as good as that.

OSHUN   [*She touches his face and hair.*] Maybe you was just that hungry. I am. It gets lonely now out here, middle of nowhere. It nice to have someone kind and strong around.

TAUREAN   I can be kind and strong.

OSHUN   I knows. Trust me.

TAUREAN   I do.

[OSHUN *leans into* TAUREAN, *runs a finger wiping juice from his face. She smiles.*]

OSHUN   Now, yes, I think now you stay with me.

[*Singing.*]

MY CHARMS BREW IN YOUR BODY, I BE YOUR ONLY
VIEW. YOUR ONLY VIEW.

[OSHUN *kisses* TAUREAN *passionately.* JAKE *enters.*]

JAKE   Well, ain't this a pretty sight.

[OSHUN *rises.*]

TAUREAN   May I have another orange, please?

JAKE   Go ahead, give him another.

OSHUN   In a bit.

TAUREAN   I never tasted oranges as good as these.

JAKE   Yeah, you right. These the best damned oranges in the world.
Who's the kid?

TAUREAN   I'm not a kid.

OSHUN   No, you not.

JAKE   What's he doing here?

OSHUN   He lookin' for work, was wondering' about the oil rigs—

JAKE   I just come off a seven-week stretch gettin' one of the new rigs up
and runnin'. All veteran riggers. We ain't hirin'.

OSHUN   I told him so. I give him some work here.

JAKE   Yeah? What else you givin' him?

[OSHUN *crosses to* JAKE.]

OSHUN   I save that for you.

JAKE   You hear that, kid? She means I'm her lover. Best damn lover she
ever did have.

OSHUN   You think so?

JAKE   [*Laughs.*] I know so, my li'l witchy woman.

> [JAKE *grabs* OSHUN, *pulls her into a rough hug, smells her hair, nibbles her neck.*]

> The kid needs to leave. Run along.

[TAUREAN *rises abruptly, pushing his chair back forcefully: it tips over.*]

TAUREAN   I'm not a kid!

OSHUN   He old enough.

JAKE   Ha. When did you start 'em so young?

[TAUREAN *takes a few steps towards* JAKE *and* OSHUN.]

TAUREAN   If you don't let her go, you're gonna find out how young I am.

JAKE   Kid, this is my grabbin'-on time, so you'll understand if I ain't about to be lettin' go. Witchy woman here about the only thing in thirty miles worth a trip.

> [*Beat.*]

> And she got the best oranges I ever did taste.

OSHUN   You mean my tree?

JAKE   [*Laughs lustily.*] I mean you *and* your tree, darlin'.

[TAUREAN *paces.*]

OSHUN   You a handful.

JAKE   You love my hands.

OSHUN   They alright.

JAKE   I'm missin' your hands, your massages. You a comfort for these weary bones.

OSHUN   What be weary, you?

JAKE   Ha! Not that bone. Definitely not that. Chère, I been thinkin' about you for almost two months. Get me through some long nights in the middle of the Gulf.

OSHUN   Sometimes you a charmer.

JAKE   Right now I'm an impatient charmer. How 'bout we stop jawin', get rid of the kid, and you get in that bed with me.

[JAKE *grabs at* OSHUN'*s breast. She pushes his hand away.*]

OSHUN   We got time for that later. You come back in a few days.

JAKE   Fuck a few days. I'm out for three weeks and I'm ready now.

OSHUN   I not. You go now.

JAKE   I don't think so. Get the fuck outta here, kid, so I can take witchy woman inside and show her how a real man cast a spell, if ya know what I mean. 'Cuz if you're thinkin' you can make it happen, trust me, she's way out of your league.

[TAUREAN *stops pacing.*]

TAUREAN   Leave her alone.

JAKE   You're a feisty crawdad, ain't ya?

TAUREAN   She said no.

JAKE   Kid, I'm lookin' to be a lover today, not a fighter. But don't push it.

TAUREAN   Maybe she don't need you anymore.

JAKE   That it, woman? You don't need me?

OSHUN   I need diff'rent things, diff'rent peoples, diff'rent times.

JAKE   Yeah? Guess what I need. Scram, kid.

TAUREAN   You scram, old man!

JAKE   I been tryin' to be nice about this, kid, but you're just not *getting'* it.

[JAKE *pushes* OSHUN *aside and lunges at* TAUREAN, *who sidesteps.* JAKE *falls, rises. They fight.*]

OSHUN   [*Yelling.*] Stop! Jake! You leave! Go!

[*The men ignore her, fighting escalates. She grabs herbs, dried flowers, and an orange off the tree. JAKE pushes TAUREAN back and grabs the knife on the table. They face off. OSHUN steps towards them.*]

JAKE   [*To* OSHUN.] What you doin' with those things?

[OSHUN *stops.*]

OSHUN   Why not we all calm down?

JAKE   I know all about you. You and that name of yours. Some voodoo love African Venus. I see you, when you think I sleeping. At that table of yours. Prayin'. Chantin'. Whatever the fuck you doin'. You ain't none of that. What we got here is you and me just passing the hours, feeding each other's needs.

OSHUN   That all you thinks?

JAKE   Not one fucking thing more. And now you think you're tryin' that voodoo shit on me?

OSHUN   Just. Like. Always.

JAKE   Bullshit. You and I, we're one in the same. Come in like a *flood* and take *what* we want. *When* we want.

OSHUN   No.

JAKE   You keep tellin' yourself that, darlin'.

[JAKE *slashes with the knife trying to strike* TAUREAN, *who falls.* OSHUN *crushes the orange, herbs, and flowers and waves them about.*]

OSHUN   [*Chants at* JAKE.] I banish all forces not in harmony with me. We are addressin' *you.*

JAKE   You hear that, kid, she thinks she's gonna hex me. Witch.

OSHUN   We are addressin' you.

JAKE   [*Growing weak.*] Not me. Not me.

OSHUN   Banish all forces hostile.

[JAKE *gets wobbly.*]

JAKE   [*Weaker.*] It's not gonna work.

OSHUN   It already is. You will understand.

> [JAKE *drops the knife.* TAUREAN *starts to rise, but* OSHUN *motions for him to stay down.*]
>
> Breathe.

[JAKE *takes a deep breath.* OSHUN *motions for him to come to her: he does.* JAKE *gently leans into her and nuzzles. He is docile now, almost childlike.*]

JAKE   You smell delicious. Like honey. I need honey.

OSHUN   I know and didn't I always give you what you needed.

[OSHUN *gets a basket, drops in the orange crush, puts in a jar of honey, hands it to* JAKE. *He takes a large wad of cash from his pocket, hands it to her. She gently urges him away from her. He exits.*]

TAUREAN   What just happened?

OSHUN   He calm down, is all.

TAUREAN   I never seen anything . . . what the hell are you?

OSHUN   You already know the answer to that.

[OSHUN *puts the money on her voodoo altar.* TAUREAN *rises. The sun continues to set.*]

TAUREAN   Will he come back?

OSHUN   [*With conviction.*] I don't want him back.

TAUREAN   What did you do to him?

OSHUN   Nature.

TAUREAN   I don't understand.

OSHUN   I know.

TAUREAN He's your lover?

[OSHUN *crosses to* TAUREAN.]

OSHUN No. A lover is someone I want to share my heart with. Someone kind and strong. That not what he was. He was just a necessity. The others, too.

TAUREAN There are others?

[OSHUN *nods.*]

Why?

OSHUN They bring me things.

TAUREAN Money. You make them bring you money.

OSHUN That not a bad thing. I buy this trailer. Food. My things. I live simple, sell what I can, advise when I can. After the storm I only gots me to rely on, take care of. Everything . . . everyone in my heart gone so—[*Beat.*]—let's just say I have many visitors what helps pass the hours. And, nature, she makes them easier to control. Some are gentle. Some just want talk. Others? Sometimes a warm body be good, even if it be a lie.

TAUREAN You said you was lonely.

OSHUN Havin' visitors got nothin' to do with bein' lonely.

[*Pause.*]

TAUREAN You asked if I wanted to know how you . . . make things special. I do need to know.

OSHUN You sure, you?

[TAUREAN *nods.*]

Why so important to you?

TAUREAN There's someone I need to connect with.

OSHUN What your name?

TAUREAN Taurean.

OSHUN Taurean? Why I know that name?

TAUREAN Used to play football for the Belle Chase Cardinals. Best running back they ever had. Got my name in the *Picayune*. Scouts came looking my junior year, but then it all fell apart. Football. Grades. All gone. I just managed to graduate. Two years ago.

OSHUN Two years? That mean you?
[*Beat.*]
Nineteen. You can't be only nineteen. You look—

TAUREAN Older.

OSHUN How that possible? *Nineteen.*

[*Pause.* OSHUN *is lost in thought before* TAUREAN *breaks the silence.*]

TAUREAN Two years. Seems like a lifetime.

OSHUN A lifetime. A lifetime.

TAUREAN I wouldn't change it, you know. What I did those last few years. Not for anything.
[*Beat.*]
But Mama still died. Cancer. I hate that she had to see this emptiness before she passed. See our memories washed away.

OSHUN You be young to know this much hurt. So young.

TAUREAN I'm not a kid.

OSHUN You got family, you?

TAUREAN Just Mama. Took care of her 'til the end.

OSHUN Through her pains?
[TAUREAN *nods.*]
Through her loneliness?

TAUREAN   Don't know that she was lonely.

OSHUN   She was. And you a good . . . *young* man. You already connect with your mama, you.

TAUREAN   How do I do that?

OSHUN   You talk to her even now?

TAUREAN   Every day.

OSHUN   Then you feel her in your heart.

> [TAUREAN *nods.*]

Trust me.

TAUREAN   I do.

OSHUN   She around, always. You not ever be lonely.

TAUREAN   You don't have to be lonely, either.

> [OSHUN *looks at him thoughtfully, picks up the bowl of oranges, crosses to the tree, leaves bowl there.*]

You coming back here with those?

> [OSHUN *picks up Saints hat, kneels in front of* TAUREAN, *brushes a strand of hair from his eyes, puts hat on his head.*]

I don't want a hat.

> [TAUREAN *takes hat off, hands it to* OSHUN. *She stands, places it in her pocket. He encircles her with his arms, nuzzling into her breasts.*]

I want you.

> [OSHUN *lingers a moment before disentangling herself. He follows after her.*]

I'll stay with you and work hard. And it won't be a lie.

OSHUN   Bring me love?

TAUREAN   I'll bring you anything.

[TAUREAN *kisses her passionately.* OSHUN *pushes him and crosses away.*]

OSHUN   I 'spose football star who takes care o' his mama through her pains be kind and strong. Like my boy, Rada.

TAUREAN   Your boy?

OSHUN   [*Nods.*] Nineteen year old.

TAUREAN   My age.

OSHUN   Played football for LSU. And he loved him his Saints.
[*Beat.*]
The storm hit just 'fore he was headin' back to school for his second year.
[*Pause.*]
The water claimed him.
[*Beat.*]
It was too fast. We was too slow. I went in after him, next thing I 'member is that hospital in Baton Rouge and his coach standin' over me. Stayed on up there a while, healin' . . . my body, but I had to come back.
[*Beat.*]
Miss him every day, but he still in my heart and I talks to him even now.

TAUREAN   I'm sorry.

[OSHUN *nods.*]

OSHUN   You finish the woodpile now, you?

TAUREAN   Anything you want.

[OSHUN *smiles at him, pats his arm.* TAUREAN *exits to the woodpile. Lights fade.*]

···scene three···

[*Lights come up on night. A towel is hung over a chair.* TAUREAN *is asleep under the orange tree.* OSHUN *kneels beside him, strokes his hair as she very slowly sings.*]

OSHUN

> A SERPENT ON MY SHOULDER
> TWINE AN ACHE WITH YOU,
> MY CHARMS, YOUR DESIRES,
> MAKE INTOXICATING BREW.
>
> [*Pause.*]
>
> TWINE AN ACHE WITH YOU,
>
> [*Pause.*]
>
> MAKE INTOXICATING BREW.
>
> My charms. Your desires. You could bring me love. But what the cost be?
>
> [*She rises, gathers herbs and jars in yard, and crosses back to* TAUREAN *as she tries to convince herself of what she already knows.*]
>
> Water as child of earth, why you bring this man . . . this *boy* to me? Sometime your will be cruel.
>
> [OSHUN *softly kisses* TAUREAN, *crosses to hose, puts it in tub, turns it on. Running water is heard.*]
>
> Give me strength not to take, but to give. Give.
>
> [OSHUN *places herbs and other ingredients into the water, hikes up her skirt, and steps into the tub, swirling in the water.*]
>
> Water as child of earth, it upon you I must put my trust. Water who cleanse my body, we are addressin' you and you will understand. I asks you to bring love for my body, my heart, and now I asks to see your ways. He a fine boy, like my Rada. So young. *Too* young. If it your will, give me strength to transfer the spell into the water and make it sleeps. No harm comin' from the cancellin' of this here spell. No further power shall it have.

[OSHUN *steps out of water, scooping some into a small wooden bowl. She crosses to the sleeping* TAUREAN *and rubs his arms with the water. He stirs, opening his eyes.*]

TAUREAN   [*Groggy.*] Where am I?

OSHUN   Been sleepin' under the orange tree 'bout an hour.

TAUREAN   What are you doing?

OSHUN   Wiping sweat from you. You work hard today.

TAUREAN   [*Sits up.*] I ate oranges.

OSHUN   And you stack the wood.

TAUREAN   And I fought an old man?

OSHUN   Me too. An old man and his ways.

> [*Pause as* TAUREAN *snuggles next to* OSHUN.]
>
> I made a bath for you.

TAUREAN   I don't want a bath.

OSHUN   [*Sniffs.*] You do, trust me.

[TAUREAN *sniffs under his arms and laughs.*]

TAUREAN   Ripe?

OSHUN   All young mens get ripe when they work hard. Have you ever done bathin' outside, you?

TAUREAN   No. But if you bathe with me . . .

OSHUN   I give it somethin' special. Outside bathin' a joyful 'sperience. My Rada did almost every day, even in the storms. I used to yell to him come in 'fore lightning strike, but he just laugh at his old mama.

[OSHUN *guides* TAUREAN *to the metal tub. She begins to undress him, lifting the T-shirt over his head.*]

TAUREAN   You're not old.

[OSHUN *runs her hands down his chest, stopping at his jeans buttons.*]

OSHUN   You should do this yo'self, bébé.

[TAUREAN *moves his hands to hers, looks at her with passion, caresses her face and arms.*]

TAUREAN   I want you to.

> [OSHUN *runs her hand down his cheek, shakes her head, then steps back, turns off hose, crosses away from him, her back to him.* TAUREAN *removes his shoes, socks.*]

> You never told me your name.

OSHUN   I know.

TAUREAN   Tell me.

OSHUN   Why it important? You leave soon, bébé.

TAUREAN   I want to stay.

OSHUN   [*Speaks to herself.*] But I must be strong. Let you leave.

TAUREAN   What's in the water? It smells good, like . . . [*Sniffs.*] mama's garden.

[TAUREAN *removes his pants and briefs. He is naked.*]

OSHUN   Rosemary oil, angelica, benzoin from the tree bark.

TAUREAN   Why all that stuff?

OSHUN   It something I do when I needs be changin' something I did.

TAUREAN   What?

OSHUN   My oranges, they soothin', sometimes more powerful than other times. They about connection. Could be lovers. Pleasure. Be family. Peace. Heart. You took it all in, and it change you. And now I change you back.

TAUREAN   I like where I am now. With you.

OSHUN   Part of me wishes I could keep you.

TAUREAN   You can. I don't want to change.

OSHUN   No matter, bébé.

TAUREAN   It does matter.

OSHUN   Get in the bath. It make you feel good.

TAUREAN   *You* make me feel good.

> [TAUREAN *embraces* OSHUN *from behind and kisses her neck. He pulls her backs to the bath, slides into it, bringing her with him.*]

This feels real. Good.

OSHUN   It feel good. But what you feel is . . . is my doin'. It nature and no further power be havin'.

TAUREAN   I don't care what it is.

OSHUN   I cares. I release it. Must have strengths to release you.

TAUREAN   No release. I'll do anything. Wear that Saints' hat even. Whenever you want, for as long as you want.

[OSHUN *abruptly rises from the tub.* TAUREAN *holds out his hands to her.*]

OSHUN   Rada's hat.

[OSHUN *shakes head "no."*]

TAUREAN   Want you.

OSHUN   No!

TAUREAN   I will love you.

OSHUN   I can't have this love.

TAUREAN   You wanted me. I know you did. I felt it when you first kissed me. Why are you fighting this now?

OSHUN   The others, *they* come to *me* and I bind them to me with my oranges. You, you *fought* me and I thought you might ease the loneliness. Might be real. But you not be real. You be *young*. *Nineteen*. I can *not* . . . *flood* over you and take what I needs. I must *give*. Must give you the life my Rada never had the chance to be livin'.

TAUREAN   I want to live with you. I don't understand.

OSHUN   You no need to. Trust me. Please. Feel the water. Feel it work into you. Feel it release you.

TAUREAN   Don't want release.

OSHUN   Do it feel good?

TAUREAN   [*Feeling release.*] Yes.

[OSHUN *pours water over* TAUREAN.]

OSHUN   Do you still want to stay, you?

TAUREAN   [*Feeling release.*] I don't know.

OSHUN   No harm may come from makin' it sleep. Please, gives me strength, make it sleep.

TAUREAN   [*Feeling more release.*] Sleep.

OSHUN   No further power shall it have.

   [*She rubs water on him.*]

   What you want now, bébé?

TAUREAN   [*Feeling more release.*] Don't know.

OSHUN   I see your ways, water as child of earth.

   [*Beat.*]

   I thinks you do. Say it. Say it.

TAUREAN   I need . . . to move on.

[OSHUN *rises, crosses to towel.*]

OSHUN   Need a powerful word.

TAUREAN   So is pain and lonely.

OSHUN   Like your mama had.

TAUREAN   And you.

   [*Beat.*]

   And me.

OSHUN   You can know those feelin's so young.

TAUREAN   I grew up fast.

OSHUN   You did.

> [*Beat.*]

> I miss people. Kind people. Real people.

> [*Pause.*]

> Time to get out.

TAUREAN   Time to get out.

> [TAUREAN *gets out of the tub.* OSHUN *hands him a towel, then crosses away from him. He dries himself, dresses.*]

> I'm not sure I understand what happened today.

OSHUN   You did everythin' right, bébé.

TAUREAN   I can take care of myself.

OSHUN   You been doin' that for two years. You needs more now. Do you still trust me? Trust Oshun?

TAUREAN   [*Nods.*] Oshun.

[OSHUN *crosses to altar, takes* JAKE's *money, crosses to* TAUREAN.]

OSHUN   I want to give you this. It gets you to Baton Rouge.

TAUREAN   Baton Rouge?

OSHUN   Go see Coach Morris at LSU. He be helpin' you get settled. I tells him you a good boy, you.

TAUREAN   I'm old enough.

OSHUN   I 'spect you are old enough.

TAUREAN   Can I take some oranges?

> [OSHUN *shakes her head "no."*]

> Will you be okay?

OSHUN   I be okay.

> [*Pause.*]

> It good you be here today, you.

TAUREAN   Oshun. Thank you for—

OSHUN   No need to thank me, bébé. It was upon you I put my trust.

> [TAUREAN *picks up his backpack and slowly exits.* OSHUN *crosses to the altar and places the Saints hat on it. She crosses to tub, takes a bowlful of water, crosses to orange tree, and pours it around the base.*]

> Water as child of earth, with these words and this potion I *release* the fruit of the land. No further power shall it have. I takes no more. I *give*. Find love myself. Put it in my own hand.

> [OSHUN *sings.*]

> I'M A VOODOO WOMAN SINCE I BEEN BORN,
> MOTHER NATURE'S BOUNTY, THE PACT I'VE SWORN,
> NOW I FIND MY OWN WAY WITH THE SKY AND EARTH,
> I USE MY GIVING STRENGTHS! JOY! CHANGE!
> REBIRTH!

[OSHUN *dances with abandon. Lights fade.*]

• • •

White or the
Muskox Play

Jonathan Fitts

To my mother, I hope you can get past the muskox

White is the darkness that never goes away.
—Richard Vetere

With special thanks to Tony Howarth and the Kennedy Center American College Theatre Festival.

Jonathan Fitts

Jonathan Fitts is a playwright living in New York City. *White or the Muskox Play* recently won the Kennedy Center's National Short Play Award and was a finalist for the O'Neill National Playwrights Conference and was the first alternate for the National Partners of the American Theatre National Playwriting Award. Fitts holds an MFA in dramatic writing from New York University. More info at www. jonathanfitts.wordpress.com.

···production history···

The play was the 2011 recipient of the KCACTF Region I One-Act Play Award and was presented as a staged reading at the regional festival in Fitchburg, Massachusetts, on January 28, 2012, directed by Tony Howarth.

The play subsequently won the Kennedy Center's John Cauble National Short Play Award and had a concert reading at the Kennedy Center for the Performing Arts in Washington, D.C., on April 19, 2012, with the following cast and director:

Director, Colin Hovde

Stage Directions, Nancy Robinette

BON   Jennifer Mendenhall

MUSKOX   Rick Foucheux

ROY   Michael Kramer

MITCH   Frank Britton

The play had a subsequent production at KNOW Theatre in Binghamton, New York, July 5–7, 2012, and a workshop at the Cape Cod Theatre Project for the week of July 23–27, facilitated by a fellowship from the Kennedy Center American College Theatre Festival.

characters

BON, Female. Many ages, ranging for eleven to forty-six. Caucasian. A woman grieving the loss of her father. She should be played by a singular, adult woman.

MUSKOX, Male. Early seventies. Not her father, but his symbol.

ROY, Male. Late forties. Bon's husband.

MITCH, Male. Late thirties. A Yup'ik man, working as a tour guide in Barrow, Alaska.

setting

The snowy tundra of Point Barrow, Alaska. Also, a pool in Florida, a suburban home in the American South, a small house in Haverhill, Massachusetts, a lanai in central Florida, a pier on the south side of Boston, the north bank of the Merrimack River.

notes

All characters with the exception of Mitch were born and raised in New England. Consider beats, where noted, as moments for discovery. Dialogue in brackets is unspoken and constitutes a silence.

• • •

[*White. So much White. Is this what the abyss looks like? I expected it to be . . . darker. Shapes rise and fall. Light rests softly on the air and its particulates. Hazy, White glares. White noise rolling in and out, licking the rocky shapes that rise and fall in the haze. A shape appears. An object of tremendous mass, density, gravity, import. Furry. Horned. Grave. It is a man in a thick fur coat. Impenetrable. Horns protrude from his fur hat. His face is so old. It has seen so much. It has been weathered by the White. The image comes into focus. Things pop out of the haze; specks of snow gently falling, rocks, a bridge, in the middle of which stands the shape . . . a man. Except he is not a man. He is a* MUSKOX *and he takes up the entire bridge. No passing. Crunch, crunch, crunch . . . an approach through the haze and snow. The* MUSKOX *does not move.* BON *materializes in the White, trudging towards the bridge in thick snow gear. It's more difficult than it looks. Under one arm, she carries a small steel jar. On her back is a large backpack. She stops to rest, panting. She sees the* MUSKOX. *The* MUSKOX *does not move.*]

BON   Move!

> [*The* MUSKOX *does not move.*]

> Come on, now!

> [BON *claps. The* MUSKOX *does not move.* BON *produces a satellite phone from her bag, dials.*]

> Hey. It's me. The bridge is blocked.

[MITCH *fades into focus, but he's many miles away.* BON *cannot see him.*]

MITCH   You owe me ten bucks.

BON   What?

MITCH   Less than three hours before you called for help. I win.

BON   Is there another bridge?

MITCH   I don't know.

BON   Can you check? It's going to be dark in a little bit.

MITCH   Sweet cheeks, you've got an hour, tops, before we go lights-out for a month. Yay, Alaska.

BON   Great. So how about a little help with the bridge?

MITCH   What's wrong with it?

BON   It's occupied.

MITCH   . . . And then I ask . . .

BON   A muskox.

MITCH   Just one?

[*A timid step towards the beast. A beastly bellow from the* MUSKOX.]

BON   One's enough. Where's the next closest bridge?

MITCH   I think there's one to the south back towards Imikpuk Lake.

BON   I don't know where that is.

MITCH   Okay. Where are you now?

BON   Just south of Point Barrow.

MITCH   Great. But *where* exactly?

BON   I don't know.

MITCH   Can you describe it?

BON   There's . . . White. A shitload of White.

MITCH   Okay. That doesn't help at all.

BON   The ocean's right there. There's gotta be another way to get across.

MITCH   There's a river, right?

BON   Yeah.

MITCH   Bring your bathing suit?

BON   Shit.

MITCH   'Cause . . . if you did . . . you'd have to show me at some point.

BON   Shut up.

MITCH   What? I'm just saying.

BON   Is it safe?

MITCH   Of course. It'd just be our little, private modeling session.

BON   The river, you dipshit.

MITCH   Oh. Yeah. Less safe. It's still moving, right?

BON   Into the ocean.

MITCH   Yeah, I wouldn't risk it. Especially so close to being dark. In this cold, getting wet is the difference between life and death.

BON   Please don't make . . .

MITCH   That's what she said.

BON   Have I told you how much I hate you yet?

MITCH   Aw. You're too sweet. Have fun. Don't die. Be home before dark.

[BON *hangs up and looks into the river from a safe distance.*]

BON   Dammit.

[*The White wind breathes and blows. Shivers.* BON *turns to the* MUSKOX.]

Okay. You really need to move now. This has been fun. Charming. But I'm done. I've got to get to the ocean. I've come this far. I'm carrying something very important.

[*She holds the steel jar before the* MUSKOX.]

This is the most important thing I've ever carried. I need to get by. Will you move?

[*The* MUSKOX *does not move.*]

Move, you fucking buffalo sunnovabitch, it's cold!

[*A threatening step towards the* MUSKOX. *Another bellow from the* MUSKOX.]

MUSKOX   It's not cold.

[*The sound pounds the White like a sledgehammer into a wall of sand.* BON *is rigid. Some of the White begins to fall away in flakes like scales.*]

BON   What did you say?

MUSKOX   It's not cold.

[*More flakes fall. They overtake the snow. They release the White. It chips away and reveals a swimming pool.*]

BON   1975.

[*A cabana of pinks and blues and Caribbean hues. A golden sun. Azure sky. Clear water. White pool.* BON *in a bathing suit. She is eleven. She stands at the edge of the pool. The* MUSKOX *steps out of his fur coat. It's much too hot, don't you think? He wears a bathing suit and stands in the pool. The fur coat and hat remain suspended, occupying the bridge.*]

MUSKOX   C'mon. You're being a baby. Once you get in, it warms up.

BON   It doesn't work like that!

MUSKOX   Who said?

BON   Mommy.

MUSKOX   Well, Mommy doesn't know what she's talking about.

BON   Mommy knows lots of things.

MUSKOX   I know plenty too. C'mon, you're making a scene.

BON   I don't care!

MUSKOX   Bonnie Elizabeth Maywell, you get in this pool.

BON   I don't want to!

MUSKOX   One . . . Two . . .

>   [*Don't make me get to three . . .*]
>   Two . . .

BON   I said I don't want to!

MUSKOX   Don't you remember how much fun we had last year? Aren't you hot?

BON   I'm fine!

MUSKOX   Don't look fine. Look like you're turning into a lobster.

BON   I'm not turning into a lobster.

MUSKOX   Sure looks like it to me.

BON   Where are you going?

MUSKOX   I'm not going anywhere.

BON   We only go on vacation before you leave for work.

MUSKOX   You're a sharp kid.

BON   I know.

[*The* MUSKOX *smiles.*]

MUSKOX   I'm going somewhere far away. Do you know where Alaska is?

BON   Up north.

MUSKOX   Way up north. Where it's *really* cold.

BON   Like the water.

MUSKOX   The water's a piece of cake. Should be no problem for a big girl like you.

[*Perhaps* BON *blushes.*]

BON   Can I come with you?

MUSKOX   If you won't even get into the water, how will you get by up north?

[BON *considers. That's fair.*]

BON   Will you catch me?

MUSKOX   I will *always* catch you.

BON   Will you hold me out of the water?

MUSKOX   I can't do that.

BON   Why not?

MUSKOX   I'm not strong enough. What do you want me to do? Walk around the pool holding you over my head like . . . I don't know . . . a stuffed pig?

BON   It'd be funny.

MUSKOX   You're getting too big for that.

BON   But it looks cold.

MUSKOX   It's not cold. Just let yourself adjust.

[BON *takes a deep breath, looks at the water.*]

C'mon. I've got you.

[*She backs up, the hint of a smile creeping across her face. The* MUSKOX *holds his arms out.* BON *takes a huge breath.* BON *runs! Towards the edge of the pool, ready to jump! As she leaps through the air,* ROY *appears in orange and camo.*]

ROY   Stage four.

[*The cabana disappears and all is* White. BON *crashes to the ground, the* MUSKOX *resumes its furry mantle. A house in southern suburbia assembles out of the* White.]

BON   November 2008.

[*The* MUSKOX *is still visible. Always visible.* ROY *reads off several blank, White sheets of paper. He carries a holstered gun.*]

ROY This don't look amazing.

BON It doesn't mean anything.

ROY You heard the doctor say "stage four"?

BON Yes!

[ROY *reads.*]

ROY This don't look amazing. Does he have . . . you know, is he able to take care of himself?

BON He wasn't drooling and wearing a diaper, if that's what you're asking.

ROY No, I mean financially.

BON Oh. I . . . I'm sure he's fine.

ROY Do Mike and Steve know?

BON Yeah, we called them after we got out.

ROY Have you guys talked about a will?

BON No.

ROY Are you going to?

BON No. We're not going to discuss it at all.

ROY Really?

BON Of course we're going to discuss it. But it's a little early, all right? He's still on two feet.

ROY [*Geez.*] I'm sorry. I, uh, printed you off some reading material. Figured you'd want to read up and whatnot.

BON Thanks. [*Ass-hat.*]

ROY How about you? You all right?

[*She looks up at him.*]

BON I'm good. [*She isn't.*]

ROY You need to talk?

BON You going somewhere?

ROY Well . . . I . . . no. I mean, I had plans to go hunting.

BON Right now?

ROY Last weekend before the season's over.

BON Right now.

ROY No, I'll stay with you if you want.

BON No. Go.

ROY I said I'll stay.

BON Go hunting.

ROY What'd you say to your dad?

BON Go. I'm fine.

ROY I'm here. Now. Talk.

BON I'm not going to make you stay if you don't want to.

ROY I want to. I'm here, aren't I?

BON Are you?

ROY Yes! What's wrong with you?

BON Stage four. If you don't get that, then leave.

ROY Look, I'm here. I'm standing here, right now for *you*. If you want to talk to me, do it. If not . . .

BON Whatever. Forget it. Just go.

ROY   You're acting like a child.

BON   Yeah, I am. But guess what. I get to.

ROY   Are you saying I can go?

BON   Yeah. Go.

ROY   I can stay.

BON   No. It's fine.

ROY   Really?

BON   Really. I'm good.

[ROY *looks at her. He turns to leave . . . At the last possible second . . .*]

BON   Roy.

[*He stops, turns back.*]

BON   [*I'm not good.*]

ROY   Yeah?

BON   [*I need to talk about this. I can't handle this alone.*]

ROY   I've got my cell on if you need me.

[ROY *fades away.* BON *turns to the audience. Bleed to White.*]

BON   Dad looked like a zombie. He'd lost a lot of weight. It wasn't like the life drained out of him or anything, you know? It's like he'd already sprung a leak and now we knew what it was. That it *was* life draining out of him. And we just had to watch. We sat in the car for an hour, and just . . . *sat* in the AC. I didn't want to cry, you know? Didn't want him to feel bad. Like he needed to protect me. But holy shit. *Holy. Shit.* I couldn't think of anything else. The inside of my head was wallpapered with it. And I looked around . . . you know, in my head . . . trying to find other things to focus on. But there weren't. The walls, the windows, they'd all been wallpapered over. Everything else was gone. It had drained out. And I started to get panicky. Almost claustrophobic. I couldn't let it out my eyes, I couldn't let it out my throat. I just had to sit there, with it in my body, pushing from the inside out. And I think Dad had to notice. 'Cause he started fidgeting. And of all things to say, he looked at me and said—

MUSKOX   Let's get some ice cream.

[*The White gives way to a very different house.*]

BON   1980.

[BON *is fifteen. A plate of meat sits before her. The* MUSKOX *steps out of its mantle, this time dressed in business attire. No coat. Perhaps sleeves rolled up. It's much too hot, don't you think?*]

MUSKOX   But only once you finish your meat.

BON   I don't like meat.

MUSKOX   It's good for you.

BON   It tastes like shit.

MUSKOX   What was that?

BON   It tastes like poop.

MUSKOX   That's what I thought. We've got to leave in five minutes if I'm going to make my flight. I can call your mom, have her meet us at Dairy Queen. C'mon.

[*Silence. Glaring at meat.*]

Tell you what. You finish half a steak and we can still go. Meet me halfway?

BON   I don't believe in eating meat.

MUSKOX   What do you mean, "don't believe"? People eat meat regardless of whether you believe it or not.

BON   No. I don't think we should kill other living creatures.

MUSKOX   Who says?

BON   Lotsa people.

MUSKOX   And if "lotsa" people said to jump off a bridge, would you?

BON   Mom lets us eat anything we want.

MUSKOX   Well, that's not always a good idea.

BON   You don't like any of Mom's ideas.

MUSKOX   That's not true. I don't like *most* of your mom's ideas.

BON   She doesn't make me eat meat.

MUSKOX   Well, she should if she wants you to grow up big and strong.

BON   Ugh. And she doesn't talk to me like *that*. I'm fifteen. I'm about as grown and big and strong as I'm gonna get.

MUSKOX   Is that so?

BON   Seems like it. When I talk to her, she doesn't remind me that I'm a kid.

MUSKOX   And I do?

[BON *decides not to speak.*]

Tough.

BON   What?

MUSKOX   You heard me.

BON   But . . . but Mom doesn't talk to me like that!

MUSKOX   I don't want to hear about what your mom does or doesn't do. We're different people. While you're here, you're my daughter. You're not my friend, or my buddy, or . . . I don't know what you think she is to you. I'm your father. So damn right I'm going to remind you of that. Half if you want ice cream.

BON   This shits!

[*The* MUSKOX *might laugh.*]

MUSKOX   It whats?

BON   You heard me.

MUSKOX   You can't use that word that way. Shouldn't use that word *at all* . . .

BON   It's not fair! You can't just come and go and expect me to be okay with it. Why can't you make up your mind? Are you here, or aren't you?!

MUSKOX   Easy. I don't expect you to be okay. I know I'm asking a lot, but I have to go if they tell me to go. That's how it is.

BON   Well, shit that.

[BON *disposes of her plate and grabs her backpack.*]

MUSKOX   And where do you think you're going?

BON   Away.

MUSKOX   Where, exactly?

BON   Wouldn't *you* like to know.

MUSKOX   You gonna at least tell me why?

BON   Because! Point is, I'm leaving. Say your good-byes now!

MUSKOX   All right.

[BON *trudges towards the exit. Stops.*]

BON   I'm leaving now.

MUSKOX   Okay. Travel by day. Steer clear of the boys down by the Merrimack.

BON   Getting dark. And there's a boy down by the river who says he loves me.

MUSKOX   He's probably lying.

[*The* MUSKOX *resumes its furry mantle.*]

BON   I don't think he is. I think he's the greatest boy I know. Much better than you. He actually loves me.

[*No response.*]

I'm going now!

[*No response.*]

Aren't you going to try and convince me to stay?

[BON *stops. She turns away, and the world fades to White. The White, Alaskan wind breathes and blows.* BON *stands opposite the* MUSKOX. *She speaks into her satellite phone.*]

How's that other bridge coming?

[*White noise.*]

Mitch?

[*Nothing.* BON *scours her surroundings. Endless White. She bends down and scoops up a handful of White snow, packing it into a ball. She throws it at the* MUSKOX. *Whumpf. The* MUSKOX *does not move. Another snowball. Another hit! The* MUSKOX *does not move. Another snowball.* BON *does not throw it. She holds it before her, offering it to the* MUSKOX.]

Want some? Tastes good.

[BON *eats some of the snowball. The* MUSKOX *does not move.*]

Not really.

[*She takes another bite out of the snowball. The world fades to a lanai in sunny Florida.*]

July 2009.

[*The* MUSKOX *steps out of its mantle dressed in shorts and a polo. It's much too hot, don't you think?*]

MUSKOX   No one.

BON   Was it the doctor?

MUSKOX   No.

BON   Who was it?

MUSKOX   [*I already said it.*]

BON   I'm not trying to be nosy.

MUSKOX   I know. How's Roy doing?

BON   He's . . . he's Roy.

MUSKOX   You're spending a lot of time down here.

BON   Of course I am.

MUSKOX   How's he doing with it?

BON   It doesn't matter how he's doing with it. This is where I want to be.

MUSKOX   I always liked him. Good man.

BON   Yeah.

MUSKOX   Is he going to come down anytime soon?

BON   If he can get off work. And we know how that goes.

MUSKOX   How about the kids?

BON   They're both off at college.

MUSKOX   What about fall break?

BON   Fall's . . . kind of far away, don't you think?

[*Will he see the fall?*]

MUSKOX   Be here before you know it. That's one thing I never got used to down south. Back in Mass, you *knew* when the seasons changed. It was hot, then one day you woke up and all the leaves had dropped. Then you wake up another day, and you can't see 'cause of all the White. Down here . . . I can't tell anymore. Nothing is separate. It just all runs together.

BON   It's not all that bad.

MUSKOX   You don't live down here.

BON   You want to keep going? Or . . . ?

MUSKOX   Yeah, let's get the sucker done.

BON   So, Uncle Wayne is going to be in charge of selling the house . . .

MUSKOX   Mm-hm.

BON   And you want the funds divided between me, Mike, and Steve?

MUSKOX   Mm-hmm.

BON   I think that just leaves personal effects. Who do you want to have what?

MUSKOX   Mm.

BON   I feel like shit saying that.

MUSKOX   Saying what?

BON   I don't want you to have to give us anything.

MUSKOX   I want to.

BON   I know. But it just feels . . . weird.

MUSKOX   It *is* weird. This isn't something that people do every day. Or plan to do. Not something I ever planned on doing, anyway.

BON   Me either.

MUSKOX   Let me see it.

   [BON *hands him the document. He looks at it with fascination.*]

   It's *very* weird. This . . . this is what will happen when I die.

BON   C'mon. Don't talk about it like that.

MUSKOX   I can no longer function, I can no longer do anything . . . but this piece of paper functions as me. It's *not* me, but someone . . . you, your brothers . . . are going to look at this after I die . . .

BON   Dad.

MUSKOX   . . . And do what it says. The last actions that I will ever begin or complete . . . and I'm holding them in my hand!

BON   I'm not comfortable talking about this!

MUSKOX   I'm sorry. I didn't mean to upset you. Don't have too many people to talk to.

BON   You didn't upset me. I'm sorry. You can talk about whatever you want to talk about.

MUSKOX   I was talking to Roy.

BON   [*What?*]

MUSKOX   On the phone. He misses you. Wants to know when you're coming home.

BON   He . . . he called you?

MUSKOX   Almost every day.

[*The world chips away to White.* BON *and* ROY's *house assembles.*]

BON   June 2009.

> [BON *is preparing to leave.*]

> Roy! I'll see you later!

[ROY *fades into focus wearing a suit.*]

ROY   Where are you going?

BON   Visit Dad.

ROY   Again?

BON   Yeah. There a problem?

ROY   No. It's just . . . you only got back a few days ago.

BON   So?

ROY So . . . he's not going anywhere anytime soon. Is it . . . do you have to go down *now*?

BON Yeah.

ROY Why?

BON [*You can't be serious.*] Are you for real?

ROY Of course I am.

BON So how can you ask why? How can you *possibly* ask why?! Are you so *dense* . . .

ROY We were going to do dinner tonight.

BON We'll do it another night.

ROY But tonight, we were supposed to . . .

BON Tonight I'm on a plane to Florida. I don't know where you are.

ROY Look, I just don't get why you can't spend time with me!

BON Because you're not leaving!

ROY I'm . . . not . . . so sure about that.

BON [*Excuse me?*]

ROY It's our anniversary. That's where I am tonight. Have a good flight.

[ROY *fades out.*]

BON Roy. Roy? ROY! YOU SUNNOVABITCH!

[*But he's gone and all that is left is White. Another house, slowly falling apart.*]

1984.

[BON *is twenty. The* MUSKOX *steps out of its furry mantle. It's much too hot, don't you think? He's dressed in disheveled business attire, soaked to the bone. It's late. He sneaks inside. The light snaps on. White light.*]

Where the hell were you?

MUSKOX I'm going to bed.

BON Why are you wet?

MUSKOX It rained.

BON No, it didn't.

MUSKOX It rained in the city.

BON Not according to Mom.

MUSKOX You shouldn't listen to your mom.

BON Do you have any idea what time it is?!

MUSKOX I don't need you to remind me. GO. TO. BED.

BON You were supposed to be on a plane to Alaska six hours ago.

MUSKOX They canceled my flight.

BON Called the airport. They said it departed on time.

MUSKOX The airline didn't cancel it. The *company* did. I'm not the Alaska guy anymore.

BON Did you get canned?

MUSKOX No.

BON Are you *going* to get canned?

MUSKOX I don't know!

BON Mom called. Said you stopped by to see her.

MUSKOX I wanted to say hi.

BON Really? That was six hours ago. Where have you been?

MUSKOX It's none of your business.

BON We were supposed to have dinner before you left. You didn't stop by to say hi to me.

MUSKOX You're capable. Empowered. Whatever the hell they call it at school.

BON That's not the issue.

MUSKOX You don't know what the issue is.

BON I think I have a pretty good idea.

MUSKOX Then what is it?

BON If I say it, you're just going to deny it!

MUSKOX I'll deny it if you're wrong!

BON And believe me, I want nothing more than to be wrong.

MUSKOX I'm going to bed.

BON Don't leave! I'm not finished!

MUSKOX I am.

[*The* MUSKOX *moves to exit.*]

BON Mom followed you to the pier.

[*The* MUSKOX *stops. Turns, so slowly.*]

MUSKOX She what?

BON Yeah. Last time I checked, you didn't have a boat. It was hours past sunset. So unless you've been taking swimming lessons . . .

MUSKOX I don't want to talk about this.

BON She saw you get in the water!

MUSKOX She's a lying bitch!

BON No, she's not! What happened? A fucking monsoon just appeared out of nowhere . . .

MUSKOX Don't swear!

BON . . . and hit *only* you?

[*The* MUSKOX *moves to exit.* BON *blocks him.*]

She said you went underwater.

MUSKOX   Go to bed!

BON   She said you didn't come up for a long time.

MUSKOX   I don't want to talk about this!

BON   What the fuck were you doing?

MUSKOX   It's none of your business.

BON   [*None of my . . . ?!*] Are you kidding me? It's *so* my fucking business it's not even funny.

MUSKOX   No, it isn't! Because contrary to your belief, the world does not revolve around you. *I* do not revolve around you. I have enough shit!

BON   So much shit that you couldn't leave a fucking note?!

MUSKOX   I didn't exactly plan on it! I came back, didn't I?!

BON   Why did you get in the water?!

MUSKOX   Because . . . because I may be getting canned. I don't know! Because I miss your mother. Because you're never here anymore.

BON   Don't you *dare* try and pass this off on me.

MUSKOX   I'm not! I'm trying to . . . All right. You know everything. You tell me what I was doing.

BON   I can't.

MUSKOX   No, you don't want to. There's a difference. Don't ask to know something if you're not ready to hear the answer.

BON   [*Why didn't you stop by to say hi to me?*]

MUSKOX   Are you ready to hear it?

BON   I . . . I . . . [*No.*]

[*Beat.*]

MUSKOX   Let me change out of these clothes. Then how about we get some ice cream? We don't have to talk about anything. Okay? And we can just be together for a little bit.

[*She swallows her tears.*]

BON   Okay.

[*And the world fades to White, the endless expanse of Point Barrow. The MUSKOX resumes its furry mantle. BON rummages through her backpack, holding the satellite phone to her ear. MITCH fades into focus, still many miles away.*]

I'm losing faith in your navigation abilities.

MITCH   Keep your panties on. Or not. You know. Whatever floats your boat. Look, why don't you come back? I'll give you a massage, we'll light some candles, eat some things. . . . We can go tomorrow. I'll come with you. We'll take the ATV.

BON   I'm staying out.

MITCH   You don't have to prove anything, you know. Do you have to go today? Right now?

BON   Wouldn't be here otherwise.

MITCH   Yeah, but why?

BON   I got out of bed today.

MITCH   Congratulations. What does that have to do with anything?
[BON *is silent.*]
Bon?

BON   Do you know how to spook a muskox?

MITCH   Um. No. Never tried. The gun should do the trick, though.

BON   No.

MITCH   Why not?

BON No.

MITCH . . . I ask again . . .

BON Unless you have a nonviolent way of moving the muskox, stop talking.

MITCH I don't know one. They're pretty fucking mean when they want to be. It's weird that there's only one. They normally travel in groups.

BON Yeah, well, we've got a loner, then.

[*She addresses the* MUSKOX.]

What's the matter? Don't have any friends to freeze to death with?

[*The* MUSKOX *bellows.*]

MITCH So, listen. I was thinking. Once all this is done, I don't want you to feel like you have to come back.

BON We made a deal.

MITCH Yeah, but given everything . . . I'm inclined to be merciful.

BON You're sweet.

MITCH If you still want to come . . . you're always welcome. But I don't want to force you here if you feel like you need to be with your man.

BON My "man"?

MITCH You know what I mean.

[BON *smiles.*]

BON Yeah. I really miss that sunnovabitch.

[ROY *fades into focus.* BON *doesn't notice.* ROY's *voice is distant, as if through a cell phone.*]

ROY Hey, Bon. It's me. I, uh. Well, I've been calling. Keep getting your voice mail. I know you've got your hands full with everything in

Alaska. I'm, uh. I'm worried about you. Wondering when I'm gonna see you next. I miss you.

[ROY *and* MITCH *fade away. The White fades to the lanai.*]

BON   September 2009.

[*The* MUSKOX *again in Florida attire. Warmer layers than before. It's getting chilly.*]

MUSKOX   How many more ways can I say it?

BON   But why?

MUSKOX   I'm seventy-three years old. If I go through with it, yeah. Maybe I'll see seventy-four. Puking and feeling like royal shit. Who'd want that?

BON   But . . . what if they came up with a cure in the next year. Wouldn't you want to hold it out as long as you could?

MUSKOX   Bon. I'm tired. I don't have the energy or the desire to hold it out.

BON   I can't listen to this.

MUSKOX   I never asked you to come down here, you know.

BON   [*You don't want me here?*]

MUSKOX   I didn't.

BON   I'm not going to let you sit down here by yourself.

MUSKOX   You've seen me more than you've seen your own husband these past two months.

BON   I told him he's welcome anytime he wants.

MUSKOX   He can't. He's got work.

BON   I've got work. I'm here.

MUSKOX   Well, not everyone's as amazing as you are.

BON Why are you defending him?

MUSKOX It's not about defending. . . . I'm just reminding you. This is *my* issue. I'm the one who's dying, you know?

BON Dad, please . . .

MUSKOX I'm just wondering who you're doing this for.

[*Daggers.*]

BON . . . What?

MUSKOX I don't want your marriage to crumble. I don't want to see the greatest man who ever walked into your life walk out of it.

BON He is, though.

MUSKOX Then go and chase after him!

BON That's what I'm doing!

[*Silence. Leaves in bright hues of orange, red, and yellow fall.*]

MUSKOX Sweetheart . . .

BON Why did you let me go?

MUSKOX [. . .]

BON I was fifteen years old. And I wouldn't eat my meat. I decided to run away. And you let me.

MUSKOX Sweetheart, I don't even remember . . .

BON That was . . . negligent. And dangerous. And . . . and a very unfatherly thing to do.

MUSKOX I'm sorry.

BON I don't give a shit about sorry.

[*Beat.*]

I'm sorry. I don't want this to be about me. This needs to be about *you*. And I feel like shit that I . . . that I left. That I'm here, now.

Talking about . . . No. I'm going to shut up. What do you want to talk about?

MUSKOX   You held on to that for all these years?

BON   Let's not talk about me.

MUSKOX   I want to know this. Thirty some odd years. If I had known . . .

BON   Why does it matter?

MUSKOX   Because it matters to you. It must've mattered a whole hell of a lot.

BON   No, it didn't. Really. It was me being stupid.

MUSKOX   You're not stupid. You're the sharpest person I know. I just don't want you to have to take this on. This isn't yours.

BON   It's not that easy, though. It's yours, sure. But it passes through me. God, it wraps me up in it. Like hairy arms. It pushes on me from the inside out. From the inside of this White, wallpapered room. I don't know exactly how to describe it. Only that it reminds me of when I left and walked down by the Merrimack.

MUSKOX   Sweetheart . . . you've got to let all that stuff go.

BON   But it's you.

MUSKOX   I know. But all this stuff you're putting yourself through. It's not like you can keep me here. No one's strong enough to do that. You're sharp enough to know that. I have to go . . .

BON   Don't! Don't.

MUSKOX   I'm worried about you.

BON   I'm worried about you.

MUSKOX   [*I'm scared as hell.*]

BON   [*Me too.*] I'm really going to miss you, Dad.

MUSKOX   I'm gonna miss you too, sweetheart.

[*They want so desperately to run and hug each other. But they can't. Because the world fades to White. The* MUSKOX *resumes its furry mantle. The woods outside* BON *and* ROY'*s home.*]

BON   October 2010.

[ROY *fades in with a handgun.*]

ROY   Are you paying attention?

BON   What? Yeah. Sorry.

ROY   We don't have to do this if you don't want.

BON   No, it's fine.

ROY   All right, it's got a little kick to it, but it shouldn't be too bad. Now, aim for that target over there.

BON   It's heavy.

ROY   Yeah. You're gonna need to practice with it. Here, let me help.

[*He helps her aim the gun, holding her.*]

BON   Like this?

ROY   You're too tense. Loosen up.

BON   I can't. I hate these things.

ROY   You've got to, or else you won't hit shit.
      [BON *breathes in . . . out . . .*]
      Better. Keep your breath steady. And then just start to pull as you exhale. You don't want to know when it's gonna go off.

BON   Okay.
      [BON *breathes in . . . out. In . . . out. . . . In . . .*]
      I can't do this.

ROY   You can.

BON I don't want to. Not now.

ROY You need to at least practice.

BON Stop it. Get off me.

ROY All right. I'm sorry.

BON Don't worry about it.

ROY Are you sure you have to do this?

BON Dad asked me to. I have to.

ROY I don't think he'd care.

BON It was in his will.

ROY Yeah, but what's he going to do if you don't?

BON Thanks for the lesson.

[BON *moves to exit.*]

ROY I just don't want you getting hurt. Alaska can be pretty rough.

BON Thanks.

ROY Do you think . . . Never mind.

BON No, what?

ROY Do what you need to do.

BON What?

ROY What do you think the chances are . . . you and I . . . after you get back?

BON I don't know.

[*Beat.*]

ROY When do you leave?

BON Next week.

ROY   And everything's set up?

BON   Everything.

ROY   All right. If, uh. If you need anything. You've still got my number, right?

BON   Yeah.

ROY   All right.

BON   All right.

[ROY *moves to leave.*]

Roy. Thank you. You . . . uh. This is a big help. You being here.

ROY   You look beautiful.

[*The world falls into White. A church assembles out of the White.*]

BON   1989.

[BON *in White. The* MUSKOX *steps out of its mantle dressed in a black tuxedo.* ROY *appears in a tuxedo, with a hint of orange and camo.*]

MUSKOX   And do you, Bonnie, take Roy as your lawfully wedded husband to have and to hold, in sickness and in health, for better or for worse, till death do you part?

BON   I do.

[ROY *steps away, his voice distant again.*]

ROY   Hey, Bon. I'm getting worried about you. Haven't heard anything in about a month. I know cell reception isn't amazing, but . . . are you all right?

[BON *turns away from* ROY. *She turns to the* MUSKOX.]

BON   Till death do we part.

[ROY *is so distant. Is he even there?*]

ROY   I'm trying to get my boss to give me next week off.

[*The* MUSKOX *and* BON *kiss passionately. Is this real?*]

I love you. I love you so much. And I want what's best for you. Whatever that is.

[*The* MUSKOX *and* BON *undress. No, it can't have happened. The world fades to White. But just because it didn't happen doesn't mean it isn't real. The* MUSKOX *and* BON *make love in the blinding White. We do not see them. They are consumed.*]

If you want me to stop calling, I will. If that's what you want. I'll let you go.

[*The world is consumed in White.*]

Just tell me.

[*Silence. Only. White. The inside of a cabin comes into focus.*]

BON   November 2010.

[MITCH *appears in the White.*]

MITCH   I can't let you go.

BON   Just tell me which way to Point Barrow.

MITCH   No. I'm not about to let you go wander off in the tundra without knowing what you're doing. You could get eaten by a polar bear, or trampled by a muskox . . .

BON   I don't want to talk about it. Not now.

MITCH   Okay, then. After we get back.

BON   I'm going alone.

MITCH   You hired me as a guide.

BON   To point me in the right direction. Consider yourself a very expensive, walking GPS.

MITCH   Easy now. I don't *have* to show you the way.

BON   I paid you.

MITCH Take it back. I don't need it. I've got guided tours out the ass. Put on that whole Eskimo song and dance about whales and caribou and shit. I make bank. We don't get a lot of White chicks except on cruises or with some shitty tourist group. So then you show up by yourself packing a .38 and a steel jar. . . . Tell me you wouldn't be curious.

[*Beat.*]

The gun. Do you know how to use it?

BON Of course.

MITCH Okay. How about this? I point you in the right direction; once you do whatever you need to do, you come back and you tell me everything.

BON How do you know I'll come back?

MITCH I'm a very attractive man.

BON [*Ha.*] I'm married.

MITCH That's what she said. And I don't know that you'll come back. But I think there's a better chance of it if I let you go.

[*Beat.*]

Now that I've fulfilled my shamanistic advice quota for the day . . .

[*Jesus. I'm turning into my father.*]

North is that way. Just follow the water.

[*He points towards the* MUSKOX. *He produces a satellite phone.*]

And take a sat phone. Cells won't work this far up. Give me a call if you need anything.

BON Thanks. I, uh. I really appreciate this.

MITCH Eh. Ten bucks says you call in less than three hours.

[MITCH *smiles and fades. All is White. The walls of hospice.*]

BON I don't want to go there.

[*The world shivers, but still all is White. The walls of hospice.*]

Please.

[*All is White. The walls of hospice.*]

October 2009.

[*The rhythmic beeping of a heart monitor. The opened mouth of a dying man; the remnants of flesh and bone struggling not to fade into White. He's losing the battle.*]

How you doing, Dad?

MUSKOX   [. . .]

[*The beeping fills the silence.*]

BON   [*She asked rhetorically.*] Can you hear me? Squeeze my hand if you can hear me.

[*Silence. The beeping is slowing.*]

Squeeze my hand if you can hear me.

[*Slowing . . .*]

Please.

[*Gone. BON cries. The MUSKOX stirs. BON does not notice. She only holds his limp hand.*]

MUSKOX   To my darling daughter, you might remember a time when you were young when I came home soaking wet. I hope you won't remember, but I know you better than that, don't I?

[ROY *fades into focus.*]

ROY   [*Hey.*]

[*He approaches* BON.]

I made it.

[*She is unaware.*]

MUSKOX   That was the day I decided to jump into the water, and you tried to catch me. Except you couldn't. No one can hold us out of the water forever. We can try, but we mostly end up looking silly.

[ROY *puts a hand on her shoulder. She doesn't feel him.*]

ROY   [*I'm here.*]

[*Another hand.*]

MUSKOX   And we get tired. No one is strong enough. To my dearest, darling daughter, I never wanted to be an obstacle for you. I wanted only the best for you. Only love. And I think I succeeded. For better or worse.

ROY   I'm here.

> [*He hugs her.*]

> Stay here. With me.

[*She puts a hand on* ROY's. *One hand remains with the* MUSKOX.]

MUSKOX   So, now, when I have to leave, I feel like I've hurt you. If it were up to me, I wouldn't leave. But I have to.

ROY   [*I won't let you go.*]

BON   [*How do you know?*]

[BON *faces* ROY.]

MUSKOX   You can come with me, to the farthest north, to the top of the world, into the deepest, darkest White . . . but you can go no further.

BON   [*Would you come here for me? To this place? To the White?*]

ROY   [*Of course.*]

BON   [*I wish I believed you.*]

MUSKOX   That is where our walk ends. To my little girl, I have to go away now.

BON   So fucking go!

> [BON's *voice shatters the world, bringing it to White.* ROY *falls away. The bridge at Point Barrow. The endless White.*]

> If you have to go away, why don't you just leave?!

MUSKOX   You have to let me go.

BON   But I can't!

MUSKOX   You have to let me go.

BON   .... But I don't want to.

MUSKOX   What do you see?

BON   I see the boy who said he loved me. He's standing across the river.

MUSKOX   [No, *what do you see?*]

BON   I see a pool. We're on vacation.

MUSKOX   No.

BON   I see a plate of meat.

MUSKOX   No!

BON   I see my father staring at the lights of the city, slowly sinking underwater.

MUSKOX   No, you don't. Look at me. What. Do. You. See?!

BON   My dad. He's wet!

MUSKOX   I'm not wet.

BON   He's cold!

MUSKOX   I'm not cold! Just let yourself adjust! What do you see?

[*Silence.*]

BON   White.

[*Her voice echoes back through the* MUSKOX.]

MUSKOX   White.

BON   Dad . . .

MUSKOX   Dad . . .

BON When did it start snowing?

MUSKOX When did it start snowing?

BON It's so beautiful.

MUSKOX It's so beautiful.

BON Oh, God.

MUSKOX Oh, God.

BON It's time to go, now.

MUSKOX It's time to go, now.

[*The handgun.*]

BON You can go.

MUSKOX You can go.

BON I love you, Dad.

[*In . . .*]

MUSKOX I love you, Dad.

[*Out . . .*]

BON I love you.

MUSKOX I love you.

[*In . . .*]

BON I love you.

[*Bang!*]

[*A bellow! Not the cry of a man but of an unmovable beast that has been moved. The furry mantle drops to the snow-covered bridge, leaving only a man, naked, frail, standing, unimposing, as man is. Such silence. BON crosses the bridge, moving past the man, carrying her urn. The man's gaze follows her, but it is nothing more than a gaze. She does not stop. She steps over the fallen, furry mantle. BON arrives at the other side of the bridge. Sea salt, cold, and White. She opens the urn and takes out a handful of White dust. The wind blows through the White. It carries the dust so far away. BON cries. Maybe she laughs. Another handful of dust. The wind pulls it away. The wind pulls the man away. BON empties the urn. The man fades away with the dust. BON is alone in the White. She exhales the breath she has held since 1975. BON crosses back over the bridge. She steps over the furry mantle. Crunch, crunch, crunch. An approach through the haze. BON does not move. ROY materializes in the White, trudging towards the bridge in orange and camo snow gear.*]

ROY   Jesus Christ, it's cold!

BON   [*Oh my God . . . Roy?!*] What the . . . what the hell are you doing?!

ROY   You didn't answer any of my calls!

BON   I get no service up here. How did you . . .?

ROY   Apparently there aren't that many White women who wander through the tundra.

BON   What about work?

ROY   Screw work. Are you all right?

BON   I'm fine.

[*You came for me.*]

ROY   Did you do it?

BON   I did.

[*You came for me.*]

ROY   All right. Good.

BON   Yeah.

[*You actually came for me.*]

ROY   Are . . . are we . . .?

BON   Yeah. We're good. Take a breath.

ROY Are you gonna be all right?

BON I don't know. Let's take it a day at a time.

[*The White begins to fade into darkness.*]

BON Sun's setting. We better get back to Barrow.

ROY And get home.

BON I have to make a quick stop first. I owe someone a drink.

ROY Oh. All right. Can I come?

BON No. Of course you can come.

ROY Does it always get dark this quickly?

BON Only once winter really begins. A month of darkness from now until January. It's the only way you can tell the seasons apart. The relationship of White to dark. Otherwise, it's easy for it all to run together.

ROY I believe it. Up here . . . White, dark . . . God, it all goes on forever. And it's so fucking cold.

BON It's not cold.

[*The White is all but gone.* BON *hugs* ROY. *Dots of White in the darkness. Stars. Or city lights?*]

Just let yourself adjust.

[*The White fades. And all is darkness.*]

• • •

The Cowboy

Patrick Holland

Patrick Holland

Patrick Holland is a director and writer for theater and film. Recently, he collaborated with Anthony Wood on the award-winning film *Baden Krunk*. Holland has worked as a director, writer, and actor at theaters large and small across Wisconsin and Chicago. He graduated from the University of South Carolina.

···production history···

The Cowboy was produced by Bunny Gumbo's Combat Theater in Milwaukee, Wisconsin, on December 17, 2011. It was directed by Katie Cummings and starred James Fletcher, Sara Zientek, Rachel Williams, and Toni Fletcher. An earlier version of the script was performed on June 10, 2006. It was directed by Todd Denning and starred John Maclay, Angela Iannone, Rachel Williams, and Allison Katula.

characters

THE COWBOY

LINDA

KIM

AMANDA

···

[*Silence. And emerging from the shadows.*]

COWBOY   [*In a black suit and black cowboy hat. The hat casts a shadow across his face.*] When you ride with the Cowboy anything can happen.

[*All three women scream silently. They all die simultaneously. Each has their own stylized death. These movements will occur throughout the show. Each woman has an area that is their own.*]

Some of you may be familiar with my work. These three certainly are. Now, let's get one thing straight from the beginning: I'm no grim reaper. In fact, my job is quite the opposite. However, and I emphasize "however" to be honest, too much of the Cowboy can be a bad thing. Or at least lead to some bad things.

[*A moment.*]

Linda.

[LINDA *stands.*]

Linda's known me for a while. I think it was high school when we met. You see, she lives a chaotic life: Work, family, men . . .

[LINDA *starts miming the essence of her life. The movements should have her going every which way. This is a stylization of her chaotic life.*]

Shit, bills, health, stress. There just seemed no way to deal with this. Now, here's where I come in.

[*He steps in her area. She holds out one of her arms as to shoot up. He puts his hand gently on the inside of her elbow. He presses gently. His touch is the drug. She reels back. Her movements become less chaotic and more euphoric.*]

In the middle of all this, I bring her euphoria. I bring her happiness. Like I said, we've been doing this since high school. She's used to me. I'm as much a part of her life as breathing. Now that things are a little more euphoric, why don't you tell them why you're here.

LINDA   I'm still figuring this all out. Things at work have gotten so complicated lately. I'm so damn stressed. And it's not just the normal work things. I'm having an affair with my boss. He's married. But we've been seeing each other for a while now.

[*Stopping abruptly. Changing tone, starting over.*]

Let me set this up a little better. I work for an ad agency. Our office is this old three-story mansion that's been converted to condos and offices. Our office shares the top floor with a condo. Business next to pleasure. We just moved into it. There are boxes everywhere. State-of-the-art kitchen, large stainless steel restaurant fridge (not even plugged in yet), skylights, balcony, view, foosball table, you know.

[*A moment.*]

It was a Saturday. I was coming into work early to get some things done. No one was supposed to be there. It was early in the morning. As I got to the office door, I heard.

[COWBOY, KIM, and AMANDA make stylized sex sounds.]

I put my key in the door.

[*The sounds stop.*]

I walked in and my boss, the man I've been having an affair with, had obviously been up to something, with someone else. I was the "other woman." And now she was. That hurt. That hurt bad. I was angry. I had just seen the Cowboy, but I was angry.

COWBOY I do what I can, but sometimes reality is stronger.

LINDA He was on the conference table, a favorite spot, naked. But where was she? All I wanted to do was find this other "other" woman. He was cheating on me. I wanted to find her. I looked everywhere: closets, under desks in offices, and then, I was standing in the kitchen and I looked out on the balcony. I peered down and saw . . .

COWBOY Two hands gripping a balcony.

LINDA I was stoned. I was freaked. And now, there was this half-dressed woman hanging from the balcony. I did what I felt. I stepped with purpose on her fingers until she let go.

COWBOY She fell three stories.

LINDA And I watched. Suddenly, I was an emotional mess. But when she hit the ground, it made a sound.

[*All make a unison grunt.*]

Her body broke. But she wasn't dead. She was still breathing. Now, I was really freaked. What had I done?

COWBOY This chick falls three stories. Hits the pavement. And is still breathing.

LINDA [*Getting more worked up. More chaotic.*] I fucking freak. It was like everything I'd repressed came out at once.

COWBOY I'm useless to her. No effect.

LINDA She wasn't dead. Shit. Was that good or bad? Shit. Shit. Shit. Shit. I stepped in from the balcony. I needed to fix this. So, I went for the nearest and biggest thing I could find. Our fridge, the stainless steel restaurant one . . . I rolled it across the floor to the edge of the balcony. This thing was heavy, but I was running on adrenaline and emotions and Cowboy. I pushed it out on the balcony. Then over the edge. It fell. And it crushed her.

COWBOY   Amendment.

LINDA   Now, this might be hard to believe, but the cord caught around my leg . . .

COWBOY   Like some kind of bad comedy.

LINDA   . . . and pulled me over the balcony. I hit the fridge and then the pavement. I was dead when I hit the fridge.

[*She repeats the death movement she did at the beginning. She ends on the ground again.*]

COWBOY   What's sad is that I always brought her euphoria. Except in her last moments. I'm no grim reaper.

[*A moment.*]

That brings us to Kim.

[KIM *stands in her area of light.*]

This one is crazy. I mean, she has done some crazy shit. You see, her life is mundane, central. Every day is a Monday.

[KIM *has a series of mundane movements. This should have a similar style to* LINDA's. *The tone can be a little lighter, though.*]

KIM   My life is so fucking boring. I file X-rays at a medical office. I live alone. Nice condo, though. I have no friends really, except the Cowboy. I used to think that moving to somewhere sunnier would make things more exciting. But then my adventures with the Cowboy started.

COWBOY   [*He steps into her area. She sticks out her tongue. And he gently presses his index finger on it. She reels from the hit.*] I make her life more fun. More crazy. We're talking pink dancing elephants here.

[KIM's *movements become more psychedelic.*]

KIM   I live for the weekends with the Cowboy. He causes some crazy shit, though. Really truly crazy shit. Remember the candy van?

COWBOY   Kim, there was no candy van.

[*Pause.*]

Tell them the latest.

KIM   Like I said, I live by myself. Cable is fun, but the Cowboy's better. And this particular day I had a strong hit. I mean, televised golf and a glass of milk couldn't settle me. Now sometimes, when the Cowboy visits, I feel like I'm in a video game. This was one of those days. He made the mundane go bye-bye. I'm also a fitness freak. I got weights. Cute workout clothes. Skimpy, but I look hot. I even got a treadmill. I kept it on my balcony. Though, as I discovered Saturday, running on a treadmill while tripping was not a good idea. In fact, they say don't drink and drive. Well, don't trip and tread. You see the Cowboy made things seem different. That was his job.

COWBOY   Job well done.

KIM   I know. So, I was tripping and on my treadmill. I turned it on and don't realize that I had royally fucked up the settings.

COWBOY   Did she mention she was tripping?

KIM   So, I got thrown off the machine . . . backwards.

COWBOY   Like those athletes who do the long jump in the Olympics . . . 'cept backwards.

KIM   I was flying through the air, off the treadmill, and off my balcony. Instinctively, I tried to grab on to something.

COWBOY   There's this balcony of an office next door.

KIM   I grabbed on for dear life. I was in my skimpy workout clothes, tripping and hanging on for life on to this balcony. Now, I don't know if it was the Cowboy or what, but all of a sudden . . .

[LINDA *stands up in her lighting area. Speaks simultaneously with* KIM.]

| LINDA   I was stoned. I was freaked. And now I saw this half-dressed woman hanging from the balcony. | KIM   I was tripping. I was freaked. I saw this half-cocked woman running toward the balcony. |

KIM   She stepped on my fingers with purpose.

LINDA   I did what I felt. I stepped with purpose on her fingers till she let go.

KIM   I let go.

[COWBOY *speaks simultaneously with* KIM.]

| KIM   I fell three stories to the pavement. | COWBOY   Kim falls three stories. Hits the pavement. |

KIM   My body made this sound when it hit the ground.

[*All grunt in unison.*]

I don't remember feeling it, though. Probably because of the Cowboy.

[COWBOY *speaks simultaneously with* KIM.]

| KIM   And I was still alive. | COWBOY   And she's still breathing. |

KIM   I can't say anything during all this. Not a sound. From the time I left the treadmill to the time I hit the pavement. Seconds. This went from a freak accident to a murder in seconds. Then this crazy bitch, the one who just initiated me into the gravity club . . . rolled this stainless steel fridge out onto the balcony. I remember it being stainless steel because of the glare the sun gave it. It reflected the sun into my eyes. Highlighting its target. Then . . .

[LINDA *speaks simultaneously with* KIM.]

| LINDA   I pushed it over the edge. And it crushed her. | KIM   She pushed it over the edge. And it crushed me. |

[*Once again,* KIM *and* LINDA *repeat their death movements from the beginning until they are on the ground.*]

COWBOY   I'm not a grim reaper. What's strange about this situation was that there was one. A situation, that is. A connection. You'll see.

[*A moment.*]

Last, but certainly not least! Amanda.

[AMANDA *stands in her area.*]

Amanda is a beautiful woman. Gorgeous. Funny. Flirty. And tired. Really tired.

[AMANDA *starts stylized movements to show her being tired, groggy.*]

But even cowgirls get the blues.

[*He watches for a moment.*]

It's sad watching someone so beautiful be so down. And that's where I step in.

[*He steps into her area. And he places his hands out. Palms facing upward. He presents them to her. She snorts in one powerful swipe. She rubs her nose. Swallows and smiles. Her movements become fast and fun. Almost like dancing at a club. She smiles.*]

Now, that's the Amanda I know. You tell them the rest.

AMANDA   [*Kind of fast, she's coked up.*] Friday night. I met these guys at this club. One was a "race car driver" and the other was a "stock broker." Yeah, like I grew up yesterday. But, I had just seen the Cowboy while "powdering my nose." I didn't care if they were the Pope. We partied all night and into the next morning. All of a sudden I'm twenty again. I end up going home with the "race car driver."

COWBOY   Truth time, honey.

AMANDA   So, it turned out, he was not a race car driver.

COWBOY   Aw, shucks.

AMANDA   It turned out he was married because he took me back to his office. And it turned out that he was good in bed, or at least on a conference table because that's where we spent the next several hours. It also turned out that he was an ad exec having an affair with one of his employees. And it also turned out that she showed up to work while we're fucking. On a Saturday morning, too! What the fuck!?!

[LINDA *stands up in her lighting area. She speaks simultaneously with* KIM.]

LINDA   I put my key in the door.   **AMANDA**   We heard her at the
I walked in.   door. I ran.

AMANDA   I looked for a place to hide. And I see this stainless steel fridge. It was restaurant-sized. And empty. Must be new. I was coked up on the Cowboy and half-naked. Seemed like a clever move.

COWBOY   Didn't see this one coming.

AMANDA   I was in there for a while. Then . . .

[KIM *stands up in her lighting area. All three talk simultaneously.*]

LINDA I was stoned.	**KIM** I was tripping,	**AMANDA** I was coked,
I was freaked.	I was freaked.	I was freaked.
And now I saw	And now I saw	And then I heard
this half-dressed	this half-cocked	the sound of
woman hanging	woman running	running toward
from the	toward the	the balcony.
balcony.	balcony.	

AMANDA   Seconds later I heard:

[*All grunt in unison.*]

Then the fridge started to move. Aw, shit. What do I do? Before I could ask myself. I was turning upside down. I felt like I was falling and floating at the same time.

[LINDA, KIM, *and* AMANDA *speak simultaneously.*]

LINDA I pushed it over the edge. And it crushed her.	**KIM** She pushed it over the edge. And it crushed me.	**AMANDA** She pushed me over the edge. And it killed me.

[*All three do their death moments as at the beginning. Silence.*]

COWBOY When you ride with the Cowboy anything can happen. I'm no grim reaper.

[*Pause.*]

I got nothing more to say.

[*Slow fade out. Letting audience take in the scene.*]

• • •

A Little Haunting

A. K. Abeille and
David Manos Morris

A. K. Abeille and
David Manos Morris

A. K. Abeille lives in Jonesboro, Arkansas; her plays have been produced in the U.S. and Canada, in English and in French. David Manos Morris is a freelance screenwriter and LucasFilm/ILM special-effects artist. He has worked on over fifty feature films. This is his first foray into writing for the stage.

···production history···

A Little Haunting was commissioned for Rough Magic Shakespeare Company's first annual "Bag of Tricks" Play Festival in Jonesboro, Arkansas. The festival ran the weekend of October 28–29, 2011. The production starred Andrue Sullivan as the MAN (with a sly credit in the program for Roberta Stevens as LITTLE GIRL, so as to not give away the twist about the body in the bed).

• • •

[*A girl's bedroom. Someone sleeping in the bed. Bedside table with lamp and book. Slippers on the floor. A man falls backward into the room.*]

MAN   Sheesh! What—?

[*Spies person sleeping in the bed.*]

Oh! Cr—sh! Sh, sh, sh, sh—

[*Whispering.*]

Okay. Okay. Okay. I can do this. I can do this.

[*Pulls out a piece of paper.*]

I just have to successfully haunt each client, and I can move up to bigger and better locations. How hard can it be? Some little girl. No sweat. Who knew that the afterlife would have ghost middle managers giving out assignments. I screamed "BOOO!" in his face. Priceless. No one's ever told me what to do before, and I don't take their crap in the afterlife either.

[*Creeps over to look at the sleeper, then whispers back toward the way he came in.*]

No problem. This'll be better than dumping little Kyle Kosinski in the trash and stealing his pants. She'll be cryin' for Momma in ten seconds. I'll be haunting movie stars and politicians in no time. Watch this!

[*Starts stalking around the bed, waving his arms weirdly.*]

Ooowoooo. Ooowoooooo!
Booooooooooo! BoooooOOOOOOOoooooo.

[*No response from sleeper.*]

Sound sleeper.

[*Looks around; takes the book from the bedside table and "floats" it around the room and over the bed.*]

Ooooooo. Oh, OOOOOOOOOO! Boo. Boo, kid. Dang. What, your parents Nyquil you or something? What!?

[*He drops the book on the floor with a thump; no response from sleeper.*]

Okay, okay—I get it, I pissed you off, you give me narcoleptic girl. No problem. Up the game.

[*Looks around; jumps for the lamp; tries to turn it on but can't find the switch.*]

Wh—crud.

[*Picks up the lamp and hovers it over the bed.*]

Little girl—little girl! Want a lamp on your—

[*Notices the lamp cord just trails, no plug on the end.*]

Great; no wonder it doesn't work. Duh. What's the matter, you reading too late, Mommy Dearest cut the cord?

[*Flips the lamp around over the sleeper's head a few times, moaning, mimes about to smash her with it in frustration.*]

Wow, are you a heavy sleeper or what?

[*Puts lamp back; spies the book on the floor, picks it up.*]

Must be one heck of a bedtime story.

[*Tries to open the book, but it is made of wood.*]

What the—? What kind of parents—? Not your business, spook! You're the haunt—haunt!

[*Ditches the book; creeps up near the bed, starts shaking the covers, then the bed itself.*]

Hauuuuuunting! Haaaaaaaaaunting! I'm haaaaunting you, little girl!

[*Shouting.*]

YOU'RE HAUNTED!

[*No response from sleeper.*]

For Pete's sake!

[*Violently shaking the bed.*]

Wake up! Wake up! No way. No way! She's dead? She's *dead*?! That's not fair. That's not FAIR! Nobody can wake the—noooo way . . .

[*He backs away from the bed, hits the wall—tries to get out of the room the way he came in, then tries the other walls, increasingly desperate.*]

Hey! Hey, let me out of here! Manager dude! Crap, man! Get me the—get me out of here! You can't stick me in here with a dead girl and I can't get out until I can scare her! Nobody can! Hey!

[*He gives up, panting, then pulls out his contract again, scanning it quickly.*]

. . . Mission support! There!

[*He pulls out a cell phone and makes a call.*]

I want to speak to a manager. There's something wrong with my assignment.

[*He pauses until his boss comes on the phone.*]

Hey to you too. Get me another client right now. You screwed up, and I'm not going to take the crap for this. No way. No way. Yeah, I know the contract says I can't move on until I scare the "present client"—but you don't get it! She's already dead or something. She's dead! She's DEAD, you idiot! I don't know, crib death or something. No, she's not a baby, I just mean—she's just lying there—died in her sleep or something—she—what? What do you mean the client's just fine and hasn't been scared at all? Hasn't been scared, man, she's frickin' dead over here!

I'll go over your head. I'll have your job. You can't stick me with this client. That's not fair! That's not FAIR! Nobody can wake the— wait, she can't hear me! Is that it? That's the deal, isn't it? She's deaf, is that it? Some equal opportunity haunting bullshit? Oh, fine. Think I feel sorry for poor little deafy girl and won't give her a real haunt? Think you're gonna stop me moving up by giving me some pity case? Idiot. I'll be your boss this time tomorrow. Listen to this!

[*Goes over to the bed, but hears the manager cut off the call.*]

Hello? Hello? Idiot.

Whatever. Here you go, deafo!

[*Shakes the mattress violently, then turns the mattress clear over, spilling sleeper out.*]

WAKE UP!

[*Sleeper is clearly a doll.*]

A doll.

[*Relieved.*]

It's just a doll—she's not dead, she's just a d—wait a minute. You said I had to—how could I—okay, that really *isn't* fair! I can't scare a little girl that isn't even—

WOMAN'S VOICE   [*Offstage.*] Lana? Have you got everything you want to put in storage?

GIRL'S VOICE   [*Offstage.*] Just about—I just want to bring the dollhouse; I need more room for my new stereo!

MAN   [*Looks around frantically, putting the pieces together.*] DOLLHOUSE?! Wait—!

[*Loses his balance as the house is lifted.*]

Wait! Wait! Booo! BoooooOOOOOOO!

WOMAN'S VOICE   [*Offstage.*] Oh, someday when you have a little girl of your own, she's going to treasure this.

MAN   When she has—hey, I can't wait until this little girl has a kid! WAIT! BOOOOOOOO!

GIRL'S VOICE   [*Offstage.*] Mom! I think we might have mice in the walls again! I hear that squeaking . . .

WOMAN'S VOICE   [*Offstage.*] Oh no—I'll call the exterminator right away; just put that right in this box, honey, and tape it up tight . . .

[MAN *falls over the doll, still protesting, as blackout.*]

• • •

Ichabod Crane
Tells All
a one-man comedy

Lawrence Thelen

Lawrence Thelen

Lawrence Thelen, formerly the literary manager and producing associate for Goodspeed Musicals, is the author of the book *The Show Makers: Great Directors of the American Musical Theatre* (Routledge). His comic opera *Pyramus and Thisbe* was presented by the 92nd Street Y, and his musical *The Third Wave* was the recipient of the Jackie White Memorial Award. His fiction and nonfiction have appeared in *Dramatics Magazine* and *Show Music Magazine*.

··· production history ···

The play has not yet received a premiere.

character

ICHABOD CRANE

scene

A lecture onstage, 1840

synopsis

In this comic one-man play, ICHABOD CRANE, at the very old age of seventy-two, gives a lecture concerning the events that led to his departure from the small town of Sleepy Hollow fifty years earlier.

to the actor

It's worth noting that nearly everything ICHABOD says about his time in Sleepy Hollow is a lie—devised over the years to make himself look better in his stories and justify his actions. He might even believe these lies to be true, forgetting long ago how the actual events played out. Despite what he says, the truth is: he was *very much* in love with Katrina Van Tassel, *terribly* jealous of Brom Bones, and *scared to death* of the HEADLESS HORSEMAN. Yet, over the years, he has created another reality to counter the stories that flowed forth following the events that suggested he was overly timid, a failed lover, or even insane. It would be invaluable to communicate some of this to the audience.

● ● ●

[*As the house lights dim, a spotlight comes up on a lectern center stage.* ICHABOD CRANE *walks to the lectern and addresses the audience.* ICHABOD *is a spry, feisty, seventy-two-year-old man. He is tall, thin, lanky, and out of proportion—looking more like a Harlequin marionette whose head is too big for the rest of his body, and whose ears and nose are too big for his head. His arms and legs are longer than they should be and don't always seem to move with the same goal in mind. He has gray hair and a sage, serious expression, which becomes almost sinister when he smiles. He is a blindly arrogant man who does a very poor job of masking his disdain for the ignorant and stupid people of the world. Yet he likes himself an awful lot.*]

ICHABOD CRANE   Good evening. I'm Ichabod Crane, and it's a pleasure to be here. I've been asked to give a lecture on the circumstances surrounding my time spent in that dreary little New York town of Sleepy Hollow, and the events that led to my departure—a story which seems to have become "legend" over the years. I appreciate the library association and the town council for asking me here so I can finally tell *my* side of the story; for many misrepresentations and rumors have been spread over the years— particularly by that most unscrupulous journalist Washington Irving—and other cynical writers who have grossly misinterpreted my character for years. Now, let me state from the outset that there was, and to the best of my knowledge, still *is* a Headless Horseman who roams the village of which I speak, and that he was in no way an apparition, a hoax, or a bit of indigestion, as some have suggested. Several have said that my timidity, my belief in the supernatural, or my failed marriage proposal to Miss Katrina Van Tassel, led to a temporary insanity—a swelling of the brain twice the normal size—which led to hallucinations conjuring up this Horseman. Well, that's simply preposterous! If my brain had swelled to such proportions, it would have exploded along the roadside like a shattered jack o' lantern.

Let me start by going through each of those points with you one by one so there's no misunderstanding. First of all, I am not a timid man. In fact, I'm quite gay, fun-loving, and gleeful. I can be raucously funny at times. And I'm quite wonderful at a party, for I can speak to nearly anyone on nearly any subject even if the person to whom I'm speaking bores me to death. I've learned to conceal my disdain very well over the years. It's all in the smile.

[*He smiles.*]

No one can be unhappy when they're looking at this face. Secondly, as far as my belief in the unknown goes—the supernatural, superstition, coincidence, and all that—it is true I believe in such things, for I have experienced them firsthand— irrespective of that ridiculous Headless Horseman event. I have seen and heard things that no man has seen or heard. Yet, that doesn't make me insane—as some have suggested—but rather *exceedingly* sane. More sane than any of you. What's more, if anyone here tonight can prove to me in facts and figures that the supernatural *does not* exist, then let him speak now or forever hold his tongue. No! I am speaking now. You can speak later!

[*He regains his composure.*]

Finally, as far as Miss Van Tassel goes, it wasn't a failed marriage proposal at all. How do these rumors get started? I never had any intention of proposing marriage to the girl. It's true that she was enamored with me, and that we spent nearly every weekend together while I was in town, and that many *assumed* I would propose to her—but the whole thing is one big misunderstanding. In the end—and let me be perfectly clear about this—it was *I* who rejected *her*, not vice versa. I have not been rejected by a woman one time in my life. Ultimately, you see, Miss Van Tassel was not my type of woman. Her table manners, for example, were atrocious. I once spent an whole evening with her during which she had a pea stuck between two teeth the entire time.

And for those of you who might believe that my real interest in the girl lay not with *her*, but with her father's well-stocked bank accounts, that too is false. True, it would have been nice not to have to confine myself to a classroom for fifty years teaching retched little monsters the basics of modern-day survival just to earn a living. But I couldn't bear the thought of returning home each evening after a long day's work to that sour expression with which she often greeted me. Not even for a sizable inheritance. Everyone has their limits, and Katrina Van Tassel was mine.

[*He takes a moment to gather his thoughts.*]

Let me start at the beginning. One day back in 1790, as a young lad of twenty-two, I came across a posting in the local newspaper for a schoolmaster. I'd had no formal training for such a position, but I'm naturally bright—as I'm sure you can tell—and had self-taught myself most everything a person needs to be successful in life. I've always been very well-read, having gone through Milton and Shakespeare and even the Bible—a ghastly piece of propaganda which, surprisingly, turned out to be quite useful in the classroom when it came to questions I didn't want to answer: "Where is the universe, Mr. Crane?"—"Read your Bible!" "Why is my uncle also my father?"—"Read your Bible!" "Where does snot come from?" Well, some questions even the Bible can't answer.

Let me, if I may, interject here my teaching philosophy for those teachers in the audience who will no doubt want to emulate me. First of all, don't give the little brats an inch or they'll walk all over you. Children must have discipline. Discipline and boundaries. They must know what they *can* do and what they *can't* do. Otherwise, they'll waste all their time—and yours—testing the boundaries and not thriving within the established structure. Now, the best way to organize this structure, I have found, is around pain. When they do what you want, you say, "good, Johnny," or "good, Sally." But if they are wrong, or bad, or disgusting, pain will rectify the situation immediately. If they miss a math problem, for instance, a wrap on the knuckles with a ruler will suffice. For more grievous acts such as spitting or smoking, I've found a good smack across the face will instantly change that behavior. And on it goes from there. It should be noted that, to date, none of my students have ever died in the classroom. I'm simply doing a parent's job. Why anyone in the world would want to have children in the first place, is beyond me—but as long as they're around, it seemed like educating them would be a sensible way to make a living.

At any rate, I answered the newspaper ad because it seemed like a good time to leave Connecticut, where I was born and raised. I had been working as a stock room manager at Anderson's Livestock, Lumber, and Feed Store for six months, and had quite a good relationship with Mr. Anderson and his daughter, Sonia, who naturally acquired a crush on me. But the dust and the hay played havoc with my sinuses, and manual labor was of no interest to me whatsoever. I've always been far more interested in using my brain than any other part of my body. And when I explained this to Sonia, her goodwill towards me went elsewhere—and, consequently, so did I.

Luckily for me, the very next day I received a letter from Baltus Van Tassel, head of the Sleepy Hollow school board and father of the aforementioned Katrina Van Tassel—the girl with the pea in her teeth. The letter included a one-year schoolmaster's contract—commencing at two dollars a week—and a one-way stagecoach ticket to get there. What a horrid way to travel—my bony little bum was sore for a week. Nevertheless, I accepted the position immediately; not because I *needed* the job, but because I was horrified at the thought of so many uneducated New Yorkers being set loose on society.

When I arrived in Sleepy Hollow it was clear the town desperately needed me. The previous schoolmaster had failed miserably as far as I could tell. The boys were working in the fields, getting their hands abhorrently muddy, and the girls were learning cooking and cleaning from their mothers. They clearly had no desire to better themselves. So I took it upon myself to do that for them.

No room and board was provided with the position, so I was taken in by the families of those I taught—I rotated weekly from house to house. Needless to say, some accommodations were worse than others. One home, for example—that of the Mullet family—was particularly gruesome. I was provided with a flea-infested cot in a dank and dirty cellar—no closet, no bureau, not even a mirror with which to perform my ablutions. Hell, everyone deserves a mirror. And my meals consisted of soup. Every day another soup: cabbage soup, parsnip soup, boiled celery soup—God forbid they should toss me a bit of meat once in a while. I'm not a glutton, but I've always had a healthy appetite. I swear I lost five pounds the week I stayed with the Mullets. Needless to say, I never went back there again.

By contrast, there was the home of Darius Vanderhoff. Now, the boy, Darius, was a lost cause—a true dirt clod—but his mother provided me with the heartiest meals I received during my tenure. Lamb stew, chicken and dumplings, pot roast. Gravy has always been one of my favorite indulgences, and Mrs. Vanderhoff knew her way around a smooth sauce. What's more, I was provided a bed in their kitchen, where many a night a second supper was to be found amid the cupboards and icebox. Mrs. Vanderhoff chalked up the lost food to a mother raccoon she had seen seeking nibbles for her young. Not wanting to spoil her feeling of goodwill toward animals, I continued to let her believe such a wild story. Through a fine bit of finagling, I was able to reside at the Vanderhoffs' home on four separate occasions. I tried for a fifth but their bankruptcy prevented it. Clearly, the nicest home I was privy to was that of the aforementioned Baltus Van Tassel—father of the daughter with the pea?—who was clearly the wealthiest man in town. There I was given my own private room—with a mirror—and three filling, though flavorless, meals a day. Mrs. Van Tassel was not what you might refer to as a gourmet. Still, I never went hungry. Their youngest daughter, Mildred, was one of my students—and upon my first stay Mildred introduced me to her older sister, Katrina, a bouncy young woman of eighteen. It was obvious that Katrina was taken with me immediately. I saw it coming, but there was nothing I could do to prevent it. I say this with all due modesty. She fawned over me the same way a squirrel fawns over a nut.

And I must say I liked it very much. So, I indulged her infatuation by staying at their home as often as possible, and visiting her on weekends as well. And each time I stayed I received more attention from her than the previous visit. Which only stands to reason; we were getting to know one another better with each passing day. As one would expect, a romance developed.

[*He smiles grandly showing he is quite proud of this feat.*]

Or, at least, that's what I let her believe. I let her indulge her fantasy with me, though I was not smitten with her at all. Oh yes, she was beautiful, with a slim, tight, little body, and a sensual, erotic smile, and all the money in the world. But she really wasn't my type. And the stories that state that my lip quivered whenever she came near me, or that I had to sit down every time she took my arm are blatantly false!

I was soon to discover, however, that there was another man interested in Katrina—Abraham Van Brunt, also known as Brom Bones. I assume he acquired the nickname because of his large, unwieldy physical resemblance to a pachyderm. Nonetheless, Miss Van Tassel had apparently had a previous, albeit short, courtship with the large fellow; and although I know not the reason for their separation, it was clear she had no interest in resuming the courtship with him once I came along. In fact, often in his presence, she would dote on me even more than usual—presumably to show him what a better catch I was, or to keep his feelings for her at bay.

Now, that's not to say they were *complete* enemies. I did happen upon them once in the pantry, where he was apparently helping her brush her hair, for it was all mussed when I stumbled upon them. And though I would have been a far better choice than he to tend her coif—knowing the intricacies of personal style and hygiene better than most—I held no jealousy whatsoever; for he was simultaneously a braggart and a bore—a seemingly incomprehensible combination that he embodied with ease. He would often bend the ear of any poor soul who happened to be near with tales of his superior and outlandish life. His favorite story being the night he outran the famous Headless Horseman of Sleepy Hollow by crossing St. Amsterdam's Bridge in the nick of time, just before he'd been forced into battle with him. Apparently the Horseman, for whatever reason, can't seem to cross St. Amsterdam's Bridge and so Brom claimed victory over the poor, helpless spirit.

But his stories held no interest for me. And his interest in Katrina brought about no jealously whatsoever. You see, it mattered not to me. I wasn't in love with her. What I did feel for her, though, was sorrow. Brom Bones was a persistent troll who wouldn't take no for an answer. I didn't want to see poor Katrina live out her days with such a beast and an ogre, and so I did what any respectable man *must* do to keep her from doom's door—I made love to the woman.

[*He again smiles grandly.*]

Oh, not in the physical sense (please!), but with words of love, with pampering looks, and by listening to her as if I was really interested. You see, it wasn't for *me* that I was doing it, it was for *her*. To save her from Brom Bones. And I must say, I played the part of the young lover quite well. Everyone was convinced that I had actually fallen for her. And the ruse worked. Daily Brom Bones got more irritable, more depressed, and more desperate. But I refused to let up. I, after all, was saving her. It was a duty; a calling!

[*Quite pleased with himself.*]

I've often fancied myself a hero because of that—sacrificing myself for the good mental health of another. Not a one of you would have done the same, I'm certain. But I've become sidetracked. Ultimately, I know all you gossipmongers want is the climax of the tale when I encountered the Headless Horseman. So, I will prolong your agony no longer.

[*As if telling a mysterious ghost story.*]

It was very late one autumn night. Van Aiken Lane was quiet and still. I could hear the church bells—a good half-mile away in the distance—strike twelve o'clock midnight. The air was cold and damp, and I shivered repeatedly as my horse made its way gingerly through the thick fog that clung low to the ground. Although there was a full moon, Van Aiken Lane was black as coal due to the long, outstretched arms of the sycamores, which had not yet lost their leaves, and the long, dangling grapevines that hung precariously low and close to my face. Every so often one would reach out and grab me around the neck!—my escape coming only when I whipped my poor gelding to trot faster than he was able. I was staying with the Dusseldorfs that week, and the closest route home from the Van Tassel residence was down Van Aiken Lane, past the Old Dutch Cemetery, and over St. Amsterdam's Bridge. Now, I'm sure you're asking yourself, "What in heaven's name was Ichabod Crane doing out alone at such a late and ungodly hour that night?" I'll tell you.

[*With lightness in his voice.*]

Earlier that evening the Van Tassels had thrown a wonderfully lavish party—presumably in my honor, although that bit of information seems to have been accidentally omitted from the invitations. The party provided me with one of the heartiest feasts I ever received in the Hollow. A true smorgasbord: kidney pie, shepherd's pie, apple pie . . .

[*Realizing he's gotten carried away.*]

Oh, and Miss Van Tassel? Yes, she was there too—by my side the entire time. In fact, the poor thing couldn't keep her hands off me. I suppose that raised an eyebrow or two, and inevitably led to the floury of rumors that ran around the room like a dog after its tail.

I had just gotten through the buffet for the second time when who walks in but that abnormally large Brom Bones. I nearly lost my appetite—a more homely and arrogant fellow I never have seen. His first stop, naturally, was to greet the guest of honor, although I received nothing more than a grunt before his attention turned to Miss Van Tassel. The giant oaf wouldn't be able to utter a proper salutation even if Good Afternoon was his first and last name. At any rate, Miss Van Tassel was clearly annoyed with his presence, for she took my arm, and with that giggle in her voice that she reserved only for me, swept me into the back parlor before I'd even finished filling my plate. I cannot say whether she needed immediate lovemaking or whether she simply wanted to gaze at me—many women do, you know—but she clearly was "in the mood." I, on the other hand, couldn't stop thinking of that chicken pot pie I had yet to sample. Nevertheless, there we were—alone— together. The woman was making protestations of love and all that when suddenly I noticed my shoe had come untied. So, I merely bent down to retie it—here, let me demonstrate.

[*He comes around to the side of the podium.*]

I knelt down to retie my shoe and . . . well, surely you can see how this could be misconstrued. Then, while I was kneeling there, who enters but the hippo himself—Brom Bones. Well, naturally, he thought I was proposing, and Katrina thought I was proposing, and I was in the midst of tying my shoe when suddenly Brom knocks me over with a blow to the ribs and off he goes dragging poor Katrina behind.

Now, it's at this point that I'm sure you expect me to say that I chased after him. But, you see, I noticed the remains of a muffin I had pocketed squishing out of my pants. Well, naturally, I had to dispose of the evidence—it was blueberry and delicious—and by the time I returned to the party, Brom had fled with Katrina in hand. All the party was abuzz and astir. Apparently, it was the scandal (and the highlight) of their social season. Though others were concerned for my well-being—looking upon me as the jilted lover—I really gave it no thought at all. Instead, I kept myself busy at the buffet—the chicken pot pie was well worth the wait, I'll have you know—where I shared small talk with a variety of incompetents until Katrina returned alone from the garden thirty-two minutes later.

Once again she whisked me off to the back parlor—where I simply *had* to take a few minutes and brush her mussed hair—and there and then she proposed a tête-à-tête alone with me following the party. Hmmm . . . women just adore me.

[*Spotting a woman in the audience.*]

You do, don't you? You've been staring at me all evening. At any rate, the party broke up and I soon found myself alone with her. Well, the poor thing nearly threw herself at me, begging that I marry her, so as to save her from a miserable life with that stuffed buffalo that had recently dragged her off. I gave it a bit of thought. But I simply couldn't sacrifice my *entire life* for the poor bedraggled waif, and I told her so in no uncertain terms. Well, the poor thing was just crushed—as I'm sure you can imagine—and crumbled into a hundred tiny tears right before my eyes. It really was embarrassing. But I was adamant. I told her I approved of her friendship but that was all there was to it. I tried to let her down easily—I didn't want to blow my chance of spending another week or two in that lavish house. And that was that. I gathered my hat and coat, and a particularly sweet-looking pumpkin from the buffet table, and headed for home.

So . . . we return to Van Aiken Lane. As I said, I mounted my nag, and in the chill of the night, he and I headed away from the Van Tassel residence and down the dark, winding, tree-lined road. The quiet of the night was interrupted only by the occasional bark of an angry dog . . .

[*He barks.*]

. . . or the hoot of a startled owl.

[*He hoots.*]

Suddenly, as my steed and I continued down the lane, I heard from behind me the hooves of another rider. I could hear it getting closer and closer; traveling faster and faster. The horse and rider were moving at a full gallop! He came up upon me. I felt a cold, damp wind brush past my face. Then, all of a sudden, the rider shouted out to me, "Good evening, Ichabod! Lovely gala, what?" and he raced on right by. It was drunken Mr. Moody, making his way home from the party. The man was so intoxicated he turned backwards in his saddle and waved me good-bye as his horse carried him 'til they disappeared down the path. I soon came upon the Old Dutch Cemetery—and the long line of headstones filled with the names of dead soldiers who'd fought in the Revolution. Van Dyke, Van Buren, Van Rhine. We walked on, grave after grave, plot after plot, body after body. Some graves had flowers, while others only weeds; still others had been obviously forgotten long ago. I could see each name clearly etched into the stones, for the road had widened, the trees had disappeared, and the full moon now shone brightly, lighting everything in shadows of gray and black. As we made our way toward the church—a short distance from the bridge—a clip-clop sound came a-tapping from behind. Clip-clop, clip-clop, closer, closer, faster, faster. Could it be another drunken reveler, I thought, racing to get past the cemetery grounds. Clip-clop, clip-clop. Faster, faster, closer, closer. The sound began to grow and grow and wild laughter began echoing in the Hollow. I kept my sights in front of me, my eyes glued to the road, when a shadow began to engulf me. The moon was growing dim as the shadow grew and grew, until it had overtaken me. A piercing cackle screeched from behind . . .

[*He cackles.*]

It was loud and long and scared the birds right out of the trees. But not I—no, not I. As I reached the edge of the bridge, I glanced behind me, and out of the mist a figure arose, and *there he was*! A horse in full stride and a horseman with no head! A large, strong, impressive presence holding in one arm what appeared to be the horseman's very own head. The horse reared up and whinnied a cry; the horseman cackled and threatened my very existence. But was I scared? Not on your life! I rode across the bridge—across which I was told the Horseman could not pass—got off my horse and stood right up to him! I said, "You go away this instant!" (Timid, my ass!) At which point, the Horseman raised his head above his head—or where his head should have been—and there it turned into a bright red ball of fire, which he hurled at me with great delight. "Ha-ha-ha!" he screamed as the gruesome appendage shot straight for my head. "Ha-ha-ha!" I said in return. "Ha-ha-*haaa*!"

[*Much calmer.*]

Now, here's where details over the years have gotten a bit sketchy. Some accounts have the ball of fire knocking my own head from my shoulders, where it shattered on the ground like a smashed pumpkin; and that my body and soul were "spirited away" by the Horseman and taken to the nether regions, never to be seen again. Well, simply put, I was not "spirited away" that night by the evil Horseman—and I am here tonight as proof of that. Nor was my head turned into a pumpkin and smashed along the roadside. What *was* smashed was the actual pumpkin I had procured from the buffet table for my late-night dessert. I merely dropped it while dodging the fireball, which had been hurled at me.

[*Back to the story with intense interest.*]

At any rate, after his head had been thrown and extinguished in a puddle, I yelled at the vision with the strength of twenty generals, "Go away, you vile creature, or I'll rip off all your other limbs!" And the great Headless Horseman rose up from the ground with a cackle and a laugh and a whinny and a fart, and the rider and its stallion evaporated into the mist and were gone—gone!—never to be seen again. You see, it was I—yes, *I*—who scared away the Horseman and not the other way around! And that, my friends, is what *really* happened when I encountered the Headless Horseman of Sleepy Hollow. The explanation of the Horseman's appearance is usually flippantly dismissed as merely Brom Bones in disguise; the idea being that he intended to scare me away from his dear Miss Van Tassel by playing upon my belief in the supernatural. Oh, what an easy and uneducated conclusion to reach, brought about by men who prefer to hear themselves talk—loudly and at length—rather than chronicle the truth.

[*With disgust.*]

Yes, I'm speaking of writers. A despicable lot—all of them! The truth is the Headless Horseman was a spirit from beyond. It's as simple as that. Some of you, I can tell, are nonbelievers. But it matters not to me. For I know the truth; you see, I was there and you were not. The Horseman was clearly a restless soul of the Revolution whose head had been blown off by a cannonball, and who had returned to earth seeking vengeance. It's all very clear, don't you see? I, however, not being responsible for the loss of the Horseman's head was never in any danger; and once he recognized that, he vanished into the night like fog in the sun.

As to my disappearance from Sleepy Hollow following this encounter—which is usually described as a frantic fleeing for my life (please!)—there is a very simple and straightforward explanation. My horse, being shaken to the bone by this encounter, raced along furiously and took a wrong turn after crossing the bridge onto Tarrytown Road—the main route out of town. By the time I realized his mistake, I had already crossed the border back into Connecticut; and, well, having already gone that far, figured I might as well return home and visit my family. The next day—having quite a reputation in my hometown—I was offered a teaching position there—one much closer to home. And it is there that I have remained for the past forty-nine years.

So, as you can see, I was an innocent bystander in all of this. I did not bring about Brom's jealousy, or Katrina's unhappy life, and I certainly didn't deserve to be chased down like a common criminal by a horseman with no head. It all remains a mystery to me. But that was many years ago. Last I heard, Miss Van Tassel married that large, bovine-shaped man and they bore seven fat little children—all of whom resembled Brom—even the girls. I can only imagine the width of her hips after seven consecutive childbirths.

[*He shudders with disgust.*]

Many years later, I heard through the grapevine that the poor dear was quite happy with her choice of men and the life that had been bestowed upon her. Oh, Katrina. How brave of you to put up such a front for the sake of the children; truly an admirable attempt to keep them from suicide or some other grizzly end. Untimely, though, Katrina Van Tassel made the biggest mistake of her life . . .

[*A cackle of disgust is heard in the distance. It is so distant it is almost inaudible.* ICHABOD *continues on without taking notice.*]

She chose a man—Brom Bones—who was completely wrong for her . . .

[*Another cackle, a bit closer.*]

And is now forced to feign love at the expense of her own wants and desires and needs . . .

[*Still another cackle, even closer.*]

Simply put, Katrina Van Tassel is a stupid woman.

[*With that, the* HEADLESS HORSEMAN *comes riding or flying into the theater and attacks* ICHABOD CRANE, *who runs for his life. The menacing spirit laughs and cackles as he attacks the aged and weak* ICHABOD. *The lights flicker and fade as the* HORSEMAN *moves rapidly about.* ICHABOD *screams with terror and just barely avoids scaring himself to death when the* HEADLESS HORSEMAN *disappears as fast as he came.*]

[**NOTE***: It's not important how the effect of the* HEADLESS HORSEMAN *is accomplished: whether through shadows, puppetry, video, or a second actor—it could even be as simple as a lighting and sound effect. What is important, however, is that it be a true moment of fright. It should take the audience by surprise and, without humor, make them sit up in their seats. They must believe that the* HEADLESS HORSEMAN *exists.*]

> There! There! Did you see it? Did you?! The Horseman . . . the Horseman! The Headless Horseman rides again! Let that be a lesson to you—all of you—especially you who don't believe. The Horseman is real—he exists—he is here. He is always here! Always! You see, I'm *not* insane! I'm *not*! I said he was real and he is! If I were you, I'd watch my step tonight. Especially while traveling over bridges. For you never know when the Headless Horseman—or any other spirit from beyond—will visit you. But remember: he brings a message—he *always* brings a message. And it's up to you to unmask it, and listen to it, and heed it. Or else be damned.

[*The lights are restored.* ICHABOD *is clearly shaken but attempts to recapture his composure.*]

> I must go, and I suggest you do the same. Go! Don't say I didn't warn you.

[ICHABOD *gathers his notes and hurries offstage. There is a subtle, distant cackle of laughter heard from the* HEADLESS HORSEMAN *as the lights fade to black.*]

• • •

Bulgarian Rhapsody

a comedy

Rich Orloff

Rich Orloff

Rich Orloff is one of the most popular unknown playwrights in the country. His short plays (mostly comedies) have had over 900 productions on six of the seven continents (and a staged reading in Antarctica). They've been published in numerous anthologies, including six times in the annual *Best American Short Plays* series. Playscripts has published sixty of his short plays in eight volumes.

Orloff has also written fifteen acclaimed full-length plays, which have been produced around the world in professional theaters, community theaters, colleges, and high schools. You can find out about his plays, both long and short, at www.richorloff.com. In his spare time, he sleeps.

···production history···

Bulgarian Rhapsody was originally produced as the climactic comedy of Rich's *Foreign Affairs*, a collection of seven short comedies set in seven different countries. *Foreign Affairs* (which also includes *Prague Summer* from *The Best American Short Plays 1999–2000*) was co-produced by the WorkShop Theater Company and the Foolish Theatre Company in New York, featuring Laurie Ann Orr Bomar, Richard Kent Green, Gary Mink, Gerrianne Raphael, Kim Reed, Greg Skura, and Baz Snider, under the direction of Holli Harms.

time

The present

place

A modest Bulgarian home

characters

> **VASILKA**, a middle-aged Bulgarian woman
>
> **TATIANA**, Vasilka's daughter, 20-ish (pronounced "Ta-tee-AN-a")
>
> **STANIMIR**, Vasilka's husband
>
> **PLAMEN**, their neighbor
>
> **DESISLAV**, Vasilka's brother
>
> **KEN**, Vasilka's American cousin

• • •

[*As the play begins,* VASILKA, *a middle-aged Bulgarian woman of modest means, is tidying the modest living room of her modest Bulgarian home. Her tidying is more a result of anxiety than need. She calls out.*]

VASILKA   Are you ready yet?

TATIANA   [*Offstage.*] Almost.

VASILKA   He should be here any second.

TATIANA   [*Offstage.*] I know, I know.

VASILKA   For our American cousin, you better look *perfect*.

[TATIANA *enters. She's dressed to give a man an unmistakable positive signal. She wears thick makeup and a dress with its top buttons unbuttoned.*]

TATIANA   How do I look? You think he'll find me attractive?

VASILKA   If he likes frigid nuns.

TATIANA   I don't want to be too forward.

[VASILKA *unbuttons some of the buttons of* TATIANA's *dress.*]

VASILKA   He'll only be in Bulgaria a few days. This is no time for subtlety.

TATIANA   But what if he prefers virgins?

[VASILKA *rebuttons the buttons.*]

VASILKA   You're right. Let's not overwhelm him.

TATIANA   I don't think they still have virgins in America.

VASILKA   Then there must not be a market for it.

[VASILKA *unbuttons a couple of buttons.*]

TATIANA   Oh, Mama. What if he doesn't like me?

VASILKA   Simple. You'll change.

TATIANA   And what if he still doesn't like me?

VASILKA   Then you'll have to get a job.

TATIANA   Mama, wake up. Ever since Communism ended, there are no jobs.

VASILKA   Did you check the newspaper today?

TATIANA   Yes. There were only seven want ads.

VASILKA   So?

[TATIANA *picks up a newspaper.*]

TATIANA "Prostitute, prostitute, prostitute, drug dealer, drug dealer, drug dealer."

VASILKA That's six.

TATIANA "Executive secretary."

VASILKA Ahh.

TATIANA "Skills include prostitution, drug dealing, and typing sixty words a minute."

VASILKA Your aunt Zelda could teach you to type.

[*There's a knock at the door.*]

Coming.

[*She checks the room one last time and unbuttons another button on* TATIANA's *dress. There's another knock.*]

Coming.

[*She opens the door. In the doorway is her neighbor* PLAMEN. *He's dressed as sophisticated as possible for a man who has no sophistication.*]

PLAMEN Hello.

VASILKA Oh, it's you.

PLAMEN This is how you greet your neighbor?

TATIANA We were hoping you were Mama's cousin.

VASILKA Stanimir's picking him up at the airport.

PLAMEN Where's Desislav? Doesn't he want to meet his cousin?

VASILKA I haven't heard from my brother in weeks.

PLAMEN Really?

VASILKA For all I know, he's dead. Or his phone's been disconnected.

PLAMEN Oh.

TATIANA How do you think I look?

PLAMEN   I can honestly say you look so beautiful that only the fear of your mother killing me prevents me from lunging at you.

TATIANA   Oh, good.

PLAMEN   [*To* VASILKA.] Does your American cousin know you're—

VASILKA   He'll find out soon enough.

PLAMEN   Are you sure he's single?

TATIANA   We don't even know if he's heterosexual.
[PLAMEN *unbuttons a couple of buttons on his shirt.*]
What are you doing?

PLAMEN   I'd rather be a gay American than a straight Bulgarian. . . . How rich do you think he is?

VASILKA   He's American.

PLAMEN   Not all Americans are rich.

TATIANA   Really?

PLAMEN   I read an article about it. Only 10 percent of Americans are really wealthy. The other 90 percent are upper middle class.

TATIANA   Mama, what's for dinner tonight?

VASILKA   I'm hoping my cousin will take us out.

TATIANA   What if he doesn't?

VASILKA   Then we'll have leftovers from last night.

TATIANA   But last night we went without food. I didn't eat anything.

VASILKA   And whatever you didn't finish, we're having tonight.

TATIANA   Mama!

PLAMEN   You better finish it tonight, or you'll have leftovers all week.

[*There's a knock on the door.* VASILKA *checks the apartment.* TATIANA *unbuttons one button.* PLAMEN *sees this and unbuttons one button.* TATIANA *unbuttons one more button.* PLAMEN *unbuttons one more button. They both start furiously unbuttoning. There's another knock.*]

VASILKA   Coming!

> [*To* PLAMEN, *then* TATIANA.]

> You, button up, or I'll kick you out. Tatiana, I want you to look like a non-virginal but shy girl who will put out for the right man.

> [VASILKA *opens the door. Her husband,* STANIMIR, *enters with her American cousin* KEN. STANIMIR *carries* KEN's *suitcase.*]

> Hello, welcome.

STANIMIR   Ken, I would like you to meet your cousin Vasilka, and our daughter, Tatiana.

> [VASILKA *smiles.* TATIANA *curtsies with a bow, revealing deep into her dress.* KEN *is overwhelmed by the view.*]

> And this is our neighbor Plamen.

PLAMEN   Hello.

[PLAMEN *curtsies, too.*]

KEN   Hi. Stanimir, you didn't tell me you had such a lovely wife and daughter.

STANIMIR   The wife's taken.

PLAMEN   Your trip must've been exhausting.

STANIMIR   Would you like a seat?

VASILKA   A drink?

TATIANA   A full-body massage?

KEN   No, thank you, Tatwana.

TATIANA   Tatiana.

KEN   Ta-tee-wana.

TATIANA   Ta-tee-*an*-na.

STANIMIR Call her Betty.

VASILKA It such a pleasure to meet you, cousin.

KEN It is an honor to finally meet you.

VASILKA When I look at you, I think, if only our great-great-grandfather were alive today. . . .

KEN I know. I could almost cry.

PLAMEN You must be a very, very sensitive man.

TATIANA In America, even heterosexuals cry.

PLAMEN Just my luck.

VASILKA So how was your flight?

KEN Well, you know how flights are. There's no leg room, and the food is barely edible.

VASILKA They have food on planes?!

TATIANA Oh, Mama, someday we must fly somewhere.

KEN I'm sure both of you can cook much better than anything you'll find on planes.

VASILKA Maybe once we could.

KEN What do you mean?

STANIMIR Surely you've read about Bulgaria in the newspapers.

KEN Actually, my hometown paper doesn't have much interna—

PLAMEN Then I'm sure the news on TV—

KEN Tells me less than my newspaper.

STANIMIR Doesn't American news media ever cover Bulgaria?

KEN I think I read a couple of paragraphs when you ousted the Communists.

STANIMIR That was years ago.

PLAMEN November 1989.

KEN So . . . What's new?

VASILKA My dear cousin, we all thought the end of Communism
would bring the beginning of prosperity.

PLAMEN Instead, most of us are worse off than ever.

STANIMIR Unemployment is rampant.

TATIANA And if you're lucky enough to have saved something, you
dare not put it in the corrupt banks.

STANIMIR And crime is so bad you dare not keep it under your pillow,
either.

KEN That's so sad.

STANIMIR At least we don't live in Romania.

ALL THE BULGARIANS [*Spitting.*] Ptui!

KEN Could I, I don't mean to trouble you—

VASILKA Ask for anything.

KEN Could I have a glass of water?

TATIANA I'll get it.

[TATIANA *curtsies, bows, and exits.*]

VASILKA She is so good at getting water.

STANIMIR Whenever she's around, men get thirsty.

VASILKA I'm sorry we cannot offer you any food.

KEN That's quite all—

STANIMIR We were going to make you a huge feast, but we have no
money.

VASILKA I was going to make you a roast chicken—

STANIMIR How dare you! Your cousin comes all the way from America, and you're telling him you're not making him a chicken? You could at least not make him a lamb.

VASILKA My apologies. Forget the chicken. I'm not making you a sumptuous roast lamb, in paprika and wine sauce.

PLAMEN Oooo.

VASILKA With fresh canned vegetables and imported potatoes.

STANIMIR And for dessert?

VASILKA I'm not making you my apricot-pear strudel.

PLAMEN Oh, I love when you don't make that!

[TATIANA *returns with a glass of water.*]

TATIANA Here's your water. Let me know if it's moist enough.

KEN Thank you, Tatiana.

STANIMIR Will you listen to him? He got her name right.

VASILKA It must be love.

KEN Actually, I, I do have someone back home.

PLAMEN and TATIANA Damn.

STANIMIR Is she a nice girl?

PLAMEN Is she female?

KEN She's very nice.

VASILKA Is she good at giving blow jobs?

TATIANA Mama!

VASILKA I just—

TATIANA You know I hate it when you brag about me.

KEN [*To* VASILKA *and* STANIMIR.] You're not—you're not trying to—I mean, we're relatives.

VASILKA You have different last names.

KEN Yes, but there are biological reasons people don't—our kids could be morons.

TATIANA Oh, Mama, just think. I could give birth to an American moron.

VASILKA And one day he could become president!

KEN I, uh, I'm sorry. If you hoped—

VASILKA You see, cousin, it's just—life is so hard.

STANIMIR Under Communism, we were miserable, year after year.

KEN Sounds awful.

STANIMIR At least we had stability. When I wake up today, I don't know if the day will be miserable or horrible. Who can live with such uncertainty?

KEN At least you have your freedom now. And can you put a price on freedom?

PLAMEN Twelve stotinkis.

STANIMIR You're overpaying.

VASILKA Americans can't understand that freedom isn't that valuable when you have nothing.

PLAMEN And in Bulgaria, the people with nothing are the lucky ones. I have less than nothing.

KEN You do?

PLAMEN The only way I could get a job was to promise my superiors a weekly bribe that's more than my wages. Every week my debt increases.

KEN Why don't you quit?

PLAMEN And lose seniority?

KEN I'm, I'm so sorry to hear about your plight, all of you.

STANIMIR   At least we don't live in Romania.

ALL THE BULGARIANS   [*Spitting.*] Ptui!

KEN   As you know, America is also going through a difficult time economically—

PLAMEN   I've heard. In America, the average household can barely afford a DVD player, a cell phone, *and* premium cable.

KEN   Do you really want those things?

ALL THE BULGARIANS   Yes!

KEN   My parents used to tell me how down to earth Bulgarians were.

STANIMIR   That's because most of us can't afford a second floor.

KEN   You know, last year, when I lost my job—

TATIANA   You lost your job?

[TATIANA *starts buttoning her dress.*]

KEN   Look, if all you're interested in is my money—

VASILKA   Cousin, we don't care about your money.

KEN   That's good, because—

VASILKA   Just to finally see your plump face and your well-fed belly—

[*There's a knock on the door.*]

STANIMIR   Who is it?

DESISLAV   [*Offstage.*] It's Desislav.

VASILKA   Thank God. He's alive!

[STANIMIR *opens the door.* DESISLAV *enters.* DESISLAV *is in good health, except that he has one leg. He uses crutches.*]

DESISLAV   Sorry I'm late.

VASILKA   Desislav, what happened?!

DESISLAV   The bus was late.

VASILKA   No, I mean—

STANIMIR   Desislav, I want you to meet Ken.

DESISLAV   It's good to meet you, cousin Ken.

TATIANA   Uncle Desislav, are you okay?

VASILKA   Why haven't we heard from you?

DESISLAV   A few weeks ago, I went to the countryside to visit my ex-cow.

STANIMIR   How is she?

DESISLAV   Bulgarian grass is so lacking in nutrients she no longer has the strength to go "moo." She just goes "mm." On my way home, I was hit by a train. Most of me survived fine, but they had to cut off my leg.

[*For a moment there's silence. Then overlapping.*]

STANIMIR   Congratulations!

VASILKA   I'm so happy for you!

TATIANA   That's great, Uncle.

PLAMEN   You lucky bastard.

KEN   Why are you all congratulating him?

PLAMEN   He only has one leg.

KEN   So?

STANIMIR   Now he'll only have to buy one shoe.

PLAMEN   A pair of socks will last twice as long.

VASILKA   Think of what he'll save on podiatrists!

DESISLAV   Not only that, but the train commission will let me ride free for six months.

TATIANA   It's like you've won the lottery.

DESISLAV   I consider myself a lucky man.

KEN   I never realized things were this bad.

STANIMIR   At least we don't live in Romania.

ALL THE BULGARIANS   [*Spitting.*] Ptui!

KEN   What's so awful about Romania?

PLAMEN   In Romania, they have laws against spitting.

KEN   I, I really wish I could make things better for all of you.

VASILKA   Just seeing you in my home, seeing you in person, knowing that each day you probably crap more nutrients than we get in our diet . . .

KEN   Look, I—

DESISLAV   My dear American cousin—

KEN   I—

DESISLAV   Don't worry. I'm not asking for money.

KEN   If I had, I'd gladly—

DESISLAV   I ask nothing for myself. For me, *nothing*. But I do have one favor to ask.
[DESISLAV *opens the duffel bag and takes out his leg.*]
Take my leg to America.

VASILKA   Could you?!

KEN   I can't take—

DESISLAV   Look at its calluses; look at its blisters. Is it too much to want one American foot? I want this leg to have the opportunities the rest of me will never have. To think that one day this leg may be slipped into Nikes and not a knock-off, to think this leg might once press on the brake of an American SUV.

TATIANA   [*Wiping tears.*] Those are beautiful dreams.

KEN Look, there are laws. What do you want me to do, take this back on the plane with me?

DESISLAV Would you?

KEN *I can't.*

DESISLAV *Why not?!*

PLAMEN There's no leg room.

DESISLAV Oh.

VASILKA Surely, cousin, you can take *one* leg.

KEN I wish I could, but—

STANIMIR I promise, we will ask nothing else of you.

TATIANA You would make my uncle so happy.

[TATIANA *unbuttons the top of her dress.*]

PLAMEN We would all rejoice in his leg's good fortune.

[PLAMEN *unbuttons the top of his shirt.*]

KEN Look, I . . . America is not this great land you think it is. Most Americans, most Americans, they prefer comfort to freedom. That's why I came here, hoping to rediscover what it felt like to hope.

VASILKA For us, cousin, hope is still a luxury item.

[KEN *looks at the group and thinks.*]

KEN Maybe if the leg was wrapped up, and if there was some certificate—

DESISLAV You mean it?

KEN I'll do my best.

DESISLAV Thank you.

VASILKA Thank you.

STANIMIR Thank you.

[*A beat.*]

Take my nose.

VASILKA Take my ear.

TATIANA Take my elbow.

KEN No—you said if—

STANIMIR Vasilka, get the carving knife.

[VASILKA *exits, as* PLAMEN *drops his drawers.*]

PLAMEN Take my penis!

KEN Stop it!

STANIMIR Just one nostril. To breathe American pollution.

TATIANA To elbow my way into American society.

PLAMEN My penis in a woman who shaves her armpits!

STANIMIR Vasilka!

[VASILKA *returns with a carving knife.*]

KEN I'm not taking anything else!

[*They start wrestling over the knife.*]

STANIMIR You can hide my nose between his toes.

VASILKA You can wrap up my ear in your stocks.

TATIANA Take any part of me you want!

[TATIANA *rips open her dress. She's wearing a red and white bra. Her panties are blue with white stars.*]

ALL THE BULGARIANS A part of me—in America!

[KEN *screams as the lights fade.*]

• • •

Change of Venue

Judd Lear Silverman

Judd Lear Silverman

Judd Lear Silverman has been produced across the country and at various international fringe festivals. Recent credits include *The Proposal* (American Globe/Turnip), *Crackers* (Blue Roses), and *Superhero Blues* (Gallery Players). A member of Charles Maryan's Playwrights/Directors Workshop and the Dramatists Guild, he is a Berrilla Kerr Playwriting Grant recipient.

···production history···

Change of Venue was developed in Charles Maryan's Playwrights/Directors Workshop in New York City, followed by a reading at Alaska's Last Frontier Theatre Conference. Its world premiere production took place in March 2012 at Full Circle Theater Company, under the direction of Nicholas Walker Herbert, performed by Francine Margolis and James Arden.

···

[*A very simple bedroom in a bordello. At rise, the room is empty. We hear a woman humming in the bathroom, though the door is closed. From the room's other door, we hear a knock. After a moment,* HERMAN *peeks in. He is 30-ish, sweet, shy, and somewhat sheepish.*]

HERMAN   Hello? Hello, is anyone here?

WOMAN   [*Voiceover.*] Hellooo!

HERMAN   Are you Natalya? They said downstairs that I'd find Natalya in Room 233.

WOMAN   [*Voiceover.*] Be right out, baby!

HERMAN   So you're Natalya, right?

WOMAN   [*Voiceover.*] Well, you'll see for yourself in a moment, won't you?! Keep your pants on, sugar.

[*Giggles.*]

Or not!

[HERMAN *enters and looks nervously around the room, unzipping his jacket as he does so. He listens to her humming, decides it is reassuring, and sits down on a corner of the bed facing away from the bathroom.*]

There's a little bar in the corner, if you wanna drink.

HERMAN   Uh, no . . . well . . . uh, no! Thanks.

WOMAN   [*Voiceover.*] It's included!

HERMAN   Thanks. Maybe later.

[HERMAN *holds up his hand to his mouth, breathes out, and tries to smell his own breath. Not great, not bad, he takes out a breath spray and does a couple of quick hits, checks again. Better. Facing away from the bathroom door,* HERMAN *does not see the* WOMAN *exit from the bathroom, dressed in a robe. She is modestly attractive, but seems friendly.*]

WOMAN   Sorry, just needed to freshen up a bit.

> [HERMAN, *though not looking at her, seems surprised and little stunned by something.*]

> Not that I've been that busy. I actually just got in a little while ago myself.

> [*Pause.*]

> Take off your coat, honey. Stay a while. I won't bite you . . . too hard . . .

> [*She goes over to the minibar and starts to pour herself a drink.*]

> You sure you won't have one? I'm pouring and, like I say, it's part of the package . . .

[HERMAN *doesn't respond or even look. She gives up, and pours. Finally, she takes a sip and turns to survey her client. Stunned, she drops her glass. The dropped glass makes him turn and look. The ensuing silence is like a sonic boom.*]

HERMAN   Shirley?!

[*He rises, stunned.*]

SHIRLEY   Herman?! What are you doing here?!

HERMAN   I could ask you the same question!

SHIRLEY   Did you follow me?

HERMAN   Follow you? You were the last person in the world I wanted to see!

SHIRLEY   What are you doing here?!

HERMAN   I would think that was obvious!

SHIRLEY   I don't believe this!

HERMAN   The question is, what are *you* doing here?!

SHIRLEY   This is a nightmare. This can't be real.

HERMAN   Oh, it's real alright. God, I don't believe this. You said you were going to work today.

SHIRLEY   I didn't lie!

[*Pause.*]

You said you were going bowling with your buddies.

HERMAN   Oh my God.

SHIRLEY   Oh my God.

HERMAN   Oh . . . my . . .

SHIRLEY   God.

[*They both sit down on opposite corners of the bed.*]

And now I've got no morning business.

HERMAN   You told me you were working.

SHIRLEY   Duh.

HERMAN   I mean . . . what are you doing here?

SHIRLEY   Isn't it pretty obvious? You?

HERMAN   Well, frankly, I wasn't getting enough at home! I didn't think we were just changing venues!

[*Pause.*]

This may just damage me forever.

SHIRLEY   There wasn't that much working for you before.

HERMAN   Why on earth . . .

SHIRLEY   Money's been tight. I know you've been doing your best, but let's face it, it hasn't been stretching. This—

HERMAN   What?

SHIRLEY   This was a way to stretch.

HERMAN   How long have you been—

SHIRLEY   Four months.

HERMAN   Four months?

SHIRLEY   Well, give or take a week. And I didn't work the holidays.

HERMAN   Jesus, Shirley, I don't know what's more of a shock—to find you here, or to know that you've been doing this for four months without my finding out! I hope you're proud of yourself!

SHIRLEY   It's not a question of being proud, Herman. You want we should lose the house? The cars? Everything we worked for?

HERMAN   Not like this! This is not the way!

SHIRLEY   Who are you to be so judgmental? You're here, aren't you?

HERMAN   To blow off a little steam, maybe. You're never interested at home. And now I know why!

SHIRLEY   Frankly, home wasn't so interesting even four months ago.

HERMAN   Have you no pride? No shame?

SHIRLEY   Actually, I have pride. You always made me feel that I wasn't any good at it. That I was lucky to even have *you*! I know it's pathetic, but here I feel valued! Here, I feel attractive, wanted!

HERMAN   That's pathetic!

SHIRLEY   That's the truth!

[*Pause.*]

Why is it that men always want what they think is illicit, illegal, dangerous? Isn't enough that women want them? Isn't it enough to have someone ready and loving when they get home?

HERMAN Most times, seems like sex is the last thing on your mind. Or so I thought. How can you do such a thing?

SHIRLEY How can you?!

HERMAN What?

SHIRLEY Coming here!

HERMAN Here? Here is just sex.

SHIRLEY Precisely!

HERMAN Like going to the gym. Or playing tennis or squash.

SHIRLEY You don't play squash.

HERMAN How would you know? You think you know everything about me? Clearly, we don't know everything about each other, even after sixteen years!

SHIRLEY Let's face it, Herman, that's not the body of a secret athlete.

HERMAN And that's the body of your everyday call girl?

SHIRLEY I'm not a call girl!

HERMAN No?

SHIRLEY No.

HERMAN Well, excuse me. I'd call you a "lady of the evening," but it's 10:47 on a Saturday morning!

SHIRLEY I think of myself as a sexual surrogate.

HERMAN Come again?

SHIRLEY A therapeutic partner.

HERMAN   Gimme a break.

SHIRLEY   People come to me when they can't—

HERMAN   Get it at home?!

[*Pause.*]

All these years . . .

SHIRLEY   You're gonna ask me to believe this is first time you've come to a place like this?!

HERMAN   No. But maybe if I'd known you were gonna put your "talents" on the market—

SHIRLEY   You'd have asked to be let in on the action?!

[*Pause.*]

You're not who I thought you were, Herman.

HERMAN   Back at ya.

[*Pause.*]

It's not like I haven't tried to make you happy, Shirley. Anything you've wanted, anything you've asked for—

SHIRLEY   What? You've gotten me?

HERMAN   Well, I certainly tried!

SHIRLEY   Don't tell me that, Herman. That only adds pathetic to your list of attributes!

HERMAN   Like you've been the perfect wife?

SHIRLEY   I've been faithful!

[HERMAN *stares at her incredulously.*]

What?! This? This isn't having an affair. This is just a job, like any other job.

HERMAN   Not quite like any other job, Shirley.

SHIRLEY Oh yeah? Name a job these days where the woman *doesn't* get screwed?!

[*Pause.*]

It's not like I'm having an affair. This is meaningless. This is mindless.

HERMAN It's a job?

SHIRLEY It's a living.

[*Pause.*]

You can't tell me you came here for a "meaningful relationship"!

HERMAN I came here . . .

SHIRLEY Yeah?

HERMAN To be a man.

SHIRLEY This makes you a man?

HERMAN Not to make me a man, to be a man. The way I don't feel in my own home!

SHIRLEY And the fault there would be—

HERMAN Shirley, I don't feel like the man in our relationship!

[*Pause.*]

SHIRLEY You feel like the woman?

HERMAN No.

SHIRLEY Well, take your pick, Herman. It's either—

HERMAN No. I mean a man in a relationship, feeling vital, feeling powerful, assertive, strong . . . a male animal!

SHIRLEY Oh, you're an animal, all right.

HERMAN You asked me! I don't feel wanted or needed or respected or . . . desired.

[*Pause.*]

SHIRLEY   You think I felt desired? You think I felt valued. I felt at best like a scratching post. "Oh, I have an itch, hold still!"

HERMAN   That's not so!

[*Pause.*]

So this is revenge?

SHIRLEY   Revenge has nothing to do with it.

HERMAN   What, then?

SHIRLEY   I told you, it was basically an economic decision. To have some independence. To have something of my own.

HERMAN   I gave you an allowance.

SHIRLEY   Like some child on a short rope?

[*Pause.*]

But also, I wanted to learn some things. About men and women. About myself. All my life I'd been such a good little girl, my daddy's little girl, your good little wife.

HERMAN   You couldn't read it in a book?

SHIRLEY   You couldn't keep it in your pants?

[*Pause.*]

I'm not proud of myself, but . . . I'm not quite ashamed, either, truth be told.

HERMAN   But you think men who come here should be, right?

SHIRLEY   I . . .

[*Pause.*]

I don't know. Now.

[*Pause.*]

I only know I'm someone different here than when I'm home with you.

HERMAN   Yeah? Well, me too. And I want to be. Someone different. Than I am at home. Someone powerful. Dangerous. Fun. Sexy.

SHIRLEY   Me too.

[*Pause.*]

HERMAN   So?

SHIRLEY   So?

[*Pause.*]

You're paying for the morning. No refunds.

[*Pause.*]

HERMAN   Really?

SHIRLEY   Really.

[*Pause.*]

HERMAN   Well, then . . . are you Natalya? They told me downstairs I'd find Natalya up here.

[*Pause.*]

Are you Natalya?

SHIRLEY   Who wants to know?

HERMAN   Hernando.

[*They stare deeply at one another a moment, all the anger, hurt, and frustration welling up into . . . something else.*]

SHIRLEY   Cash or credit?

[*She opens her robe to him.*]

• • •

The Wager

Neil LaBute

Neil LaBute

Neil LaBute writes for both stage and screen. His works include *Bash*, *Mercy Seat*, *The Shape of Things*, *The Distance from Here*, *Fat Pig*, *Autobahn*, and the very recent *This Is How It Goes*.

··· production history ···

The Wager was written for and produced by Theater Breaking Through Barriers as part of a collection of one-act plays about disability, under the heading *More of Our Parts*, performed June 21–July 1, 2012.

• • •

[*Silence. Darkness. A city street. Quiet now as it's getting late (or early, depending on how young you are). A couple (GUY and GAL)—dressed for a night out—comes down the street, both a bit wobbly from a night of partying. Nearby is a* HOMELESS DUDE, *sitting in a wheelchair with a small cart nearby piled high with bags and shit, etc. He's pretty much minding his own business. For now.*]

GUY   No, no, no, come on, seriously. Can we go now? Please?

GAL   *Baby*—can't we just hang a little longer? It's Sheila's birthday! I don't wanna . . .

GUY   Seriously, it's—

[*Checks watch.*]

Sweetie, it's 1:45 in the morning and I gotta work tomorrow! I mean today. I have to be at work in, like . . . six hours.

[*Kisses her cheek.*]

Six.

GAL   Me too!

[*Beat.*]

Well, class. I have class tomorrow. Or today. Or . . . whatever!

GUY   Uh-huh. At three. In the afternoon. And it's an art class, by the way, which is painting and pottery and . . . that sorta deal. It's basically *crafts*. Like what kids do . . .

[*The* HOMELESS DUDE *has worked his way over to them by this point—dragging his cart along beside him with a cane.*]

HOMELESS DUDE   Hey, man, what's up?

GUY   Nothing's up, dude. I'm having a private conversation with my girlfriend. Why?

HOMELESS DUDE   That's cool . . .

GUY   Yeah, thanks for the *endorsement* there.

HOMELESS DUDE   She's pretty.

GAL   Honey, let's go. Come on.

[*Silence. The* GAL *wants to go and tugs on the arm of her boyfriend. He, however, is staring at the* HOMELESS DUDE.]

GUY   No, hold it. He stopped us, let's see what he wants . . .
  [*To* HOMELESS DUDE.]
  So?

HOMELESS DUDE   Hungry, bro, that's all. Can you help a brother out tonight? It's cold being out here on the street . . .

GUY   I'm an only child, so first things first: we're not *brothers*, ya got that? Bro?

HOMELESS DUDE   It's cool . . . that's cool. Okay.
  [*Beat.*]
  Anyway, can you help me out a bit? Anything you can spare. Know what I mean?

GUY   No, what? You people always want something, so it's impossible to keep up . . . What do you want? Tell me.

HOMELESS DUDE   Some *bread*, man! You know that . . . *Mon-ey!* Come on . . . just some change.

GUY   Oh, just some change—because we must have cash, we're young and white and all that shit, so we must be rich.

GAL   Clark, please. I'm cold.

GUY Sorry.

[*To* HOMELESS DUDE.]

My girlfriend's cold, so I can't really get into it with you right now, like I was gonna, but hey, it's your lucky night . . . I'm gonna teach you the value of money—or in your case, *food stamps*.

[*The* GUY *reaches into a pocket and produces a dollar bill. He holds it in his hand and points to it, using his head to gesture.*]

GAL Baby, stop . . . what're you doing?

GUY I'm giving this dude a job.

GAL What?

GUY I'm *offering* this *gentleman* the chance to earn a living wage . . .

[*Smiling.*]

And learn a little about capitalism, too, while he's at it.

GAL Yeah, while I'm standing here freezing.

GUY Gimme a minute!

[*To* HOMELESS DUDE.]

Hey, *Denzel*, come over here a sec! How 'bout a little wager?

HOMELESS DUDE What'chu mean?

GUY Here. My two hands. I've got money in there. One dollar . . . that's a least a chicken leg at KFC . . . maybe even a slice of watermelon. You want it?

[*The* HOMELESS DUDE *looks at the guy, unsure at first what to say. Finally he blurts out:*]

HOMELESS DUDE Hell yeah!

GUY Good, but you gotta earn it. Okay? Easy.

HOMELESS DUDE Whatever, man, just gimme it . . .

GUY Not so fast! Hold on there and don't go touching me, either. You're dirty.

GAL Clark, don't! My God . . . why're you . . . ?

GUY What?! Just stop, please? Okay? It's not *racist*, it's a fact. Look at him—I'd say it to anybody. It's not a *black* thing . . . it's a *soap* thing. The man is filthy!

[*The* GAL *just shrugs her shoulders and shifts her weight from one high-heeled shoe to the other.*]

GAL Maybe I'll just go . . .

GUY Where? You didn't even bring a *purse*—don't think I didn't notice—so I'm the money guy tonight and now this dude wants some—for free—just because he's so, so *great* or something and so, fine, I'm now giving him the chance to have some . . . do you mind? Can you hold on for a few more minutes without complaining just once in our entire dating life?

GAL Clark! Don't talk to me like that.

GUY Okay! Here. God.
[*Takes off jacket, puts it over her shoulders.*]
Better? Now can I get on with this, please?

GAL . . . Yes. Go on.

GUY Thank you.
[*To* HOMELESS DUDE.]
Women, huh?
[*The* GUY *waves a dismissive hand at her, in effect telling her to "be quiet." He turns back to the* HOMELESS DUDE *and holds up the dollar again.*]
Okay, look, you pick the hand it's in and the money's yours.
[*Smiles.*]
However: you get it wrong and I get to punch you. One time. Anywhere I want.

HOMELESS DUDE   *What the fuck*?! Hold up, now . . . just hold on . . .

GAL   No! Stop it, Clark, just stop it!

GUY   I'm not doing anything! I'm suggesting a bet—if anything happens . . . it's because this guy goes for it.
[*To* HOMELESS DUDE.]
If you've got the guts, go ahead.
[*The* HOMELESS DUDE *looks carefully at both of them.* GUY *flashes the money at him, smiles. He puts his hands behind his back and mixes it up again. His fists come back out front.*]
. . . What's it gonna be, *Denzel*? You up for this or not?

GAL   Stop calling him that!

GUY   How do I know that's not his name? They like names like that.
[*To* HOMELESS DUDE.]
So what is it, then? T'Shawn? Julius? *Magic*, maybe?

GAL   Clark, now you're just being . . .

HOMELESS DUDE   It's Clark. Just like you, man.

GUY   Bullshit! It is not!

HOMELESS DUDE   'S true. I was born Clark Jackson . . .

GUY   Okay, well, at least you've got a classic last name. I was gonna say . . .

GAL   Please, can we just go? Just give the guy some money and let's head home . . .

GUY   Nope. Ol' Clark and me are gonna finish this first.
[*To* HOMELESS DUDE.]
You ready to try or are you a coward, too . . . on top of being a fucking *beggar*? Hmmm?

HOMELESS DUDE   Fine. I'll try it.

GUY Good!

[*Hides dollar.*]

Go for it, buddy. You take a really good guess now . . .

[*The* GUY *holds out both hands. Turning them over slowly. The* HOMELESS DUDE *studies both fists. About to choose one, then the other. Finally goes with the right. The* GUY *reluctantly opens his hand to show the crumpled legal tender. The* HOMELESS DUDE *scoops up the bill, happy with himself. The* GAL *rolls her eyes.*]

GAL All that for a *dollar!* Don't be such a *bully*, Clark. Now let's go . . .

[*The* HOMELESS DUDE *wheels himself away, counting his good fortune this evening. Or morning. The* GUY *calls him back.*]

GUY Wait, man, hold up!

[*Smiles.*]

We got a bet going and we just got started—double or nothing?

[*The* HOMELESS DUDE *studies him. Looks at the single in his hand.*]

GAL No, no, no! I'm not standing here for . . .

GUY Stop! Just—I'm almost done.

[*To* HOMELESS DUDE.]

Again? Here, let's make it at least interesting.

[*Without hesitation, the* GUY *pulls a twenty off his roll and folds it up into a tiny square.*]

There. Now you got something to play for! If you've got the stomach for it . . .

GAL God, I can't believe you're acting so . . .

GUY Believe it! I'm sick of being stopped all the time, every five minutes, them asking for my money, a cigarette, whatever. Time for it to stop!

[*To* HOMELESS DUDE.]

So: up to you, *Cassius Clay*—I made the bet. Are you man enough to take it?

HOMELESS DUDE . . . Hell yes . . .

GUY   Cool. But remember, it's double or nothing this time, so that's two punches. Just so we're clear.

[*The* GUY *smiles at the* HOMELESS DUDE. *Puts his hands out. The* HOMELESS DUDE *studies his hands, then wheels himself back over and picks one. The* GUY *opens his hand—empty palm. Before the* HOMELESS DUDE *can even react, a sharp right jab to his cheek knocks him sideways out of the chair and flat on his back.*]

HOMELESS DUDE   Aaawwwgghhh!

GUY   Tough luck, buddy. Nice try, though. And now here's number two . . .

HOMELESS DUDE   Please, man, please, no! Please!

GUY   Come on, don't be such a . . .

GAL   Clark, stop! STOP IT NOW! STOP!

[*The* GAL *is so persuasive in her yelling that* CLARK *stops an inch from hitting the* HOMELESS DUDE. *She grabs his arm and he turns to her.*]

GUY   *What?*!

GAL   If you touch him once more—I mean, even *breathe* on him or whatever—I'm so outta here that you'll never see me again. And I mean ever. For all time.
[*Beat.*]
Look at you, what you're doing . . . my God, you are acting like an, an animal! A *jungle* animal who's gone nuts in the head. I'm serious! I've had my doubts about you, I mean, in the last few weeks, you have gone outta your way to be rude and mean and, and a real *scumbag* to waiters and cops and even people we know . . . I do not get what has gotten into you, seriously, I mean, like, ever since we slept together you have not been the same guy I met at that wine bar . . . I don't *get* it but I'm definitely *aware* of it.

[*Beat.*]

Now, I need ya to suck it up and be the guy I fell for . . . just turn away from this or I'm telling you now . . . I'm outta here if I have to walk all the way back to Fulton Street on my own! I will and that'll be the absolute end of us. You got that? I am deadly serious here—we're done if you don't follow me outta here right now. Up to you.

[*Beat.*]

Be a real man, someone I'm proud of, or keep being this . . . asshole that you're working so hard at tonight! And *Cancun* is off . . . just so you know. No way would I ever go to a foreign country with you now until you take a few anger management classes and maybe even some racial sensitivity thingy—a *seminar* or whatever. I'm just really not feeling safe around you and, so, just . . . prove me wrong or I walk away. Right now.

[*Beat.*]

I mean it, Clark. Now.

GUY   Come on. *Mandy.*

[*Beat.*]

That's bullshit. I mean . . . you're not . . . gonna . . .

GAL   [*Bursts out crying.*] I guess that's my answer . . . okay! You are being such a bastard to me . . . fine! I've wanted to break up with you for a while now and this is the perfect excuse! I don't even need one for a, a freak like you, but fine . . . you want one, then you got one! That is it and I am done with you! You hear me?
I'm . . . I'm . . . done! Good-bye!

[*And with that, she's gone. Tottering off on her heels into the night.*]

[*The* GUY *looks at the* HOMELESS DUDE.]

GUY   Now look what you've done! Damnit! I'll deal with you in a second . . .

[*The* GUY *curses to himself and starts to go after her as she disappears out of sight.*]

Mandy! Come on, stop for a—*Mandy*, I was just trying to *help* the guy! Come back!

[*The* HOMELESS DUDE *rubs his cheek. Checks to make sure his dollar bill is safe as the* GUY *returns. He's pissed off. The* GUY *makes his way back to the* HOMELESS DUDE, *who turns and looks up at him. A long pause between them.*]

. . . Okay, for you, buddy—now you're gonna get it.

HOMELESS DUDE   Get what?

GUY   Duh.

[*Breaks into a big grin.*]

Your money!

[*Hands him fifty bucks.*]

And thanks! You done good, my man.

HOMELESS DUDE   Pleasure, bro . . .

GUY   No kidding!

[*Beat.*]

You know how hard she was making it to break up with her? Damn, I was having to be such a dickwad!

[*Plops down next to him.*]

It was exhausting!

HOMELESS DUDE   Sorry, man . . . I know how girls can be . . .

GUY   [*Nodding at this.*] Not enough to just have laughs and get a pizza and, and, like, make out on a semiregular basis! Who's not happy with that? I am! All guys are!

HOMELESS DUDE   Sounds good to me.

GUY   Exactly! Guys want that! But not girls . . . They want all that other . . . I mean, some gals just don't ever get the message, no matter how many *flares* you fire up there into that night sky. Two, three dozen, it doesn't matter. They just do not get it. Especially the beautiful ones! I mean . . . yes, okay, you're great-looking! You still don't shut up at night . . . you still like bad movies and you still leave your shit all over the house!

[*Beat.*]

I dunno, man, I *really* do not know. Girls are weird . . .

[*The* GUY *shakes his head, then counts out some money into the* HOMELESS DUDE*'s hand.* HOMELESS DUDE *studies it.*]

HOMELESS DUDE Absolutely.

[*Counting.*]

I thought we said sixty. When we talked about it earlier.

GUY Did we?

HOMELESS DUDE Yes, you said sixty plus anything that I won off you. During the bet.

[*Beat.*]

It was you who said it, bro, not me.

GUY Okay, then, *bro.* Sixty it is.

[*About to give him more money.*]

Hey, you wanna play for it? Double or nothing?

[*The two men look at each other and slowly smile—there is a moment of pure male understanding between them.*]

HOMELESS DUDE Nah. I'm good . . .

GUY Okay. Your loss.

[*Beat.*]

You outta here now or what?

HOMELESS DUDE Yep. Probably gonna buy me a room tonight and watch the game. The Knicks're in town and so—anyways, it's getting cold out.

GUY Yeah, no kidding! And I lost a jacket in all this, too—*Calvin Klein*!
[*Beat.*]
. . . Oh well. Worth it, I s'pose.

[*The* GUY *checks his watch.* HOMELESS DUDE *starts to shiver a little as he looks up at the guy.*]

HOMELESS DUDE Be seeing ya . . . gotta go. Freezing my butt off down here.

GUY Yeah, sorry, here . . . lemme help you back up into your chair. Least I can do!
[*The* GUY *helps the* HOMELESS DUDE *back into the wheelchair.*]
There you go—and I'm not being rude, but you being *handicapped* totally helped out with the sympathy card. That was awesome!
[*Holds out his hand.*]
Thanks again, man . . . I really couldn't've done it without you! Seriously, I've tried!

[*They both snicker at this and shake hands. Linger a bit.*]

HOMELESS DUDE Yep.
[*Beat.*]
Hey, you wanna go get a meal or something? I know it's late, but . . .

GUY Ummm . . . no, that's okay.
[*Smiles.*]
Gonna go back to that bar—there's a couple cute girls in there tonight, gonna check 'em out.

HOMELESS DUDE Ha! You white boys never learn!

GUY That is true! We never do—but we keep on trying, so that's something. Right?

[*The* GUY *checks his watch. He starts to head back inside. He stops for a second, looking off in the direction that his girlfriend has gone. He hesitates, then turns and goes off down the street.*]

HOMELESS DUDE   Amen to that, brother. Amen to that!

[*The* HOMELESS GUY *smirks and then turns back to his money. Begins to count it. Suddenly, he stands up and gathers his things. He goes to his cart and attaches it to the wheelchair. He then pushes them both off into the opposite direction. He is definitely walking now without a care in the world. Walking and whistling. Silence. Darkness.*]

• • •

A Waffle Doesn't Cure Insomnia

Erica Bennett

Dedicated to Jon Lee Cope

Erica Bennett

Erica Bennett is a playwright and tenured librarian at Fullerton College, Fullerton, California. Her plays include *Water Closet* (2011, White Horse Theater Company), *Freed* (2009, the Laguna Beach New Play Festival), and *Jolly and Bean* (2009, Newport Theatre Arts Center). Her short documentary *Mendez v. Westminster: Families for Equality* aired (PBS) in 2010. Bennett received her BA in theater arts from California State University, Fullerton, studying acting under Donn Finn and Jose Quintero. She was featured in Benicio Del Toro's short film *Submission*. She worked as a writer's and development assistant for nearly ten years in dramatic television production on such shows as *The Young Riders*, *Gabriel's Fire*, *Under Suspicion*, and *The Big Easy*.

Bennett holds a Master of Library & Information Science degree from UCLA. She is a member of the Dramatists Guild and the Orange County Playwrights Alliance.

···production history···

A Waffle Doesn't Cure Insomnia was given a staged reading for the Orange County Playwrights Discovery series in *Love, War & Loyalty* at the Empire Theatre in Santa Ana, California, the home of Theatre Out, on Saturday, December 1, 2012. Featuring Jeffrey Kieviet and Jennifer Pearce, as Heyzeus and Mou-Mou, respectively, the staged reading was directed by the author.

characters

> **HEYZEUS CHRISTOS**, 19, any gender, any ethnicity. A disco queen.
> **MOU-MOU**, 27-ish, female, any ethnicity. A heroin addict.

setting

The Splendid Dance Hall ladies restroom

time

Winter 1984

···

[*Splendid Dance Hall ladies room. The long horizontal mirror hanging above the sinks is indicated; characters look out at the audience when they check themselves out. At rise: disco music pounds from the other side of the closed door.* HEYZEUS *checks himself out in the "mirror." He poses. Another pose. Changes his pose again.*]

HEYZEUS [*To his reflection in the "mirror."*] You ever wonder what the world wants from you?

[*Changes pose.*]

Not me. Damn, I don't even know who the hell I am; standing here looking at you in the mirror.

[*Changes pose.*]

However, I can assure you, the world isn't so much as thinking even a little bit about you.

[*Changes pose.*]

Me, on the other hand? I may not be a narcissist, however, I am Heyzeus Christos. I am not "the" Jesus Christ, fool, but—

[MOU-MOU *enters, slams and locks the door behind her.*]

MOU-MOU   Girl, I've been looking all over the place for you!

HEYZEUS   Where else would I be? Duh.

MOU-MOU   Kisses—

[MOU-MOU *crosses to* HEYZEUS. *They air-kiss.*]

HEYZEUS   Kisses.

[MOU-MOU *checks herself out in the "mirror."*]

MOU-MOU   What's got you down all of a sudden? Frowny. Didn't your mother ever tell you—"Be careful—"

HEYZEUS and MOU-MOU   "Someday your face will freeze that way."

MOU-MOU   I mean, one minute you're the dancing queen in a room full of glittering balls, the next minute, you're the lady in—

HEYZEUS   I am Heyzeus Christos.

MOU-MOU   Heyzeus. Christos. Jesus Christ. Ain't life hard enough, but to be chained around the neck by the freaking Son of God? Change your name again, baby, unless you're a born-again something or other and believe the world revolves around your dick and shit and not me.
    [*Beat.*]
    I am so out of it.

HEYZEUS   [*Re: her chest.*] Nippy-nippy.

MOU-MOU   Don't name-call me, sweet cheeks. Like my new boobies? Thought I'd try thirty-eight, double-D on for the holidays. What? I themed it. Don't you get it? It's frigid on the dance floor?

HEYZEUS   They look like two rocks sitting on your chest. Loosen your bra straps. Put a little bounce in your step or the boys'll only think you're fake from the neck down.

MOU-MOU   Hey, I may be a stupid slut—

HEYZEUS   You ever think about life, Mou-Mou? Anything besides Barry Gibb?

MOU-MOU   Yummy. Curly hair to his shoulders. Tight. Oh, alright. I am always considerate of others. Other than that, you're right, I only think about myself.

[*Beat.*]

With Barry Gibb. Where's my gloss?

HEYZEUS   Day after day, party after party, is this all there is?

MOU-MOU   Hold on.

[*Listens. Beat.*]

I'm hearing violins.

[*Beat.*]

Oh my God, it's your birthday! I totally forgot it's your birthday! Happy Birthday, Heyzy—

HEYZEUS   Hey-zeus—

MOU-MOU   Here. You can have my bra.

HEYZEUS   Don't flash me.

[MOU-MOU *elaborately removes her bra through her blouse without revealing herself.*]

MOU-MOU   Here's your bounce. Jealous much?

HEYZEUS   Mou-Mou, I am expecting presents, but I want more from life than meaningless encounters, casual sex, and a minimum-wage job that makes me cover up my very own self.

MOU-MOU You really thought that chicken joint'd let you expose a little ankle?

HEYZEUS Why you think I got the butterfly tattoo? 'Cause I like the pain?

MOU-MOU Not even just a little?

HEYZEUS I'm serious.

MOU-MOU Answer? For one: you dropped out of junior college.

HEYZEUS Who thought you'd need to pass chemistry to get a cosmetology license.

MOU-MOU They are called chemicals.

HEYZEUS What?

MOU-MOU Dye? Like my hair? The stuff that makes my hair blonde?

HEYZEUS Oh, I know that. Peroxide. See, I did too learn something in college.

MOU-MOU What do you think peroxide is? A chemical. Two: you moved out of Ricky's house and are living on the street.

HEYZEUS And your couch.

MOU-MOU And my shower. Yes, baby, I know, but you need an address to get a job. And a phone number. By the way, Ricky loved you.

HEYZEUS I'm not good in the diapers and shoulders to cry on department. Now shoes, and we're talking.

MOU-MOU I totally appreciated you were with my brother when he died.

[*Pause.*]

HEYZEUS He was my first.

MOU-MOU Love?

HEYZEUS   Trick.

MOU-MOU   Three: You're Peter Pan.

HEYZEUS   How's that?

MOU-MOU   Peter Pan. The boy who never grows up.

HEYZEUS   I'm nineteen-years-old today and I found a purple lesion.

[*Pause.*]

MOU-MOU   How about waffles?

HEYZEUS   A waffle doesn't cure insomnia.

MOU-MOU   Girlfriend, no lie, I am totally going to have a waffle right now.

HEYZEUS   I bet yours won't have peanut butter on it.

MOU-MOU   No, but totally a waffle. This is the Splendid Dance Hall. Read the stamp on the back of your hand. Where "Anything is possible!"

HEYZEUS   Sounds like a fortune cookie.

MOU-MOU   Whatever it is, it's true.

HEYZEUS   When you're alive.

MOU-MOU   That's right. When you are alive.

HEYZEUS   Don't you get it?

[HEYZEUS *shows* MOU-MOU *the purple lesion on his arm.*]

MOU-MOU   It's like we're twins. Totally. Waffle twins.

[MOU-MOU *shows* HEYZEUS *a cluster of angry red needle tracks on her arm.*]

HEYZEUS   Let me see your other arm.

   [MOU-MOU *sticks out both arms.* HEYZEUS *grabs them, looks.*]

   You're using again. Mou-Mou!

MOU-MOU   You know me. I might fall, but I get right back in the saddle.

HEYZEUS   I love you so much.

MOU-MOU   Insomniac waffle twins.

HEYZEUS   I am so tired.

MOU-MOU   You'll sleep at my place tonight?

HEYZEUS   Okay.

MOU-MOU   Stella misses you.

HEYZEUS   I hate it when your cat uses my chest as a scratching post.

MOU-MOU   She's making bread.

HEYZEUS   Tell her to stop.

MOU-MOU   You tell her.

HEYZEUS   I'm not dead yet.

MOU-MOU   That's my girl.

[*They hug.*]

HEYZEUS   Last time I got the buttermilk and they were kinda meh.

MOU-MOU   Mine are frozen, yet homemade waffles that I think are about six months old. Truly.

HEYZEUS   Oh, crispy. Nice.

MOU-MOU   With a liberal amount of syrup.

HEYZEUS   Real maple syrup. Does L.A. get snow or earthquakes in January?

MOU-MOU   I really don't know.
   [*Beat.*]
   You want to go?

HEYZEUS   I do.

MOU-MOU   Tomorrow. We'll go tomorrow.

[*Pause.*]

HEYZEUS   Fuck me.

MOU-MOU   What?

HEYZEUS   I don't want to think about dying. But when Ricky—and then—I don't know. I'm nineteen. Jesus H. Christ. My life. My mother! You've got to promise me you won't tell my mother.

MOU-MOU   You know I will. Irene'd kill me, I kept this from her.

HEYZEUS   But not my dad.

MOU-MOU   Are you kidding. I don't want him to go to jail for murder.
       [*Beat.*]
       I'll leave telling him up to your mother.

HEYZEUS   Do you think he'll forgive me?

MOU-MOU   Your dad?

HEYZEUS   Yeah.

MOU-MOU   For what, baby?

HEYZEUS   For being a "homosexual."

MOU-MOU   Baby, there's no blame for being gay.

HEYZEUS   I know, but—

MOU-MOU   I mean it. Get that thought out of your head.

HEYZEUS   I'm a freak.

MOU-MOU   [*Sing-song; plugs her ears.*] Na-na-na-na-na. I can't hear you.

HEYZEUS   But I need you to listen.

MOU-MOU   Heyzey, I'm nothing but an old junkie, but it seems to me your feelings are normal. For you. Just like my nearly nonexistent feelings are normal for me. And what's good for the preacher man is good for him, if that's what you mean.

HEYZEUS Yes.

MOU-MOU So all of this is about your born-again religion.

HEYZEUS I'm going to hell.

MOU-MOU I wouldn't know hell from hell on earth. I walked out of my family's church when I was fourteen-years-old and never looked back.

HEYZEUS Don't you fear God?

MOU-MOU Where was he when the old man down the road raped me for the third time on my way to school? Pulled me behind his shed. Left me like a dirty rag, lying in the mud. No sir, no more church for me.
[*Beat.*]
Heyzy, didn't you take Jesus as your personal savior?

HEYZEUS Yes.

MOU-MOU Then you're in. Into heaven. According to what I've been told.

HEYZEUS I've sinned.

MOU-MOU Why so much doubt, you're a believer? Didn't he die for your sins?

HEYZEUS You believe it?

MOU-MOU I "think" it's a crock-o'-shit, but I'm not you. I'm okay without the myth. But if it makes you feel better, I do think I heard that story in Sunday school. Honestly, my brain is like a sieve and I could be remembering it wrong. You okay?

HEYZEUS Sure.

MOU-MOU You want God to believe you, you're going to have to say "sure" with a little more conviction.

HEYZEUS   And I didn't make cheerleader.

MOU-MOU   Neither did I, baby, neither did I. And I was behind the pool house with the basketball coach during the homecoming game.

[*Beat.*]

May I unlock the door now?

HEYZEUS   Yes. I mean, I am ready to dance.

MOU-MOU   Smith or Jones?

HEYZEUS   Smith.

MOU-MOU   Come here. Let's fix your face. You've gone and streaked it. No more crying, deal?

[MOU-MOU *reapplies* HEYZEUS*'s blush.*]

HEYZEUS   I'm not. It's sweat.

MOU-MOU   No more glistening then.

HEYZEUS   Yes, dear.

MOU-MOU   Laverne or Shirley?

HEYZEUS   Laverne. Bridget or Bernie?

MOU-MOU   Bridget. [*Pause.*]

HEYZEUS   I've missed your happiness.

MOU-MOU   We're going to live forever, don't you know?

[*Beat.*]

Heyzeus, I may not be here, but I'm always here for you. Waffles, then clinic?

HEYZEUS   Ain't disco grand?

[*Blackout.*]

• • •

Wife Shop

Angela C. Hall

Angela C. Hall

Angela Hall is a playwright/performer/dramaturg from Dublin, Georgia. She holds a BA in English and an MFA in playwriting. A published poet and short fiction writer, she has taught creative writing at Georgia College and Georgia State University and currently is an instructor at the University of Georgia. Her one-act play *Greenlight*, produced by Rising Sun Performance Co., recently ran Off-Off-Broadway at Hostelling International. She is currently working on a full-length play exploring the disturbing history of lynching in the American South.

···production history···

Wife Shop was first workshopped as part of a course at Augusta State University. It received a fully staged university production on April 17–18, 2009, at Georgia College and Georgia State University as part of its *24 Hour Play Festival*. And it made its world premiere as part of the Georgia Fine Arts Academy's Café Apollinaire at Ciné Labs in Athens, Georgia, on April 9, 2012, with the following cast:

ROCKO   Michael Thorton

BUMPY   Dane Troy Alexander

FOXXY   Arleshea Wright

WIFE   Hannah Rose Broom

GERALD, MICHAEL   George Pate

···

[*Scene opens with a sign that reads "BUMPY'S USED WIFE SHOP." There is a "MODEL BLACK WIFE" on display. The "wife" is in 1970s garb, think Foxy Brown or Coffy from the popular Pam Grier blaxploitation films. BUMPY, a man in his 40s–50s, is making small adjustments to the model. He hangs a sign around her neck. The sign reads "LIKE NEW—FOXXY—STANLEY MODEL BLK1978." There is a slash through the $10,000 price and a new price at "50% Off—$5,000" is listed.*]

BUMPY   Hello, my darling. My goodness. You look dee-licious. Just dee-licious. I'm feeling good about finding you a husband. Got up feeling like today is your day.

[BUMPY *kisses* FOXXY. *The phone rings.* BUMPY *picks up.*]

Thanks for calling Bumpy's, authorized Stanley repair, where one man's trash is another man's treasure . . . okay . . . calm down, sir. When did you buy her? Uh-huh

[*Pause.*]

. . . And do you have a receipt?

[*Pause.*]

I'm sorry. I don't take returns after ninety days . . . did you say clearance? Items on clearance are sold as is. No warranties at all.

[*Pause.*]

I can't tell you what to do with her, sir. Quite frankly, you bought her over a year ago. You're lucky she lasted this long.

[GERALD, *a wiry, somewhat mousy young white man enters Bumpy's.* GERALD *appears quite nervous.*]

BUMPY Welcome to Bumpy's . . . where one man's trash is another man's treasure. How can I help ya?

GERALD I'm looking for a wife . . . reasonably priced.

BUMPY Well, you've come to the right place. We carry only the best. We got used models, refurbished models, and shelf pulls. We're also a certified Stanley repair shop.

GERALD Right.

[*Nods.*]

I'm not sure how this works. This is my first wife. I've been saving up.

BUMPY Good. Like I said, Bumpy carries only the best. Shelf pulls and used models come with ninety-day warranties. Clearance wives are sold as is. They're on clearance for a reason. Our refurbished models come with a standard six-month warranty, but some models are eligible for extended warranties.

GERALD Okay.

[GERALD *can't seem to take his eyes off* FOXXY.]

I like this one.

BUMPY *That* one?

GERALD I like the black models with the . . . you know . . . the—

BUMPY With the what?

GERALD   You know.

> [*Spreads his hands to indicate wide hips.*]

> Curvy, shall we say. And she seems to fit the bill.

> [GERALD *looks* FOXXY *up and down, nearly salivating. Clearly itching to touch her, perhaps even sniffing her hair.*]

> She certainly seems to fit the bill.

BUMPY   You? You gotta be a special man to handle this much woman.

GERALD   Don't worry about me, Mr. Bumpy. I may be small, but I'm strong.

BUMPY   Back in the '70s when Pam Grier was kicking ass, I couldn't keep 'em on the shelves. Now I can't give 'em away. I got a few more stacked in the back. The Stanley BLK-1978.

GERALD   Any others?

BUMPY   Stanley has the brand-new BLK model. They're calling her the Rachelle O-Come-Uh. She's really something. Got lots of style and grace, can be tough as nails, but wants it every night. The kicker—expensive. I'm saving up. I've got one in stock, a shelf pull. But she's missing the—

GERALD   Okay. Where is she?

BUMPY   In the back here. I'm touching her up before I put her on the floor.

[*The two men peer behind a curtain.*]

GERALD   She's not black.

BUMPY   I know. That's what she's missing.

GERALD   But that's what I want.

BUMPY   This is a shelf pull. It's routine for them to having missing parts, and it just so happens that—

GERALD   So she's just Hillary Clinton. No thanks.

>   [*Beat.*]

>   Can I test her out, Foxxy, I mean?

BUMPY   What do you mean "test her out"?

GERALD   I mean, can I . . . *touch* her?

BUMPY   Not unless you're taking her home, pal.

GERALD   Oh . . . okay. I just wanted to feel her skin. Just a little touch.

[GERALD *reaches out to touch* FOXXY. BUMPY *slaps* GERALD's *hand.*]

BUMPY   I told you. You touch her, you buy her. But I guarantee you'll be happy. This is the last model. Came out in '78, so she has two switches.

GERALD   Yeah?

BUMPY   Yeah.

[BUMPY *turns on* FOXXY.]

FOXXY   . . . You sorry-assed, short-dicked motha—

BUMPY   Don't let that scare you off. Like I said, she's got two switches. It's a little finicky, though. The button gets jammed. Here, let me—

[BUMPY *presses the remote control.* FOXXY *will go in and out of character, vacillating between the brazen, stereotypical head-rolling black woman, to a more genteel character.*]

FOXXY   Hi, honey, I made your favorite for dinner . . . and look, I even crocheted these new socks . . . Can't you do anything right? Damn! I'm not gonna put up with this shit! Cook your own goddamn dinner. She-it! And cut the goddamn grass already. Do a bitch have to do everything around this motherfucker? I feel like I'm walking through the jungles of Africa. I've ironed up enough clothes for the entire week, sweetheart. I figure we'll go to church on Sunday, then a nice meal at Olive Garden. Or maybe even a picnic. Oh, that would be lovely, don't you think? Shit, a bitch is tireder than a field slave. Don't just stand there looking at me. Go get me a glass of water or something, motherfucker.

[BUMPY *frantically pushes the buttons and shakes his head.*]

BUMPY   I'm sorry. I didn't know it was quite this bad . . . I thought I'd fixed it enough to—

GERALD   No. I . . . I like it.

BUMPY   Yeah?

GERALD   [*Nods excitedly.*] Oh yeah. I'll take her.

BUMPY   Good. Good. I'll just get her all ready for you, and you can come by and pick her up this afternoon.

[*The two men shake hands. As* GERALD *exits,* ROCKO *enters. An African American male,* ROCKO *is clearly a regular. He and* BUMPY *have a familiar way with each other.*]

ROCKO   Whassup, Bump?

BUMPY   How ya doing, Rock? Any particular model this time or—

ROCKO   No. I don't care. You ask me this same question every time I come in here, Bump. Just white . . . that's my only requirement. She can be dumb as a doorknob and wear a goddamn tutu on her head. I don't give a shit. I'll just look around if you don't mind.

BUMPY   Go ahead.

[ROCKO *exits.* BUMPY *busies himself readying* FOXXY *for pickup.*]

ROCKO   [*Yells from offstage.*] Hey, Bumpy?! What about the model in the window?

BUMPY   What about her?

ROCKO   How much?

BUMPY   Look at the price tag.

ROCKO   I see the price tag, nearly 5 G's for a burned-out Pam Anderson look-alike? Come on, Bump, that's highway robbery.

BUMPY   I'm not cutting any deals. You've shopped here a thousand times, Rock. You know how this works. No haggling. The price you see is the price you pay.

ROCKO   A brotha should get a discount as much money as I've put in your pocket. How 'bout a layaway?

BUMPY   You know I don't do layaways.

ROCKO Well, you should.

[MICHAEL, *a young white man, enters with a "wife" in tow. She is strapped to a hand truck. She wears a dress and heels. At this moment, ROCKO also re-enters. He looks at MICHAEL's "wife."*]

ROCKO   What about this one?

[MICHAEL *pulls his "wife" close to him, but the "wife" seems to "eye" ROCKO.*]

MICHAEL   She's mine. I'm looking for a part.

[BUMPY *speaks without looking up.*]

BUMPY   Hi. Welcome to Bumpy's, where one man's trash is—

[BUMPY *finally looks up, stops mid-sentence, taken aback by the model "wife" in front of him.*]

Oh my God.

[BUMPY *walks around the model, looking at her closely.*]

Is this a . . . it can't be. A Stanley AJT1963? My God, Stanley made the best wives. Look at the craftsmanship. Perfection. And this model . . . everything a man could want. There aren't many on the market. I never thought I'd see one in person. The envy of every man. Cooked, cleaned, sex five times a week, all while raising the babies and—[*Shakes his head.*]—damn. I'm speechless.

MICHAEL   Yeah, my dad bought her for me. He kept her in tip-top shape till I was ready for a wife. But now . . .

BUMPY   Your dad's a good man. A good man.

[*Beat.*]

My goodness, she looks like new. What's wrong with her?

MICHAEL   I dunno. I think she's . . . depressed.

BUMPY   What? They don't get depressed.

MICHAEL   Apparently they do.

BUMPY   No. They don't. I've been in this business for over thirty years, and this model—

MICHAEL   I'm telling you.

[*Beat.*]

Turn her on. Go ahead.

[BUMPY *uses the remote and turns her on. The model's face saddens as if she's about to cry, but trying not to, followed by a whimper that before long turns into loud sobs and outright wailing.*]

BUMPY   Whoa, whoa! Shut it off! Jesus! I've never seen that before. I've never seen this model *emote*.

MICHAEL   So what do I do?

BUMPY   You're supposed to say something if they flip out like this. Hold on. I'll get the old manual.

[BUMPY *runs offstage and returns quickly with the manual and begins to read.*]

It says you can reset her. Okay . . . Say "honey" twice, as if you're cooing to a baby, then rub her hair and gently put her head on your shoulder. Kiss her forehead as if she is a six-year-old girl. And then hand her $10 and tell her to go buy herself a nice new hat.

[MICHAEL *follows the instructions, but there is no response from his "wife."*]

Okay, if that doesn't work . . . try *putting* a new hat on her head. Then say, "Look, just like Jackie O. would wear." Then kiss her again on the forehead, this time cup her face in your hands. Touch her nose and wink.

[*Again* MICHAEL *follows the directions. This time, the* WIFE *takes the hat off her head and throws it across the room. Both men jump, clearly afraid.*]

What the fuck?!

WIFE   I don't want a goddamn hat. I want a—*divorce.*

BUMPY   That word's not in her vocabulary. I mean, that she's been programmed not to know the words "divorce," "alimony," or "cunnilingus."

WIFE   I'm real, douche bag.

MICHAEL   No, you're not.

WIFE   Yes. I am.

BUMPY   They love male attention. Watch this.

[BUMPY *tries to kiss her. And she slaps him.*]

WIFE   What the fuck are you doing?

MICHAEL   My dad bought you for me, and kept you in storage until—

WIFE   No, he didn't, dumb ass. He paid me to "pretend" to be a model wife.

MICHAEL   That's a lie.

WIFE   He hired me to take care of you because . . . well, because you're a loser. And couldn't get a woman to marry you if you were the last man on God's green earth.

MICHAEL   That is a filthy lie.

WIFE   You're dumb as nails. You're a slob, and you slow-cook ribs . . . for a living.

[WIFE *takes out a pack of cigarettes and lighter.*]

MICHAEL   Hey . . . stop that.

> [MICHAEL *snatches the cigarette out of her mouth. Then she jumps at him as if she's going to hit him. He flinches, and* WIFE *laughs.*]

> Where'd you even get a cigarette?

WIFE   Tommy's.

MICHAEL   What the fuck is Tommy's?

> [*Slow realization.*]

> The truck stop? Tommy's truck stop?

> [WIFE *gives him a look that clearly says, "Yes, that Tommy's."*]

> That place is just a hangout for . . . oh my God!

WIFE   I make more in the cab of Big Mike's semi than you do in a week at that grease trap.

MICHAEL   What?!

[BUMPY *covers his mouth as if he's about to vomit.*]

BUMPY   You're a disgrace to Stanley's classic model #42358-AJT1963.

MICHAEL   When do you go to Tommy's truck stop?

WIFE   While you're at that shit job.

MICHAEL   Barbecue is king in the South. KING!

WIFE   You smell like pork . . . all the time.

MICHAEL   I do not.

WIFE   It's nauseating.

MICHAEL   [*Wimpily.*] I do not.

WIFE   Sometimes I think I'm screwing Piglet.

MICHAEL   I *do not*.

[MICHAEL *covertly tries to sniff himself.* BUMPY *and* ROCKO *sniff him as well.*]

ROCKO   You *do* smell like pork, my friend.

>[ROCKO *then provides* WIFE *with another cigarette.*]

>Here you go, sweetness.

WIFE   Thank you. Finally . . . a gentleman.

[ROCKO *and* WIFE *get closer and* MICHAEL *gets in between them.*]

MICHAEL   Hey . . . what do you think you're doing? Get your hands off my wife, and do not give her cigarettes. She does *not* smoke. The Stanley model 1963 model does not smoke.

>[MICHAEL *again snatches the cigarette from* WIFE. MICHAEL *stomps and grinds it into the ground. Then gets in* ROCKO's *face.*]

>There's your cigarette, *my friend.* How do you like that, huh?

[ROCKO *simply pulls another and hands it to* WIFE *again.*]

ROCKO   Hey, you wanna get outta here?

WIFE   Do I ever.

[MICHAEL *frantically presses remote-control buttons, then takes out a $10 bill.*]

MICHAEL   Just get a nice hat . . . a pill box, like Jackie O. . . .

[*At this moment,* FOXXY *springs back to life.*]

FOXXY   Who you talking to, mothafucka? I don't want no goddamn hat. Jackie O., my ass. Oh, a hat, how lovely. I can wear it to church with Gerald on Sunday. Beautiful, just beautiful.

MICHAEL   I'm not talking to you. Bumpy, can you please shut that thing off?!

BUMPY   I'm trying.

[BUMPY *frantically presses buttons while aiming the remote at* FOXXY.]

MICHAEL   [*Pleading.*] Please. Here's $10, just get yourself a nice hat.

BUMPY   [*Looking to* MICHAEL.] Stop saying it! She's not the Stanley Model AJT1963.

FOXXY   Yeah, stupid ass. She ain't worried 'bout no goddamn hat. Tell this sucka to take that hat and stick it up his ass, honey.

[WIFE *snatches the $10 and puts it down the front of her dress.*]

MICHAEL   Hey, give that back.

FOXXY   She ain't giving back shit, limp-dicked motherfucka. $10 won't buy a bitch a goddamn hat no way. She-it!

MICHAEL   Doesn't she have an off switch?

BUMPY   What do you think I'm trying to do?!

WIFE   Come and get it . . . I dare you.

[ROCKO *gets in* MICHAEL*'s face.*]

ROCKO   Yeah. We dare you.

FOXXY   You heard the man, he double-dog dare you.

[ROCKO *and* WIFE *exit hand in hand.*]

• • •

The Interview
a short play

A. R. Gurney

A. R. Gurney

A. R. ("Pete") Gurney has been writing plays for over fifty years. Among them are *The Dining Room*, *The Cocktail Hour*, *Love Letters*, *Sylvia*, *Big Bill*, *Mrs. Farnsworth*, *Indian Blood*, *The Grand Manner*, *Office Hours*, and *Black Tie*. He taught at MIT for many years before turning to writing full-time. Besides plays, he has written three published novels, several television scripts, and the librettos for two operas. Gurney is a member of the Theatre Hall of Fame and the American Academy of Arts and Letters, and has honorary degrees from Williams College and Buffalo State University.

··· production history ···

The Interview was written for and produced by Theater Breaking Through Barriers as part of a collection of one-act plays about disability, under the heading *More of Our Parts*, performed June 21–July, 1 2012.

set

Two straight-backed chairs, side by side, to simulate an automobile

cast

> **HOWARD**, a father, in his forties
>
> **KEN**, his son, late teens

···

[*At rise,* HOWARD, *in the "driver's seat," is reading a newspaper, occasionally glancing off because he expects someone. After a minute or so, he sees someone coming, folds his paper, puts it aside.* KEN *comes on, opens the car door, settles into the passenger side, unzips his backpack, all the while taking his time.*]

HOWARD [*Finally.*] So?

KEN [*Getting something out of his backpack.*] What?

HOWARD [*Louder.*] How did it go?

KEN Oh.
   [*Putting his hearing aids into his ears.*]
   Hold it, Dad.

HOWARD I just want to know how the interview went.

KEN [*Hearing aids almost in.*] It went OK.

HOWARD [*Noticing the hearing aids' activity.*] Did your hearing aids bother you during the interview?

KEN No.

HOWARD   Batteries let you down or something?

KEN   No. They're fine.

HOWARD   So why are you fussing with them now?

KEN   What?

HOWARD   [*Louder.*] I'm just asking if you had to adjust your hearing aids during the interview?

KEN   Oh. No.

HOWARD   You didn't?

KEN   No.

HOWARD   But you were fussing with them now.

KEN   I was just putting them back in.

HOWARD   Why?

KEN   [*Somewhat impatiently.*] So I can hear you, Dad.

HOWARD   I see.

> [*He "starts" the car, then stops.*]
>
> Now wait a minute. Were you wearing them during the interview?
> [*Pause.*]
>
> I'm asking you a question, Kenny.

KEN   What?

HOWARD   Were you wearing your hearing aids during the interview?

[*Pause.*]

KEN   No.

HOWARD   What?

KEN   [*Dryly.*] Hard of hearing or something, Dad?

HOWARD   Why weren't you wearing them?

KEN   I didn't want to.

HOWARD   You chose not to wear your hearing aids during a crucial personal interview for one of the finest colleges in the country?

KEN   Right.

HOWARD   Why?

KEN   What?

HOWARD   You heard me, Ken. I asked you why you didn't wearing your aids.

KEN   Because I wanted to come across without them.

HOWARD   "Come across"? What do you mean, "Come across"?

KEN   Be myself.

HOWARD   Kenny, my dear friend, we are talking about your future. If they admit you there, it could make a major difference in your life afterwards.

KEN   I know that, Dad. But I had to see if I could do it.

HOWARD   And did you?

KEN   I did OK. After all, it was just one on one, she and me, in her office. Nobody interrupting, no extra chatter echoing around the room. And I kind of knew the drill. So I could really concentrate. And read her lips and see her expressions and all that stuff.

HOWARD   I notice you're wearing them now, quick enough.

KEN   [*Patiently.*] Yes, Dad, because you're driving the car and looking at the road, so I can't always read your whole face when you're talking.

HOWARD   Fair enough. The point is, the interview went well.

KEN   It went OK.

HOWARD   Anyway, she must have known you were hard of hearing.

[*He starts up the car.*]

KEN   Why do you say that?

HOWARD   Well, I mean your guidance counselor at school must have sent on the information . . .

KEN   No.

HOWARD   [*Putting on the "brakes." They both lurch forward.*] No?

KEN   I asked him not to.

HOWARD   You asked your school guidance counselor not to send out the information about your handicap?

KEN   Yes.

HOWARD   Not to any of the colleges you applied to?

KEN   Right.

HOWARD   Kenny, for God's sake, why?

KEN   Because I don't want to be a special case.

HOWARD   Oh, Ken.

KEN   I've got good SATs, I've got good references from my summer job. . . .

HOWARD   Working with disabled kids, I might add.

KEN   So what? And I was runner-up in the interscholastic high hurdles last year. So the colleges can judge me on all that stuff.

HOWARD   Do you plan to wear your hearing aids when you get to college?

KEN   At times and places of my own choosing, Dad. But I don't want to get accepted because I'm some disadvantaged deaf kid who needs special care.

HOWARD   Well. So be it. It's your life.

> [*Starts up the car again. Both lurch back.*]

> Besides it sounds like you got away with it anyway.

KEN   What do you mean?

HOWARD   You said your interview went well.

KEN   I said it went OK.

HOWARD   Just OK?

KEN   Up to a point.

HOWARD   [*Clawing at the wheel.*] I'm pulling over to the side here.

> [*Stopping the car.*]

> What point?

KEN   Well, toward the end of the interview, we both got slightly offtrack.

HOWARD   Go on.

KEN   It was weird, actually. She was talking about the summer reading requirement, which happened to be *Tinker, Tailor, Soldier, Spy*, and I thought she was talking about my senior science project at school.

HOWARD   How could that happen?

KEN   I think we got our signals crossed on the word "mole."

HOWARD   Mole?

KEN   There are moles in chemistry measurement, Dad. And there are moles in the British Secret Service.

HOWARD   Ah. So you misunderstood each other.

KEN   We got all tangled up.

HOWARD   So what did you do?

KEN   I got up and left.

HOWARD   You walked *out?*

KEN   I had to, Dad. I mean, I was polite, and said thank you and shook hands, all that, but I had to leave. I knew we were in trouble, and it might get worse, so I got out while the getting was good.

HOWARD   She must have thought you were nuts.

KEN   I don't know what she thought.

HOWARD   You could have said, "Excuse me, but I'm hard of hearing."

KEN   I didn't want to say that.

HOWARD   Well, sir.

[*Reaching into his pocket.*]

I'm sorry but I'm going to do something about this.

[*Takes out his cell phone.*]

KEN   Dad, no.

HOWARD   Sorry, Kenny, I have to. Your future is on the line here.

[*Punches a number; speaks into phone.*]

May I have the admissions office, please?

KEN   Please, Dad.

HOWARD   [*Hand over mouthpiece of phone.*] What was the name of the woman who interviewed you?

KEN   I won't tell you, Dad,

HOWARD   [*Into phone.*] Hello. This is Howard Klein. My son Kenneth was just there for an interview. . . . May I speak to whomever interviewed him. . . . Ah. Ms. Novak. Thank you.

KEN   Oh, Dad, I can't stand this.

[*Gets out of the car, stands off upstage somewhere.*]

HOWARD [*On phone.*] Ms. Novak, I'm the father of Kenneth, whom
you just interviewed. . . . Yes, he told me. He's embarrassed about
that, and I'll tell you why. He's very hard of hearing, Ms. Novak,
and he didn't want you to know it. He's a bright, wonderful boy,
and sweet athlete, but I think you should know—what? . . . Yes, all
right.

[*Looks off.*]

Hold on. I'll see if I can arrange that.

[*Leans across, opens the "car door."*]

Ken! Kenny!

[KEN *looks at him.* HOWARD *holds out the phone.*]

She wants to speak to you.

[KEN *approaches the car slowly.*]

KEN Why?

HOWARD Who knows? . . . Come on. Hurry. She's waiting.

KEN [*Taking the phone, standing outside the car.*] Hello? . . . Yes . . .

[*Listens carefully.*]

Really?

[*More listening.*]

Thank you, Miss Kovak. Good-bye.

[*Snaps the phone shut, hands it to* HOWARD.]

HOWARD What did she say?

KEN [*Getting into the car.*] She said she could tell I was deaf all along.

HOWARD Does that upset you?

KEN Not at all.

HOWARD Good.

KEN You know how she could tell?

HOWARD   How?

KEN   She said I leaned toward her on everything she said and my whole face responded actively.

HOWARD   That's true enough. That sounds like you.

KEN   And she said—sure you want to hear this, Dad?

HOWARD   Of course I do.

KEN   She said that when I talked I was equally expressive, as if I was reaching out to her in a special way. Something like that.

HOWARD   Sounds like a lovely lady.

KEN   She said that if more candidates could talk that passionately and listen that intensely, her job would be much easier.

HOWARD   Wow! Sounds like you nailed the interview, Kenny.

KEN   I guess I did.

HOWARD   [*Starting up the car, pulling out of his parking place, driving.*] Well, let's get home. Your mother will be thrilled to hear this.

KEN   Miss Novak said something else too, Dad.

HOWARD   I'm all ears.

KEN   She said that if I decide to come there next year, I might consider majoring in drama.

HOWARD   Drama? Why drama?

KEN   She said that the best actors speak intensely and listen intensely, as if their lives depended on it, and that's what I did in my interview. So I should try acting.

HOWARD   Well, when you get to college next fall, you can tell Miss Novak or better yet, the Dean, that you hope to concentrate intensely on chemistry rather than drama, and that you'll need to sit in the front row, and probably have to record the lectures besides. May I assume you'll do that?

KEN   Maybe.

HOWARD   [*Turning toward him.*] What?

KEN   Keep your eyes on the road, Dad.

[*They drive on.*]

• • •

Come Again, Another Day

Cary Pepper

Cary Pepper

Cary Pepper has had work presented throughout the United States and in Europe. *How It Works* won the 2012 Ashland New Plays Festival and was a finalist at Dayton Playhouse's FutureFest 2010. *The Maltese Frenchman* was a finalist for the National Play Award, *And Jonah Rose Up* was a semifinalist in the Dorothy Silver Playwriting Competition, and *The Walrus Said* won the Religious Arts Guild Playwriting Competition. *Small Things* won the Tennessee Williams/New Orleans Literary Festival 2006 One-Act Play Contest, aired on National Public Radio, and has been published in *Best American Short Plays 2005–2006*. *House of the Holy Moment* was part of the 2008 Bay One-Acts Festival and has been published in *Best American Short Plays 2007–2008*. His work also appears in *Audition Monologues for Student Actors II* and *Scenes and Monologs from the Best New International Plays* (both Meriwether Publishing).

Cary is a member of the Dramatists Guild, a founding member of the San Francisco Bay Area playwrights group ThroughLine, and a member of the Marin Playwrights' Lab.

···production history···

Come Again, Another Day was initially produced in New York City by the SoupStone Project (1987). Most recently, a reworked version was presented by Happy Dog Productions in Berkeley, California, in October 2011, with Ron Dritz as Martin and Joe Lucas as Ivan Foley. It was directed by Hal Gelb.

characters

IVAN FOLEY, 40 years old

MARTIN, about 50 years old. Well-dressed. A gentleman.

setting

The living room of Ivan Foley

time

The present

• • •

[IVAN *comes in, dressed in a suit, which he immediately begins to take off as he moves about the room, muttering angrily.*]

IVAN   Goddamn bastards! Stupid pricks! For two months you give 'em your best while they sit there and sip it through a straw! . . . Then they narrow it down to you and some other bimbo, and throw you against each other for another month while they make up their minds. . . . Finally, they name a day when they'll tell you who beat out the other, then they cancel the final interview, say they need more time, and they'll call in an hour! Sure! What do they care! They're safe and secure behind their desks! They've got a job! What do they care about what you're going through!? How many times do they expect you to pour yourself through a tube? How many times do they think you can!? . . . They'll call in an hour! . . . Suppose I wasn't here to get the call? Then what? . . .

Would they panic? . . . Would they sit by their phone all day, dialing and dialing until they got me in? Or would they just call the other guy? "What the hell, one's as good as the other!" . . . Goddamn, inefficient, inconsiderate, insensitive . . .

MARTIN   [*Stepping from the shadows.*] Sleazebags.

[IVAN *jumps at the sound of* MARTIN's *voice and wheels around, very frightened.*]

IVAN   Jesus!

[IVAN *shudders as he regards* MARTIN. MARTIN *smiles at him.*]

Who the hell are you!

MARTIN   Martin.

IVAN   Martin. . . . Martin who?

MARTIN   Just . . . Martin.

IVAN   Just Martin. . . . How'd you get in here?

[IVAN *can barely contain himself as he virtually hops around in fear, not wanting to remain in any one place for too long, yet not sure just where will be safe.*]

MARTIN   There are ways.

IVAN   Well, what do you want?

MARTIN   To talk. Would you care to sit down?

IVAN   Yes! I would care to sit down! . . . No, I don't want to sit down! And I still don't know who you are.

[MARTIN *starts to answer.*]

And just "Martin" doesn't do it! Or is that your last name?

MARTIN   Just Martin.

IVAN   All right, "just Martin," what do you want?

MARTIN   To talk.

IVAN   About what!?

MARTIN You. What you're like. Who you are.

IVAN Why?

MARTIN Because there's time.

IVAN Oh, really? Time for what?

MARTIN To talk. There's some extra time.

IVAN Extra time before what?!

MARTIN Before I have to kill you.

IVAN WHAT?

MARTIN I'm here to kill you. And there's some extra time before I have to do it. I thought we'd talk.

[*Pause.*]

IVAN You're here . . . to . . . kill me? . . . What is that supposed to mean?

MARTIN I really don't know how to make it much clearer.

IVAN You're here to kill me . . .
[MARTIN *nods.*]
WHY?

MARTIN I don't know . . . I never ask.

IVAN Ask? Ask who?

MARTIN The people paying me.

IVAN You're being paid to kill me?
[MARTIN *nods.*]
ME?
[MARTIN *nods.*]
By who?

MARTIN   I never divulge the name of a client.

IVAN   They've got the wrong person.

MARTIN   Ivan Foley . . . ?

IVAN   Yeah . . .

MARTIN   373 E. 33rd Street . . . ?

IVAN   Yeah . . .

MARTIN   Apartment #23 . . . Social Security # 170-46-3782 . . .

IVAN   What are you, from the IRS?

MARTIN   Born: July 7, 1956 . . . Father: Henry . . . Mother:
Susan . . . Black hair, brown eyes . . . height: 5 feet,
6 inches . . . weight: 145 pounds . . . Birthmark on the
inner right thigh . . .

IVAN   You from my doctor? . . . So I'm Ivan Foley, birthmark and all! So
why does someone want me dead?

MARTIN   I imagine it must be something you've done.

IVAN   What?! . . . To who?

MARTIN   I never divulge the name of a client.

IVAN   Well then, fuck you! And as a matter of fact, get the hell out of
here!

MARTIN   I'm the one in control here, Ivan.

IVAN   The fuck you are!

[IVAN *goes to the door and throws it open.*]

Get out!

[IVAN *takes a few steps back into the room, coming closer to* MARTIN, *only
to find* MARTIN *has drawn a gun, which is equipped with a silencer. Drawn
up short,* IVAN *freezes at the sight of the weapon and stares at it.*]

Jesus . . . Christ!

[*Pause while* IVAN *continues to stare.*]

God . . . damn!

MARTIN Close the door, Ivan.

IVAN Hey, wait a minute . . . let's talk about this.

MARTIN That's what I want to do . . . talk.

IVAN Yeah, yeah . . . let's talk.

MARTIN But first, close the door.

IVAN The door?

MARTIN Yes. The door.

IVAN The door . . .

MARTIN The door.

IVAN The door.

MARTIN Close it. And please don't do anything stupid, or I'll be forced to kill you right now.

IVAN [*In a daze.*] Uh-huh . . . uh-huh . . .

[IVAN *goes to the door, closes it, and comes back into the room.*]

MARTIN Sit down, Ivan.

IVAN [*Dutifully sitting.*]

What the hell is going on here?

MARTIN Someone has put out a contract on you. I'm carrying it out.

IVAN Why? . . . Don't I have a right to know what I did?

MARTIN You know. You just can't remember.

IVAN They've got the wrong man.

MARTIN   The description matched.

IVAN   Maybe the description matched, but that still doesn't mean I did it. Maybe I was there, and someone saw me . . . But I still didn't do it . . . Or maybe I did it. But they don't have to kill me for it. I mean, how bad could it have been . . . whatever it was I did? But I never did it!

MARTIN   If they say it's you, it's you. They're very thorough.

IVAN   Who is? Who are they? Don't I have a right to know that?

MARTIN   What difference does it make? If someone puts out a contract on you, what's the difference if it's the Mafia, the government, or the Parking Violations Bureau?

IVAN   It's right that I should know! It just is!

MARTIN   Maybe . . . That's what everyone always asks.

IVAN   And you never answer?

MARTIN   I never divulge the name of a client.

IVAN   Well, you've got a hell of a nerve!

MARTIN   I do a job. Just like you.

IVAN   I don't have a job!

MARTIN   Sorry.

IVAN   Is this someone I owe money to?

MARTIN   Do you owe money to anyone?

IVAN   No.

MARTIN   Well then, it couldn't be that, could it?

IVAN   So what the hell can it be?

MARTIN   I told you, I don't know.

IVAN   Well, how can you kill someone without knowing why? Aren't you just the least bit curious?

MARTIN   Not really . . . It's got nothing to do with me. It's nothing personal.

IVAN   Oh, so it's like going to the supermarket and picking out a can of peas!

MARTIN   It's a job.

IVAN   Well, mister, if there is a hell, you are sure going to spend some hard time down there. And someday it's going to be reversed. . . . I'd sure like to see how smug you are when that happens.

MARTIN   That will depend on who's holding the gun. A person, or a sleazebag.

IVAN   Which are you?

MARTIN   A person.

IVAN   I think you're a sleazebag!

MARTIN   That's because I'm going to kill you. If we met under other circumstances, you might like me.

IVAN   You want to give it a try?

MARTIN   Personally, I wouldn't mind. But this isn't a personal matter.

IVAN   Somehow, I keep forgetting that.
[*Pause.*]
So what happens now? You just pull the trigger, and that's it?

MARTIN   If you like . . . But there's still some time.

[*Long pause.*]

IVAN   And . . . ?

MARTIN   I thought we'd talk.

IVAN   Talk about what?

MARTIN   You.

IVAN   Why? It's nothing personal.

MARTIN   It's very rare that I get to talk to any of my . . . assignments.

IVAN   Must be a lonely job.

MARTIN   It can be.

IVAN   So what's going on here that's special?

MARTIN   You came home early. You weren't due back until three.

IVAN   What is this? They know my schedule?

MARTIN   They're very thorough.

IVAN   So if my interview wasn't canceled, I'd come walking in here, at three, like I was supposed to, and you'd have just opened fire?

MARTIN   Something like that.

IVAN   So am I supposed to be grateful?

MARTIN   I am. It's given us this chance to talk.

IVAN   What is this thing you have with talking?

MARTIN   I love to learn about people.

IVAN   Why? So you can kill them better? . . . Sleazebag!

MARTIN   I'm not a sleazebag. I use what I know to make it easier for others when I do my job. If I used what I know to torture people, I'd be a sleazebag.

IVAN   Hey, look, really, are you just crazy, and it's simply a matter of time until the drugs wear off? Or is there some way we can talk this over and find a way out?

MARTIN   We should talk . . . But there's no way out that I can see.

IVAN   But we can try.

MARTIN   See what a good idea talking was?

IVAN   I sure do . . . OK . . . Tell me more about this difference between people and sleazebags.

MARTIN   People know how to live together in a tough world and not hurt each other. Sleazebags are greedy and selfish. They'll do anything they have to, to get what they want.

IVAN   Uh-huh . . . Which is the biggest group? Or are they both about the same size?

MARTIN   Sleazebags are biggest, by far.

IVAN   And I guess they should be eliminated, right?

MARTIN   Right!

IVAN   But the good ones, the people, they should live, is that it?

MARTIN   Right!

IVAN   Well, Martin, I'm not a sleazebag!

[*A short pause, while* MARTIN *regards* IVAN.]

MARTIN   Sorry . . . a deal is a deal.

IVAN   Well, how much are you being paid? Maybe I can meet it. Maybe I can do better!

MARTIN   I don't do things that way.

IVAN   At least give me a chance to beat their price! That's only fair!

MARTIN   You should have called me before they did.

IVAN   I didn't know any of this was going on!

MARTIN   Neither did I, until I got their call.

IVAN   OK . . . But if they can hire you, I can hire you back, right? And everything is even. You could make a good living not killing anyone . . . just going back and forth, and letting everybody buy you off!

MARTIN   That would be breaking a contract.

IVAN   So what?!

MARTIN   Breaking a contract makes you a sleazebag.

IVAN   I don't care if you're a sleazebag or not! I'll pay you not to kill me!

MARTIN   I don't do business that way.

IVAN   [*To himself.*] This is great . . . I'm locked in a room with an overly principled psychotic!
[*To* MARTIN.]
So what am I supposed to do now?

MARTIN   Talk.

IVAN   All right . . . Let's talk about not killing me!

MARTIN   I had something a little different in mind.

IVAN   So you think of a topic!

[IVAN *gets up and begins to randomly wander about the room.*]

MARTIN   If you're looking for something to throw at me, don't do it.

IVAN   [*All "innocence."*] I wasn't looking for something to throw at you.

MARTIN   Yes, you were. But it won't do you any good. I'm very fast.

IVAN   Oh, people have tried that before, huh?

MARTIN   It's a common ploy.

IVAN   But it doesn't work.

MARTIN   Never.

IVAN   Tell me, what else do people try?

MARTIN   Lots of things. But I'd much rather talk about you.

IVAN   You want a drink? Some coffee? Anything to eat?

MARTIN   No, thank you very much. . . . People try that, too. And I'd prefer you don't leave this room.

IVAN   I can't believe this is happening to me!

MARTIN   We all have to die at some point.

IVAN   That's so easy for you to say! You're just gonna do your job and walk, and I'm gonna be lying here and never know another thing, ever!

MARTIN   You're right. It's very scary.

IVAN   Thanks a lot. Sleazebag!

MARTIN   I'm not a sleazebag.

IVAN   No, you're just a prick! Go around killing people you don't even know. . . . The world certainly needs a lot more of you!

MARTIN   You don't know me.

IVAN   How can anybody ever get to know you? You always kill them first! Tell you what . . . I'll get to know you—all you like. You want a friend, I'll be your friend. You want to talk, you can come over every night, we'll talk. We'll do anything you want.

MARTIN   Anything?

IVAN   Oh, Jesus! . . . Yeah, anything.

MARTIN   Ivan . . . what is it you think I want?

IVAN   Martin . . . I don't know.

MARTIN   Then what makes you think you can do it?

IVAN   You're right . . . You're right . . . Maybe I can't do it . . . But then we can't be sure, because I don't know what it is.

[*Pause.* MARTIN *regards* IVAN *in silence.*]

But you can tell me! You can tell me what it is, and then we'll know if I can do it.

[*Pause.* MARTIN *continues to regard* IVAN. *Then:*]

MARTIN   Ivan, I'm not crazy.

IVAN   No one said you were!

MARTIN   You're talking to me as if I am. You're patronizing me.

IVAN   [*Patronizingly.*] No, I'm not. I'm just trying to figure out what it is you want so we'll know if I can do it or not.

MARTIN   You're doing it right now.

IVAN   [*Still patronizing.*] Oh, am I? Well, that's good. That's good if I'm doing what it is you want right now.

MARTIN   I mean, patronizing me.

IVAN   Well, what the hell is it you want me to do?!

MARTIN   Just be yourself. Do what you'd do normally.

IVAN   Normally, I wouldn't be sitting here with someone who says he's about to kill me! What do you want me to do, put on a goddamned "Normal Act"? What the hell would anyone do normally," face to face with someone who wants to kill them?

MARTIN   I don't want to kill you. I have to.

IVAN   The man is playing with verbs! You don't have to do anything you don't want to! And you may not want to kill me, but you're sure as shit not breaking your back not to!

MARTIN   I haven't done it yet, have I?

IVAN   'M I supposed to fall down and kiss your feet?

MARTIN   I'm simply pointing out that in most cases you'd already be dead.

IVAN   Well, fucking gol-ly!

MARTIN   There may be a reason.

IVAN   What do you mean?

MARTIN   A reason we've been given this extra time. A reason you came home early.

IVAN   The reason I came home early is those bastards canceled my interview!

MARTIN   Well, there could be a reason for that.

IVAN   You mean, like . . . fate? Like . . . something is supposed to happen with this time we've been given?

MARTIN   That hasn't occurred to you?

IVAN   Uh . . . no.

MARTIN   It occurred to me . . . As soon as I heard your key in the door, I had to make a decision. Kill you then . . . or wait.

IVAN   So why'd you wait?

MARTIN   It occurred to me that it might be worth taking some extra time with you.

IVAN   And I still don't know which way I'm better off.

MARTIN   Well, the choice has been made. Try using the time to your advantage.

IVAN   How?

MARTIN   You might try talking me out of it.

IVAN   You said that couldn't be done.

MARTIN   You could try.

IVAN   How?

MARTIN   Give me a good reason why you should live.

IVAN   If I can do that . . . give you a reason . . . you won't kill me?

MARTIN   Well, I can't make any guarantees . . .

IVAN   But maybe you won't kill me.

MARTIN   It's certainly worth a try, isn't it?

IVAN   Right . . . A reason why you shouldn't kill me . . . Well, it just isn't a good thing to do. It's a sin . . . I mean, every religion in the world has a rule against killing in it, so it's got to be a bad thing. No matter which God they believe in, they all put it in that you shouldn't kill each other.

MARTIN   I'm not religious.

IVAN   OK, forget the religions. . . . Every society has rules that you can't do certain things, and killing is always one of them. Always! I mean, it's just recognized by . . . everyone! . . . as a very bad thing to do! It's . . . universally frowned upon!

MARTIN   I'm not concerned with society.

IVAN   Well, killing is crazy! Sane people just don't go around killing other people! Whether it's for a price, or because it's Monday and it's raining!

MARTIN   Is it any more sane to get into a ring and beat another man senseless while everyone watches and cheers? Or smash someone to the ground to get possession of a ball? Or drive a car in circles to see how fast it will go? People do insane things all the time. And half the time they're getting paid to do them.

IVAN   But everyone else says those things are OK!

MARTIN   [*Shrugs.*] Maybe it's everyone else that's crazy. . . . What other arguments can you give me?

IVAN   Got any samples?

MARTIN   Most people claim their family.

IVAN   I have no family. You must know that, too!

MARTIN   That was just an example.

IVAN   How about, I just don't want to die? I didn't do anything, I'm not guilty of anything, I just don't want to die! How's that for a reason!

MARTIN   No one wants to die. I'd suggest something a little more unique.

IVAN   Why? Because you say so?

MARTIN   Because you should. It's important.

[*Suddenly,* IVAN *leaps at* MARTIN. *But apparently* MARTIN *is expecting it, and anyway he's too fast. As* IVAN *leaps,* MARTIN *steps out of the way. Now he's standing at a safe distance from* IVAN, *the gun aimed directly at him. They stare at each other,* IVAN *waiting for* MARTIN *to pull the trigger. Long pause.*]

That wasn't very smart. Or safe.

IVAN   Yeah, it could have gotten me killed! . . . What am I supposed to do, cower like a trapped rabbit until you decide to put an end to it?

MARTIN   You could try talking to me.

IVAN   And you could try walking out of here! See, neither of us seems to be getting what we want! "Give me a good reason not to kill you!" . . . Suppose I did come up with one? Would you just leave?

MARTIN   But you didn't come up with one.

IVAN   So what does that mean? I deserve to die? You think just because you didn't . . . Wait a minute! I do have a reason!

MARTIN   What is it?

IVAN   I have to make a phone call.

[*Pause.*]

MARTIN   To whom?

IVAN   The interview I had today . . . the one that got canceled. They said if I didn't hear from them by two-thirty, I could call them. It's two-thirty now. I want to make the call.

[*Long pause.*]

I've been after this job for almost three months now. It's down to me and one other guy. I went through a lot to get to this point. I'd like to know if it paid off.

MARTIN   Why? If they tell you you didn't get it, you'll only be depressed. . . . And if you did get it, I'd imagine you'd only be more depressed, considering . . . me.

IVAN   I still want to know. Even if it doesn't matter anymore. You buy a lottery ticket, you don't not check the numbers.

MARTIN   Personally, I'd advise against it.

IVAN   Personally, you're going to be around tomorrow. And personally, I don't give a shit what you advise.

[IVAN *goes toward the phone.* MARTIN *snatches it up before he can get to it. With fierce, quiet determination.*]

I'm going to make that call!

[*Pause.*]

MARTIN   What's the number?

IVAN   555-4731.

[MARTIN *dials the number, waits until the phone is answered on the other end, then hands the receiver to* IVAN.]

Hello . . . Mr. Martin, please. . . . This is Ivan Foley. Oh . . . Well, when will he be back? I see. Well, he told me to call him at two-thirty. Did he leave any message? Oh . . . Yes, I would like him to call me when he gets back in. He's got the number! Thank you very much.

[*He hangs up.*]

The prick! He tells me to call him at two-thirty, and he's out to lunch! If he knew he was going to be at lunch, why'd he tell me to call? And if he tells me to call at two-thirty, the least he can do is make sure he's finished stuffing his face by then!

MARTIN   Now that's a sleazebag.

IVAN   She said she'd have him call when he got in.

MARTIN   He'd better call soon. You don't have much time left.

IVAN   Now wait a minute! You have your job! The least you can do is let me see if I got mine!

MARTIN   I contracted for three. Earlier is all right, but later is no good.

IVAN   That's being extremely compulsive!

MARTIN   Isn't it funny, how at a given moment something can become so important that nothing else matters . . . like this phone call. . . . Or right now your Mr. Martin might be agonizing over his decision between two job applicants, not even tasting the food in his mouth. . . . On the other hand, perhaps he's just frustrated because the waitress isn't bringing his shrimp salad on rye fast enough, or his hamburger isn't well done.

IVAN   [*Who has been deep in thought.*] Hey, wait a minute. . . . His name is Martin . . . your name is Martin. . . . He's not in his office, though he said he would be. . . . You're here. . . . All that information you know about me could have been gotten from my job application. . . . Are you . . . ? . . . You're not him, are you? . . . Jesus! . . . Are you him?

MARTIN   You've never seen him?

IVAN   No. The interviews were all conducted by subordinates. I was supposed to meet him for the first time today. But that was canceled . . . Unless . . . Jesus! Is this the interview? . . . Is this one more bizarre test you're putting me through after everything else?

[*Pause.*]

I'm right! That's why you didn't shoot when I walked through the door! There aren't even bullets in that thing! You wouldn't use it if I made you! You're Martin, from Stone & Malloy, and when this is all over you're going to rip off your mask and yell "Surprise!" Jesus, what you guys won't do to get the right man for the job! What about the other guy? He being tested the same way?

MARTIN   I wouldn't know. But I can tell you this: there most definitely are bullets in this "thing," and I most certainly do intend to use it.

[*Pause.*]

IVAN   You're serious! . . . Jesus, you're serious! Wait a minute . . . Hold it! . . . It's something else! You were hired by the other guy! He's paying you to get rid of me so he'll get the job! That's it, isn't it?

MARTIN   I never divulge the name of a client.

IVAN   But that is it . . . It's me or him. And he wants the job so badly he's willing to kill me. What a rotten thing to do!

MARTIN   What a desperate thing to do.

IVAN   But he's done it, hasn't he?

[*A pause. They regard each other.*]

Well, you owe me that phone call! Both of you! If he's so desperate that he went this far . . . and if you're so sick that you're going along with it . . . the least the two of you can do is let me find out if I won or not.

Because I did it all on my own, without calling in someone else to take out the opposition!

[*Short pause.*]

OK . . . Two can play at that game. I can't buy you off . . . I can't pay you not to kill me . . . But I could still hire you, couldn't I?

MARTIN   To do what?

IVAN To kill someone! Why else would I want to hire you? I want you to kill him. The other guy. After you do me, you go on over there and blow his fucking brains out!

[*Pause.*]

MARTIN Ivan . . . He didn't hire me to kill you.

[*Pause while* IVAN *takes this in.*]

IVAN He didn't . . . ?

> [*MARTIN shakes his head.*]
>
> You're not from Stone & Malloy . . . ?
>
> [MARTIN *shakes his head.*]
>
> This isn't the interview?
>
> [MARTIN *shakes his head.*]
>
> And you're not working for the other guy . . . ?
>
> [MARTIN *shakes his head.*]
>
> SHIT!
>
> [*The phone rings.*]
>
> That's the call!

[IVAN *starts for the phone. But* MARTIN *calmly picks it up first.*]

MARTIN Hello? . . . Yes. . . . All right.

> [IVAN *stares at* MARTIN, *torn between his obsession with the call, his sense of complete violation, and his fear of the gun.* MARTIN *hangs up. Pause.*]
>
> That was for me.

IVAN For you? You're getting phone calls here? I don't believe it! What do you do, leave forwarding numbers?

MARTIN Sometimes.

IVAN You're really something! You come here to kill me, and you give your friends my number?! Well, you still owe me that phone call! My call!

[MARTIN *sits down.*]

MARTIN   The contract's been canceled.

IVAN   What?

MARTIN   The contract's been canceled.

IVAN   You're kidding.

MARTIN   No.

IVAN   Why was it canceled?

MARTIN   I didn't ask. They told me it was called off, and I accept it. I don't have to kill you.

[IVAN *breathes an enormous sigh of relief as he takes this development in.*]

IVAN   That's . . . that's great!

[*Pause.*]

MARTIN   But I'm going to anyway.

IVAN   What?

MARTIN   I'm going to kill you anyway.

IVAN   Ah, come on now! What the hell are you talking about? You said it was nothing personal!

MARTIN   That's right.

IVAN   That's right! So why the fuck are you going to kill me?

MARTIN   Because you couldn't give me a reason not to.

[IVAN *stares at* MARTIN, *incredulous.*]

IVAN   I don't believe it! I just don't believe it!

MARTIN   I said it was important. You couldn't do it. And if you didn't have a good reason to live then, you still don't have one now.

IVAN   Says who? . . . The contract's been canceled! The deal is off! The shop is closed!

MARTIN   This is a freebie.

IVAN   Yeah? Well, won't your bosses be a little teed off at you for not doing what you're told?

MARTIN   They just said the contract was canceled. They never said not to kill you. For all they know, the job was already done.

IVAN   You are some sick animal! You talk with someone for a few minutes, and you decide you're going to kill them!

MARTIN   You can learn a lot about a person in a few minutes.

IVAN   Wait a minute! I see it all now! You are crazy! There never was a contract on me. You're just some street lunatic who picked my apartment at random, and now I'm paying the price! This isn't something that's organized, or paid for. This is just some freaky bit of city madness that's found me. . . . Like the sickos who push people onto subway tracks, or walk down the street hacking up total strangers with meat cleavers. . . . You manage to keep the insanity off you for years and years, and then one day, for no reason at all, out of nowhere, it suddenly finds you. . . . I'm right, aren't I? This whole thing . . . You're just improvising as you go along. There was no contract. . . . That call was just someone calling to shoot the shit and it turned out to be a lucky dramatic touch. It's all you, right? . . . I mean, you can tell me. You're still sitting there with the gun.

[*Long pause.*]

MARTIN   It's real, Ivan. All of it. There really was a contract. And it really has been canceled.

IVAN   And you're really going to kill me anyway.

MARTIN   Unless you can give me a good reason not to.

IVAN   Back to that again! What am I supposed to do? Beg? Is that what you want me to do? . . . OK, you want me to beg, I'll beg.

MARTIN   I don't want you to do anything.

IVAN   I know. Including live. . . . Well, I'll try begging.

[IVAN *sinks to his knees.*]

Martin, I'm on my hands and knees to you. . . . I'm begging you not to kill me. . . . I'm begging you . . .

[*As* IVAN *speaks, he inches closer and closer to* MARTIN *until he is literally at his feet.*]

Please don't kill me. . . . Please don't do it.

[*Suddenly he grabs the chair* MARTIN *is sitting on and hurls it over backward, sending* MARTIN *to the floor.* IVAN *leaps on top of* MARTIN, *and after a brief struggle manages to wrestle the gun away from him. Then* IVAN *scrambles to his feet, putting a safe distance between him and* MARTIN.]

All right, you sick son of a bitch! Get up!

[MARTIN *rises, remaining totally expressionless.*]

And don't do anything stupid, or I'll be forced to kill you right now! Hey, Martin, is this a first? Did this ever happen before?

MARTIN   This is most certainly a first.

IVAN   Well, how does it feel to have things reversed? How does it feel to be on the other end of the gun?

MARTIN   That will depend. On whether you're a person, or a sleazebag.

IVAN   Oh, I can be a real sleazebag when I want to be. A real sleazebag.

MARTIN   Then I suspect this will be quite unpleasant.

IVAN   I suspect it will. . . . Now, who sent you?

MARTIN   I never divulge the name of a client.

IVAN   Not even if I do your body a little damage? Say, like shoot off an earlobe?

MARTIN   You can shoot me wherever you like. I'm not going to tell you anything. And personally, I don't think you're capable of doing something like that.

IVAN   Oh, I'm capable, all right! Given the right motivation I'm capable of anything!

MARTIN   I hope so.

IVAN   Who sent you, Martin?

[MARTIN *is silent.*]

All right, give me your wallet.

MARTIN   I never carry a wallet when I'm working.

IVAN   So you're just some person out of nowhere, who I'm going to kill.

MARTIN   I'm just a person.

IVAN   But you don't seem to think I'm going to kill you. Well, you've already gotten a few surprises today. Now, you give me a good reason why I shouldn't kill you.

MARTIN   No.

IVAN   What's the matter? Don't you want to play that game anymore?

MARTIN   You'll be able to discount all my reasons, just like I did yours. And if I should come up with one you couldn't discount, you wouldn't accept it anyway.

IVAN   You got that right!

MARTIN   Besides . . . you should kill me.

IVAN   What?

MARTIN   I was going to kill you.

IVAN   Yeah, but you're crazy.

MARTIN   That's neither here nor there. I was going to kill you. . . . You should kill me. That would be the wise thing to do. The safe thing.

IVAN   There's plenty of time to do that. . . . Let's talk.

MARTIN   Yes, of course. . . . But the situation could reverse again. I might get the gun back from you.

IVAN   Maybe I don't want to kill you! Maybe there are other things I want to do with you!

MARTIN   I'm sure there are. But I'd recommend killing me. It's a simple situation.

IVAN   For you, all this may be simple! For me, it's pretty damn complicated!

MARTIN   And scary. . . . I'd suggest you . . .

IVAN   I'd suggest you shut up!
   [*Pause.*]
   I'm going to call the police and let them deal with you.

MARTIN   No, I couldn't allow that.

IVAN   I'm the one in control here.

MARTIN   If you reach for the phone, I'll walk out. The only way you'll be able to stop me will be to shoot me. . . . I don't think you want to do that.

IVAN   I'll shoot you in the leg.

MARTIN   I'll keep going.

IVAN   I'll shoot you in both legs!

MARTIN   If you can.

IVAN   I will if I have to!

MARTIN   If you call the police, you'll have to.

[*Pause.*]

IVAN   Who are you?!

MARTIN   Your problem now isn't getting information. It's deciding what to do with me.

IVAN   I can do anything I want with you!

MARTIN   Well . . . If you let me walk out of here, you can never be sure I won't come back tomorrow. Or the next day. Or the day after that. You'll never be able to walk down the street and feel safe again.

[*Short pause.*]

IVAN   Then I should kill you.

MARTIN   That's what I've been telling you.

IVAN   But you're trying to convince me to do it. . . . You're working at it.

MARTIN   I got careless. I made a mistake.

IVAN   You're not even going to try to talk your way out of it?

MARTIN   There is no way out of it.

IVAN   You're not trying!

MARTIN   Was I going to let you out of it? A mistake has been made. There's only one thing to do.

IVAN   You want me to kill you!

MARTIN   Do I?

IVAN   Yes! That's why you didn't shoot when I came through the door! All this bullshit about talking . . . You've been waiting for this to happen all along! You want me to kill you. Well, I'm not going to be sucked into this. I'm taking you somewhere they may be able to help you. Or at least keep you from doing this to someone else. Let's go. Walk. Out the door.

MARTIN   The door?

IVAN   Yes. The door! Walk!

MARTIN   No.

IVAN   I'm giving the orders now! I said walk!

MARTIN   No.

[IVAN *makes a tentative movement toward* MARTIN *in an attempt to be threatening. But* MARTIN *isn't threatened. In fact, he subtly readies himself for another struggle. . . .* IVAN *senses this, realizes* MARTIN *just isn't afraid of him, and retreats. Then, at a safe distance again, he aims the gun at* MARTIN.]

IVAN   WALK!

MARTIN   No. If you don't like it, shoot me.

> [*Long pause.*]
>
> But you can't, can you? You can't pull the trigger. Not even to wound me. You have the gun, but the only way it will help you is if you use it. And you can't. I'd say you have a problem.

IVAN   I can't believe this! . . . I can't take care of myself! It's no good! It's all no good!

> [*Pause.*]
>
> What the hell am I supposed to do now?

MARTIN   I'd suggest you kill me before the situation reverses again.

IVAN   What for? If it doesn't reverse here, it'll only reverse somewhere else. A man violates your home, threatens your life . . . you'd think you'd at least be able to do something back to him. . . .

> [IVAN *looks at the gun.*]
>
> The only way I'd be able to use this was if you attacked me . . . Maybe . . . Even then, I'm not so sure. How's that for an ability to survive?

MARTIN   Not so good.

IVAN Not so good. You were right. I do deserve to die. I've been existing through the good graces of others. I've been allowed to go on simply because that right has never been challenged. No wonder I couldn't give you a good reason not to kill me. . . . And now, even if you walk out and never come back . . . what will I do? Wait for it to happen again? Just go on existing, until someone decides otherwise?

MARTIN Do you want to hold on to the gun?

IVAN Thanks . . . I don't even want it in the house.

[*Pause.*]

If I give this back . . . will you kill me?

MARTIN I might.

IVAN Suppose I took the bullets out.

MARTIN I could reload.

IVAN And if I kept the gun, and just told you to go, you might come back later and kill me anyway.

MARTIN I might.

IVAN So it really doesn't matter what I do, does it?

[IVAN *handles the gun, toying with it as if he could be contemplating using it on himself.*]

MARTIN Careful with that. . . . The safety is off.

IVAN It doesn't matter. . . . Nothing does any more. . . . It just does not matter.

[IVAN *handles the gun without thinking or seeing. . . . His hands simply move over the buttons and levers, until he becomes aware that his finger happens to be firmly resting on one of them. Randomly, he squeezes. . . . The bullet clip pops out, falling harmlessly into his hand. He stares at it as he holds it.*]

Hmmph! . . . You push one button, the thing goes off with a roar and destroys you. You push another, it throws up its insides and becomes harmless. And you go on with whatever you're doing. . . . It's all in which button you push. It's as simple as that.

[IVAN *lets the gun drop to the floor.*]

You were going to kill me, and I can't bring myself to hurt you. . . . What does that mean?

[*Pause.*]

MARTIN   You're not a sleazebag.

[*Pause.*]

IVAN   So I'll be a dead person.

MARTIN   [*Indicating the gun.*] You're sure you don't want to keep that? Just in case?

[IVAN *shakes his head.* MARTIN *slowly picks up the gun. He reaches into his pocket and takes out a new clip of bullets. He inserts the clip into the gun.* IVAN *watches this disinterestedly, as if merely curious to see what happens next in a movie, no longer concerned with what* MARTIN *does. The gun is now loaded. . . .* MARTIN *stands facing* IVAN, *the weapon aimed casually at his chest. Long pause.*]

IVAN   What are you waiting for?

MARTIN   You want me to kill you?

IVAN   I want this to be over. I don't care how anymore. If you're going to kill me, do it, and get out of here. If you're not going to kill me, don't do it, and get out of here. My life is being decided by other people. Whether I have a job or not . . . Whether I know if I have a job or not . . . Whether I live or die. . . . You can't live like this . . . With no control . . . A person has to . . .

MARTIN   Take control back.

IVAN   How?

IVAN   A moment at a time.

[*The phone rings.* IVAN *remains motionless until, after five or six rings, the phone falls silent again.*]

MARTIN   That could have been your call.

IVAN   So what?

[*Long pause.*]

MARTIN   Well, good-bye, Ivan.

[IVAN *braces himself for the shot.* MARTIN *puts the gun away and moves toward the door.*]

IVAN   You . . . You're not going to . . . kill me?

MARTIN   No.

IVAN   Why not?

MARTIN   I've changed my mind.

IVAN   But . . . I didn't give you a reason not to.

MARTIN   Yes, you did, Ivan . . . Yes, you did.

  [MARTIN *is at the door. The phone rings.* IVAN *remains motionless.*]

  Answer the phone, Ivan.

IVAN   The phone?

MARTIN   The phone . . . Answer your phone.

[MARTIN *leaves.* IVAN *slowly goes to the phone and picks it up.*]

• • •

Take My Land . . . Please

John F. Richardson

John F. Richardson

John F. Richardson—a Southern California native and graduate of USC—is currently a member of New Voices Playwrights Theatre and Orange County Playwrights Alliance. Over the past six years, a dozen of his one-acts and full-length plays have been given staged readings and full productions.

···production history···

Take My Land . . . Please premiered as part of *Summer Voices 2012: Eight One-Act Plays* produced by New Voices Playwrights Theatre at Stage Door Repertory Theatre in Anaheim, California, on July 28, August 4, 5, and 11, 2012. Director: Yvonne Robertson

> **CHIEF CONEY**   Richard Comeau
> **MARGO**   Ginger Francis
> **PETER MINUIT**   Kyle J. Spiller

characters

> **CHIEF CONEY**, 30–40, an Indian chief
> **MARGO**, 25–35, Chief's secretary
> **PETER MINUIT**, 40–50, Dutch businessman

setting

A pristine Manhattan shoreline

time

May 1626. Thursday.

···

[*At rise: a beach. At left is a large upright fishing pole stuck into the ground. At right is a primitive-looking kiosk. A sign at the front of the kiosk reads, "Manhattan Realty—Best Deals of 1626!"* MARGO *stands inside the kiosk holding a clipboard. She is dressed as a business professional in skirt and heels. A single upright feather protrudes from the back of her head.*]

CHIEF CONEY   [*Stands at center dressed as a sideshow barker complete with striped vest, straw hat, and bamboo cane. A single upright feather protrudes from the back of his hat. Broad New Yawk accent.*] Lots! Lots fowr sale! How much? Prices so low ya can't friggin' believe it! Fuggetaboutit!

I'm talkin' dirt cheap here! Yowr own mutha wouldn't give ya this good of a deal! Hey, I'm practically givin' 'em away! Lots here! Boy, do I got lotsa lots!

PETER MINUIT   [MINUIT *wears a traditional Pilgrim costume with a broad white collar. MINUIT pulls a child's wagon on which is stacked three boxes. From the open box on top we can see some of the contents, which have been haphazardly thrown in: Frisbees, beach balls, rubber tomahawks, plastic squirt guns, and a multitude of cascading Mardi Gras bead necklaces. MINUIT steps over to the kiosk and makes an elaborate bow to MARGO.] Goedemorgen!* Ah, excuse. English, yes? . . . I bid ye a good morning, fair lady. I am a duly authorized representative of the Dutch West India Company, entrusted with the negotiation of a transaction of no small significance and wouldst ask ye a small favor in assisting me with its completion. Prithee, can ye tell me whether ye be the correct party from whom to secure rights to yon property?

MARGO   [*Likewise New Yawk accent.*] Huh?

PETER MINUIT   Ah! What a dullard I am! I forgot to bring a translator!

CHIEF CONEY   Margo. What's Fancy Pants want?

MARGO   Beats me! He's talkin' double Dutch. It sure ain't English!

PETER MINUIT   English! Ye speak English!

MARGO   Yeah. How 'bout that. Now we both do.

CHIEF CONEY   Hey, Dutch boy! What's with the getup? It's a clam bake, not Happy Thanksgivin', fer chrissakes! And anyway, deliveries are in the rear! Geez! Looks like the party committee really screwed the pooch on this one!

PETER MINUIT   Allow me to make myself known. I am Peter Minuit, Third Director General of New Netherland.

CHIEF CONEY [*A la John Wayne.*] Well, nice to meet ya, *pilgrim.* Minuet, ya say? Yeah. We heard of ya, haven't we, Margo? Let's show 'im.

[*The* CHIEF *and* MARGO *proceed to dance a minuet to the tune of Beethoven's Minuet in G major.*]

Dum. Dee-dum. Dee-dum. Dee-dum. Dee-dum. Dum. Dee-dum. Dum. Dee-dum.

[*To audience.*]

And they say we ain't cultured!

PETER MINUIT No! No! *Peter Minuit!* Minuit with two I's!

[*The* CHIEF *and* MARGO *stop dancing.*]

CHIEF CONEY How ya doin', Peter Minuet with two eyes?

PETER MINUIT Please to understand. I have no time for merrymaking. I am a businessman looking to buy land.

MARGO Mister Minuet, today is yowr lucky day! Chief Coney here is the Delaware tribe's top realtor! He's won awards as the highest-grossing realtor in the county fowr the last three years!

CHIEF CONEY Thanks, Margo. Margo's my personal secretary. I don't make a move without her. She's my Gal Friday, ya might say. Even though today's Thursday.

PETER MINUIT I am honored to make your acquaintances. Perhaps we can get straight to the matter at hand. As you can see, I have brought a generous supply of provisions with which to negotiate.

CHIEF CONEY I like a man who comes prepared to do big business. It's like fishin' the bay here. Ya wanna catch the big fish. Ya gotta bring the big pole. Whaddaya think, Margo?

MARGO I think . . . I think we got a big fish on the line right now!

CHIEF CONEY Really? Looks pretty calm out there to me.

MARGO He's closer than ya know! If ya land 'im, there'll be enough dinner fowr the both of us! It'll be a *Dutch treat* . . .

CHIEF CONEY Oh. Ohhh! Yeah, I gotcha. Margo, I think it's time to break out the good stuff.

MARGO Comin' right up, Chief!

[MARGO *goes behind the kiosk and brings out a folding tray with a bottle and three shot glasses. She takes the bottle and pours some into each glass.*]

CHIEF CONEY Here's mud in yer eye!

PETER MINUIT Oh no! I cannot! As my uncle Erik always says, one should never drink spirits before conducting business.

CHIEF CONEY Guy sounds like a regular killjoy! Hey, I think we all got a Dutch uncle like that around the ol' neighborhood. Am I right?

MARGO Right, Chief!

CHIEF CONEY Down the hatch, Petey!

PETER MINUIT But—

MARGO Ya wouldn't want to insult the entire Delaware Nation now, would ya?

[MINUIT *reluctantly drinks. Both the* CHIEF *and* MARGO *throw the contents of their glasses over their shoulders.*]

CHIEF CONEY That's the stuff! Chateau Firewater, Tuesday before last!

[*To* MARGO.]

Hit us again!

[MARGO *pours.*]

PETER MINUIT [*Coughing.*] Oh, I really must protest—

CHIEF CONEY Ah-ah-ah! It's bad luck to stop in the middle of the Businessman's Toast ritual!

MARGO It's true!

[MINUIT *drinks, and the* CHIEF *and* MARGO *dispense with their drinks as before.*]

CHIEF CONEY We'll make ya a Delaware brave yet!

MARGO Well, he's already got plenty of Dutch courage!

CHIEF CONEY Nice one, kiddo! Hit us again!

[MARGO *pours.*]

MARGO The third toast ensures a profitable transaction for all parties concerned.

PETER MINUIT Oh, screw it!

[MINUIT *drinks, and the* CHIEF *and* MARGO *dispense with their drinks as before.*]

CHIEF CONEY Excellent! And now on to business!

PETER MINUIT Yes! Please!

CHIEF CONEY So, what was youse lookin' fowr? Something cozy fowr a summer bungalow getaway? No, wait! Don't tell me. Yer a family man, am I right? Yoow'll be wantin' the deluxe-size lot with plenty of room fowr a front lawn, a backyard, and that sprawling dream house youse always promised yerself.

PETER MINUIT I need more than that. The land is for commercial purposes.

CHIEF CONEY Hey, I like the way this guy thinks!

MARGO Petey's good people!

CHIEF CONEY Yoo bet!

> [*To* MINUIT.]

> Well, yowr in luck, my friend. 'Cause this whole area's already zoned for it! So, what sorta business ya got in mind?

PETER MINUIT Fur trading.

CHIEF CONEY Uh-huh . . . Is that what the kids are callin' it these days? Hey, look. I'm not here to judge. I'm here to sell ya land. What youse do with it is yowr business. Am I right?

MARGO Right, Chief!

CHIEF CONEY Listen, this ain't no Roanoke Lost Colony boondoggle. I mean, if youse wanna build temples to worship lobsters in— hey—that's *yowr* lookout! So, how many lots ya gonna need? One through forty-eight all got great ocean views. Hell, who am I kiddin'? They *all* got great ocean views!

PETER MINUIT I wish to purchase them all.

CHIEF CONEY All?

MARGO All?

PETER MINUIT All of Manhattan Island. In exchange I offer ye the entire contents of any two of yon three boxes.

CHIEF CONEY Two boxes, ya say?

PETER MINUIT A very fair trade. Ye may freely examine the contents of all boxes to verify the generosity of my offer.

CHIEF CONEY Hmmm . . . Whaddaya say we make this a little more interestin'? Margo. The shells.

[MARGO *takes the tray and goes behind the kiosk. She brings the tray back, which now contains three large seashells and a small rubber ball.*]

PETER MINUIT Another tribal ritual?

CHIEF CONEY Hey, yoo catch on quick! A little somethin' to spice up the proceedin's. It's a game of chance we call the Peanut Shuffle. If ya can guess which shell the peanut is under after Margo shuffles 'em around a bit, I'll *give* ya lots one through forty-eight.

PETER MINUIT For free?

CHIEF CONEY   Yeah, but if ya guess wrong, *we* take that heavy-lookin' bottom box there for free.

PETER MINUIT   The rubber tomahawks and the Mardi Gras beads? I don't know . . .

CHIEF CONEY   Look at the upside. If ya win, yer way ahead on the deal. And if ya lose, ya still got the other two boxes fowr which to conclude a "generous" transaction fowr the whole shebang.

MARGO   It's easy. Go ahead. Give it a shot.

PETER MINUIT   Oh, why not! Yes!

[MARGO *places the ball and moves the shells very slowly. She stops.*]

MARGO   Where's the peanut?

PETER MINUIT   Under this one!

[MARGO *reveals.*]

MARGO   Winner!

CHIEF CONEY   Nice goin', Petey! Ya just got yerself some prime real estate fowr nuthin'! Wanna go again? I'll put up lots forty-nine through ninety-six against the middle box.

PETER MINUIT   The arrow-through-the-head and the rubber chickens? . . . Alright! Yes!

[MARGO *moves the shells as before.*]

MARGO   Where's the peanut?

PETER MINUIT   Here!

[MARGO *reveals.*]

MARGO   Winner! Winner again!

CHIEF CONEY   It's a fun game, isn't it?

PETER MINUIT   Oh yes! Very fun!

CHIEF CONEY   Yeah. Youse gettin' to be a regular pro at this! So, let's cut to the chase, shall we? This time let's play for the whole kit and caboodle. Ya obviously got an edge on us, so whaddaya say we even the odds and make it even more interestin'? Double or nuthin'. Ya win this time and ya get all the lots scot-free.

PETER MINUIT   Oh! That wouldst be a blessing!

CHIEF CONEY   But if *we* win—

MARGO   Yeah, right! Like there's any chance of that happenin'!

CHIEF CONEY   I'm just sayin'. *If*—on the off chance—we were to win. We'd take back the land that youse already won along with all three boxes of goods.

MARGO   No way! Are youse nuts?! He'll clean us out! Can't ya see he's on a streak?

PETER MINUIT   Hmmm . . . Mind you, it is an enticing offer. But—

CHIEF CONEY   Yeah, maybe yer right, Petey. Maybe we should stop. Those boxes do look pretty heavy. Better let me relieve ya of some of that stuff fer a trade. After all, I am a sucker fowr them Mardi Gras beads . . .

PETER MINUIT   Alright! I'll play! Shuffle the peanut!

[MARGO *moves the shells around very quickly.*]

MARGO   Where's the peanut?

PETER MINUIT   I—I . . . I don't know!

CHIEF CONEY   C'mon, Peter Two Eyes. Whaddaya say?

PETER MINUIT   Here!

MARGO   [*Consoling.*] Oh, Petey!

CHIEF CONEY   That's a shame!

MARGO   That's a shame!

PETER MINUIT I'm ruined!

CHIEF CONEY Look, Petey, I feel bad about this. I really do. Gaining yowr goodwill and trust is worth more to me than any stretch of land. I still wanna sell ya every one of them lots. Tell ya what I'm gonna do. I'm gonna make ya a very, very, *very* special one-time offer. Ya got any spare change on ya?

PETER MINUIT Just this. Sixty guilders. I was saving up to buy discount booklets for the ferry.

CHIEF CONEY Say again? Sixty whaddaya call 'em?

PETER MINUIT Pardon. In your people's language—[*New Yawk accent.*]—twenty-fowr bucks.

CHIEF CONEY Nice. Well, how 'bout this? Gimme the cash and all of this—all of Manhattan—is yowrs.

PETER MINUIT Do ye mean it, truly?!

MARGO The Chief's as good as his word.

[MINUIT *has become a man transformed. He walks down front as in a trance.*]

PETER MINUIT [*To audience.*] I, Peter Minuit, am about to purchase all of Manhattan Island for a mere sixty guilders! Who could have imagined it? True, they are but primitive savages. They have no negotiating skills. They know nothing of business transactions. As they say, it is taking candy from a baby. Still. This is a miracle! When historians write of this moment, I will be remembered as the shrewdest businessman of all time!

[MINUIT *turns back to* CHIEF CONEY *and hands him a leather pouch.*]

I wish to purchase all of Manhattan Island with these sixty guilders!

CHIEF CONEY Welcome to the neighborhood, pal! Margo, I believe it's time for us to head on back.

PETER MINUIT What? Are ye leaving now?

CHIEF CONEY Yep. The Welcome Wagon takes it from here. Protocol. You understand. Stick around. It should be fun.

MARGO Be sure to try the sponge cake. It's dee-lish!

[CHIEF CONEY *picks up a* "SOLD" *sign from behind the kiosk and hands it to* MINUIT.]

CHIEF CONEY Here. Ya betta take this and stick it in the ground somewhere out there in the middle, just to make it official.

PETER MINUIT Yes! Thank ye! Oh, thank ye!

[MINUIT *hugs* CHIEF CONEY *and* MARGO *and then quickly runs off.*]

CHIEF CONEY Let it not be said that Chief Coney of the Canarsee ever missed an opportunity to turn a quick profit. Outta nuthin' no less!

MARGO Yowr too modest!

CHIEF CONEY Now let's pack up and get the hell outta here before the Delaware find out I just sold their land to Little Lord Fauntleroy!

MARGO Friggin' Delaware!

[*Blackout.*]

• • •

YouTopia

Chaney Kwak

Chaney Kwak

Chaney Kwak writes comedies of manners across genres. His writing appears in *Zyzzyva*, the *New York Times*, *Condé Nast Traveler*, and other publications. He is working on a full-length play about Berlin.

··· production history ···

Performed in June 2012 at the InspiraTO Short Play Festival, Toronto, Canada.

characters

MARGARET JUNIPER, late 20s, in her last trimester

SMITH WINSTON, late 20s/early 30s, handsome in a budding real-estate mogul kind of way

KENZO TOYAMA, flamboyant, Eurotrashy, and self-proclaimed "ageless"

FRILL FREEMAN, 20s, sweet, sunny, slightly simple

DOCTOR, male, voice only

scene

A wedding reception somewhere in America

time

Summer evening, in very near future

···

[SMITH, FRILL, *and* KENZO, *each sporting a wrist device, are seated around an elegantly set table at a wedding. They are typing on an invisible touch screen in the air.* MARGARET, *heavily pregnant, waddles to the empty chair next to* KENZO.]

MARGARET Is this "Table Hashtag Freedom"?

KENZO [*Without looking up.*] Yeah.

[*With great difficulty,* MARGARET *lowers herself into the empty seat.* FRILL *notices her.*]

FRILL Oh my God, are you okay?

MARGARET I'm fine.

FRILL   Hi, I'm Frill.

MARGARET   Margaret.

FRILL   It's so good of you to come . . . in your condition.

MARGARET   What condition?

FRILL   You know . . . you're . . .

KENZO   Fat?

FRILL   No! Carrying another life!

SMITH   Congratulations!

MARGARET   I'm not knocked up.

[*Awkward silence.*]

FRILL   Oh dear, that'll teach me not to open my mouth before checking people's profiles.

SMITH   [*Typing in the air.*] Huh, I'm not seeing you at this table.

MARGARET   What do you mean? I'm right here.

FRILL   You forgot to check in.

MARGARET   I'm not on Foursquare.

    [SMITH *and* FRILL, *speechless, stare at* MARGARET. *Even* KENZO *stops typing.*]

    I don't carry any connection.

FRILL   But . . . why not?

MARGARET   Because I don't want to.

SMITH   Then how do people know who you are?

MARGARET   I tell them.

FRILL   How do your friends see you?

MARGARET   I wave at them.

SMITH Fascinating!

FRILL Does your . . . shape have anything to do with your lack of connection?

MARGARET My shape? My . . . ? Oh! Of course, I'm pregnant!

FRILL Why did you lie?

MARGARET It was a joke.

FRILL I don't get it.

SMITH I think this is irony. I learned about it in history.

FRILL Oh, wasn't there a song about it in the last century?

MARGARET No, this isn't ironic, and neither was that song.

SMITH Then what is irony?

MARGARET It's . . . oh, never mind.

[KENZO *giggles at something he sees on-screen, then types away.*]

FRILL The bride told me this table's named "Freedom" because it's the singles' table. Isn't it neat?

KENZO [*Still typing.*] Speak for yourself. I think I just found a hot new boyfriend—he's supposed to be about fifty feet . . .

[*Looks around.*]

Above me? That's where I like 'em!

FRILL Are you friends with the bride or the groom?

MARGARET Both. I introduced them.

KENZO So you are the cave woman who forced them to meet in person. You're practically a legend, darling.

MARGARET Oh?

KENZO Yes, let's see each other again in something . . . more comfortable.

MARGARET   What?

KENZO   Not you, honey. I'm chatting on MeetMarket.

[*Back to his screen.*]

No, just some pregnant thing.

FRILL   It was a beautiful wedding, wasn't it? I'm so glad they had a physical ceremony.

SMITH   I read it was just as good in 3-D.

FRILL   Who said that?

SMITH   Rate-my-wedding-dot-com.

MARGARET   Do you think I can get a glass of water? I'm not feeling well.

FRILL   Of course. Let me text the waiter.

[FRILL *types in the air.*]

SMITH   Tell me. Why don't you carry connection?

MARGARET   Because once you're online, you can kiss your privacy good-bye.

FRILL   But privacy means having secrets.

MARGARET   No, privacy means being offline.

KENZO   Go offline? *Ma cherie*, that's a vulgar thing for a lady to say!

MARGARET   Going offline is good for your soul.

KENZO   Huh?

MARGARET   I'm sure you can do it, too.

KENZO   I can also hold my breath underwater, but that doesn't mean I go around asking for a drowning, hello? Privacy is so passé.

SMITH   Invisibility is selfish. We, the people, share all.

MARGARET   Is that the newest tagline?

FRILL   It's gone viral this year.

MARGARET   You know what else is viral? Herpes.

SMITH   I don't understand. Why hold back?

MARGARET   Because I'm not someone's entertainment.

FRILL   We're living in an evolved society. You have nothing to be ashamed of. We, the people, share all.

SMITH   We are living in YouTopia.

MARGARET   It's pronounced "utopia."

SMITH   No, YouTopia, because you make it happen!

MARGARET   Very clever. Are you going to trademark it?

SMITH   Of course not! That's the beauty of YouTopia. Everything belongs to the community.

[SMITH *stands tall, full of optimism and pride.*]

We share everything—images, music, words. No one monopolizes knowledge. We no longer hide behind cowardice.

[*He walks over to behind* FRILL *and places his hands on her shoulders.*]

No more anonymous comments, no more hate speech . . .

FRILL   No more sexism!

KENZO   And no more gay bashing since all the fanatics turned out to be self-haters. Now we see exactly who's sleeping with who.

FRILL   No more war! Now that we know everything about everyone, we can prevent conflicts before they begin.

SMITH   Isn't this a fantastic time to be alive? We're all equal before technology. All you have to do is consent to be part of it.

FRILL   Privacy isolates you. Join us. No one should be lonely.

MARGARET   But I'm not. I have my books. Soon I'll have my baby. And I even meet people—in person! Although . . . that's getting harder.

SMITH   Your experience is so unique. Don't you think you owe it to the community to share your story?

MARGARET   I owe nothing.

KENZO   Selfish!

MARGARET   Once you unveil every part of you, you strip yourself of dignity.

SMITH   No, you become honest with the world.

MARGARET   When we're bare and vulnerable, what will the machines do with all that they know of us?

KENZO   Oh, you poor, obsolete thing! There's no sinister plot. Technology liberates us.

FRILL   The algorithms understand us better than we do, so we don't have to waste time trying to find ourselves.

SMITH   Our parents' generation spent their twenties meditating in Delhi, taking drugs in Amsterdam, writing plays in Berlin . . . and where did their "path to self–discovery" lead them?

FRILL   Not very far. They were the least productive generation in modern history, weren't they?

KENZO   Look, in today's world, you're either visible or you don't exist. Which is it going to be?

MARGARET   You know my choice.

[MARGARET *flashes her bare wrist.* KENZO *and* FRILL *coil back, and* SMITH *sits down, defeated.*]

KENZO   What do you have to hide?

MARGARET   Nothing.

KENZO   I don't believe you.

[KENZO *presses a button in the air and a flashlight explodes on* MARGARET.]

MARGARET   Don't you dare upload my picture.

KENZO   Why not, paranoid pansy?

FRILL   We're at a wedding! Can't we just enjoy the moment?

KENZO   I am!

[MARGARET *swings her hand where* KENZO *is typing. Smugly, he leans back and continues blogging.*]

MARGARET   I'm entitled to my privacy!

KENZO   Not if your thought-terror can endanger the community.

MARGARET   Thought-terror? What the . . .

FRILL   [*Helplessly.*] We the people agree that thought-terror should be prevented. The word's gone . . .

MARGARET   Viral?

FRILL   [*Delighted.*] Yes!

KENZO   Don't worry, dear. I'm just putting you on my micro-mobile blog. I only have about a million followers.

MARGARET   I don't want to be on your micro-mother-mobbing-mobile blog, and I don't need connection devices strapped on me, and I hate this Me-me-me-topia!

KENZO   [*Clapping as if saluting an opera diva.*] She's positively mad! Brava!

FRILL   Oh dear, it must be the hormones. Where's that water?

SMITH   [*Googling.*] I think she might be suffering from . . . "hysteria"?

MARGARET   How typical! When a woman has an opinion, you tell her she's crazy. Guess what—you are crazy.

KENZO The present evidence suggests otherwise, sweetheart.

MARGARET Tell me. Who keeps an eye on the one who watches you?

FRILL Everyone! We the people agreed to see and be seen.

MARGARET This is just like *1984*.

FRILL What's that?

SMITH Here, Wikipedia says that's the year Mark Zuckerberg was born.

[*A moment of reverent awe among* FRILL, KENZO, *and* SMITH.]

KENZO Look around—life is great! We're finally free—from violence, from shame, from inhibitions.

MARGARET Do you call this free? You're all chained to your keyboards!

KENZO Excuse you, mine's an Apple iBoard!

MARGARET iBoard, shmiboard, I'll give your strap-on a taste of the floorboard.

KENZO That's it. I'm reporting you to the People's Forum.

[MARGARET *grabs* KENZO*'s wrist.*]

You can't do that! You're violating my freedom of speech!

MARGARET Freedom of speech ends when a person's privacy is invaded.

[KENZO *and* MARGARET *wrestle over his watch.* FRILL *and* SMITH *are at a loss.*]

KENZO No, it ends when you violate another citizen's right to speech. That means your freedom of speech should be stripped, pronto!

[KENZO*'s argument convinces* SMITH. *He restrains* MARGARET. *He looks around, embarrassed, at the unseen wedding guests who are watching them.*]

MARGARET   God!

FRILL   Everything will be all right.

[*A splash under the table.*]

MARGARET   My water just broke.

[KENZO *rushes, squats in front of* MARGARET, *and points his wristwatch at her crotch.*]

MARGARET   Get your iPerv away from my birth canal!

[MARGARET *pushes* KENZO *away, but he persists. She pulls his head and strangles him with her thighs,* 007 Golden Eye *style.*]

KENZO   [*Gasping for air.*] That is not . . . the kind of behavior . . . you want to have attached . . . to your newborn!

FRILL   He has a point. Think of your child's brand! Her corporal identity begins the moment she's born.

SMITH   The minute her sonogram's posted!

[MARGARET *lets* KENZO *go.*]

KENZO   [*Recovering from* MARGARET's *grip.*] I plan to attach an infra-camera on my surrogate.

FRILL   Oh, that's a good idea.

SMITH   Why didn't I think of that?

KENZO   I should tweet about it.

MARGARET   God, enough about Twitter, you twat! Some help?

[FRILL, SMITH, *and* KENZO *snap to it and begin typing.*]

SMITH   Is there a doctor around . . . Not one!

FRILL   I'll call mine.

MARGARET   [*Sprawling over her chair.*] Oh my God, I'm contracting!

KENZO   Quite the contrary. You seem to be expanding!

[*A dial tone. Then the characters look up, as the doctor's image is presumably projected in front of them.*]

DOCTOR'S VOICE   Hello there. Whoa, you're in labor!

MARGARET   No shit, Sherlock!

[*Screams in pain.*]

DOCTOR'S VOICE   I'm going to need to examine your cervix.

FRILL   I'm so sorry.

[FRILL *puts her wrist up* MARGARET's *skirt.*]

DOCTOR'S VOICE   Oh, you're dilated. We need to get this party started.

SMITH   [*Typing away.*] I'm on it. How to assist birth with an online doctor!

KENZO   [*Filming the whole scene.*] Your child will thank me for this publicity.

SMITH   Technology is saving your life!

MARGARET   What kind of world . . . is my baby . . . being born into?
[KENZO *is elated;* SMITH *is feeling heroic. Watching* MARGARET's *pain being broadcast, however,* FRILL *doesn't seem so sure anymore.*]
Utopia?

KENZO, FRILL, SMITH   YouTopia.

[*Blackout.*]

• • •

acknowledgments

It goes without saying that the authors in this book are the ones who make this book what it is. They deserve all the credit, and I truly thank them for their talents. But I also need to thank several people who helped me locate these excellent pieces of theater; folks who spread the word so nicely and passed some very good discoveries my way include John Patrick Bray, Steve Feffer, Guadalupe Flores, Kevin Donovan, and Julius Novick. And thanks to everyone who submitted their work for me to read and review, making this project, once again, a joyful but also challenging undertaking.

Thanks always to the folks at Applause Theatre & Cinema Books, especially John Cerullo, Bernadette Malavarca, and Carol Flannery. Thanks also to June Clark, my agent, for supporting this project. And thanks to Jean and Erin, voices of sanity always in my corner.